TOP 10 FOR BOYS

2014

Paul Terry

WHAT'S INSIDE?

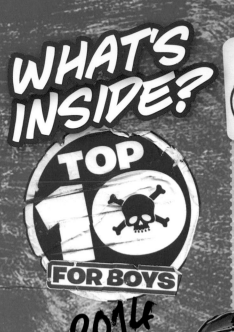

TOP 10 FOR BOYS 2014

ONE
HIGH-OCTANE MACHINES

Extreme Speed 10
Bigger The Better 14
High Performance 18
Cash Machines 22
Armed & Dangerous 26
Top Secret 30
Your Shout 34

TWO
ANIMAL KINGDOM

Out For Blood 38
Most Hunted 46
Rapid Movement 50
Sizing Things Up 56
Highly Evolved 62
Millions Of Years Ago 66
Your Shout 72

Produced for Hamlyn by
SHUBROOK BROS. CREATIVE

Written & Researched by Paul Terry

Top 10 Of Everything was devised and
created by Russell Ash

An Hachette UK Company
www.hachette.co.uk

First published in Great Britain in 2013,
by Hamlyn, a division of
Octopus Publishing Group Ltd
Endeavour House
189 Shaftesbury Avenue
London WC2H 8JY

www.octopusbooks.co.uk

Copyright © Octopus Publishing Group Ltd 2013

Russell Ash (1946-2010) was the originator
of the *Top 10 Of Everything* annual, and
his passion for facts, eye for detail,
and pursuit of the curious fascinated
and entertained millions of readers. His
invaluable database has continued to
inform this edition.

ISBN 978-0-600-62345-8

A CIP record for this book is available
from the British Library.

Printed and bound in China.

SIX
MUSIC MASH-UP

Chart Toppers 170
Fan Forum 178
Price Tag 186
On Stage 192
Your Shout 198

SEVEN
EPIC STRUCTURES

Skyscraping 202
Mass Appeal 208
Great Lengths 212
Designed To Deliver 218
Bizarre Builds 222
Your Shout 226

THREE
GAMING GALAXY

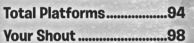

Digital Development........ 76
Gold Coins...................... 80
Download Focus 86
Beyond The Console 90
Total Platforms................ 94
Your Shout 98

FOUR
SPORT ZONE

Just For Kicks 102
Leap Of Faith 108
In Full Swing................... 112
Throw Down.................... 118
Muscle Movement 122
Engine Thrust 126
Extreme Danger.............. 130
The A-Teams 136
You're On Your Own 140
Your Shout 144

FIVE
FORCES OF NATURE

Land Demolition 148
Savage Oceans 152
Heaven-Sent.................... 156
Around The World........... 160
Your Shout 166

EIGHT
MOVIE SHOWTIME

Blockbusters................... 230
Before The Big Screen ... 238
The Making Of 244
Star Talent 248
Your Shout 252

NINE
ONLY HUMAN

Dare To Go 256
Power Play 262
Dangerous Minds............ 266
Body Work....................... 270
United We Stand.............. 274
Fictitious Figures 276
Your Shout 280

TEN
INFINITE SPACE

Astro Orbits.................... 284
Galaxy Watch 292
Mega Rocks 296
Voyages Of Discovery . 298
Sci-Fi Station................. 302
Your Shout 308

Your Shout Round-up........310
Your Shout Answers 312
Index 314
Picture Credits &
Acknowledgements......... 320

WELCOME!

Hey there! Thanks for picking up this book! What can you expect from these pages? Well, where do we BEGIN?! Firstly, we are Team T-10. We will be bringing you an incredible collection of AMAZING facts and info...

When we say "amazing", we are NOT kidding around! The range of facts within these pages is unlike anything you've ever experienced before. Team T-10 doesn't just care about the top dogs... we go way, WAY beyond the number ones. You will discover what the Top 10s are in virtually every subject that YOU care about. High-tech machines... gigantic dinosaurs... astounding sports stars... the mysteries of outer space... and that barely scratches the surface. You are about to uncover thousands of facts and eye-popping figures which will mean you'll never look at the world in quite the same way again. But it doesn't end there... This is YOUR book and it's an interactive experience! Check out how it works by reading these two intro pages, and then... LET'S ROCK!

GETTING THE MOST OUT OF YOUR T-10

Top 10 is an interactive book that needs your input to make it a one-of-a-kind copy. Here's how the cool content works...

FRIENDLY CONTENT

This is the first ever T-10 that is exclusively for boys! So, we've only added content that is relevant to you. All games and movies are rated 12 or under, meaning you can check out absolutely everything that's featured in the media realm of the T-10 universe!

IT'S YOUR TURN!

Here at T-10 Towers, we'd love to hear your comments and any ideas that you have for new lists that you and your friends would like to see in the next edition.

Please contact the publisher or visit the website at...

www.octopusbooks.co.uk/top10

BEEN & SEEN

This is a simple check-list based on the related subject. How many things have you seen on these lists? Those ones get that all-important tick!

Check out this example of what Team T-10 has "Been & Seen", when it comes to this list within the Forces Of Nature zone:

SAVAGE OCEANS
LARGEST SHIPS SUNK BY NATURE

BEEN & SEEN

Tick the natural phenomena you've seen with your own eyes!

- ☐ **TORNADO**
- ☑ **ICEBERG**
- ☑ **LIGHTNING**
- ☑ **COSTAL ROCKS**
- ☑ **BLIZZARD**
- ☑ **HIGH WINDS**
- ☑ **SNOWSTORM**
- ☑ **HAILSTORM**
- ☐ **GIANT WAVE**
- ☑ **CORAL REEF**

GIVE IT A TRY...

When you see a "Give It A Try..." panel, this is your chance to get active and try something different!

Here's what to look for. This is an example of a "Give It A Try..." from the Sport Zone. These are scattered throughout the book. See how many you can do, and get your friends involved too!

GIVE IT A TRY... ON THE SPOT

Next time you're with your friends and family in a park, set up some kicking challenges to see who has the most accuracy. A great way to do this is with a penalty shootout.

SHUFFLE UP

This is one of T-10's most fun features: you get to rework the lists according to your opinions! "Shuffle Ups" become your very own Top 10 Unofficial lists.

We really want you to stamp YOUR personality on this copy of T-10. So, when you see a "Shuffle Up", really have a think about what would be in YOUR ultimate Top 10 on that subject. Take a look at this example of Team T-10's fave music artists on Facebook. We've even added a few in that weren't on the original list. Remember, these are your lists, so you can add in what you like!

SHUFFLE UP

Who would you have at number 1? Now you've seen the Top 10 most "Liked" music stars on Facebook, why not list them in order of your favourites?

1	LINKIN PARK
2	30 SECONDS TO MARS
3	KATY PERRY
4	LADY GAGA
5	RIHANNA
6	MICHAEL JACKSON
7	BAND OF SKULLS
8	SHAKIRA
9	THE BLACK KEYS
10	LIL WAYNE

FAN FORUM

Team T-10 are massive fans of many musicians and singers, but how many of YOUR favourite pop and rock stars are in their fervid community?

MOST 'LIKES' ON THEIR OFFICIAL FACEBOOK PAGE

SHUFFLE UP

CHECK IT OUT!

YOU RATE!

The best part about the interactive stuff is the "You Rate" button. These allow you to customize categories and come up with YOUR ultimate T-10 lists. Check out how it's done...

WHAT TO LOOK FOR?

You'll notice that these "You Rate" buttons pop up all over the book. Most Official T-10 lists will have one.

YOU RATE!
1 to 100

RATING LISTS

When you spot a "You Rate" button, you are being invited to rate the number 1 on that list from 1 to 100. The more you love it or think it's amazing, the higher you'll score it. For instance, Team T-10 thinks Sherlock Holmes is pretty awesome, so we've given him a "You Rate" of 76.

MOST MOVIES IN A FRANCHISE

It's pretty common for a popular character or franchise to enjoy multiple movie successes, but these 10 make all the others look like they're not even trying...

	FRANCHISE/CHARACTER	TOTAL FILMS
1	Sherlock Holmes	37
2	James Bond	25
3	Star Trek	12
4	Batman	8
5	Harry Potter	8
6	The Avengers	7
7	Star Wars	6
8	X-Men	6
9	Superman	6
10	Ice Age	4

YOU RATE! 76

BATMAN XTREME FACT

A total of five different actors have portrayed the Caped Crusader on the big screen between 1966 and 2012, but Christian Bale has donned the batsuit the most for Christopher Nolan's trilogy of Batman Begins (2005), The Dark Knight (2008), and The Dark Knight Rises (2012).

COMPILING YOUR LISTS

The "Your Shout" zone at the end of each category is your chance to compile the ratings you have given throughout that section. Go back through your scores and write the 10 number 1s you scored highest in the chart provided. Here's an example of Team T-10's Movie Showtime ratings...

	NAME	"YOU RATE" SCORE
1	THE AVENGERS	98
2	AVATAR	82
3	SHERLOCK HOLMES	76
4	TRANSFORMERS	72
5	BATMAN	65
6	PIRATES OF THE CARIBBEAN	61
7	MIB 3	59
8	DR. WHO & THE DALEKS	52
9	DANIEL RADCLIFFE	42
10	TITANIC	27

HIGH-OCTANE MACHINES

Here at T-10 Towers, the screech of wheels and the scream of engines are music to our ears. This zone will take you on a pulse-racing journey into worlds where metallic monsters dominate land, sea and air. Whether it's the most advanced stealth fighter or the fastest car, we've got it covered. Time to buckle up...

EXTREME SPEED

Technology has given mankind the ability to experience speeds that used to be the stuff of science fiction. Start your engines as we look at the fastest machines on Earth...

TOP 10 FASTEST IN THE AIR

If you've ever flown in an airplane, you may have experienced a sense of great acceleration on take-off, but nothing like the speeds these craft can achieve...

	AIRCRAFT	PILOT(S)	DATE	LOCATION	TOP SPEED (KPH)	(MPH)
1	Lockheed SR-71 Blackbird	Eldon W Joersz, George T Morgan	Jul 28, 1976	Beale Air Force Base, CA (USA)	3,529.6	2,193.2
2	Lockheed YF-12A	Robert L Stephens, Daniel Andre	May 1, 1965	Edwards Air Force Base, CA (USA)	3,331.5	2,070.1
3	Mikoyan Gurevich Ye-166	Georgii Mosolov	Jul 7, 1962	USSR (Russia)	2,681	1,665.9
4	McDonnell-Douglas F-4 Phantom II	Robert G Robertson	Nov 22, 1961	Edwards Air Force Base, CA (USA)	2,585.1	1,606.3
5	Convair F-106 Delta Dart	Joseph Rogers	Dec 15, 1959	Edwards Air Force Base, CA (USA)	2,455.7	1,525.9
6	Lockheed F-104C Starfighter	WW Irwin	May 16, 1958	Edwards Air Force Base, CA (USA)	2,259.5	1,404
7	McDonnell F-101A Voodoo	Adrian Drew	Dec 12, 1957	Edwards Air Force Base, CA (USA)	1,943.5	1,207.6
8	Fairey Delta 2	Peter Twiss	Mar 10, 1956	Chichester (UK)	1,822	1,132
9	F-100C Super Sabre	Horace A Hanes	Aug 20, 1955	Palmdale (USA)	1,323	822.1
10	Douglas F4D Skyray	James B Verdin	Oct 3, 1953	Salton Sea (USA)	1,211.5	752.8

CHECK IT OUT!

With huge leaps forward in technology leading to developments like the internet and computer-generated imagery (CGI), you'd think that 2013 fighter jets would trump anything over a decade old. But, amazingly, the 49-year-old Lockheed SR-71 Blackbird is still the fastest military jet ever since it took to the skies back in 1964!

FACT FLASH! TOP SPEED **2,193** MPH

GIVE IT A TRY...
SONIC PAPER PLANES

You may have made paper planes before, but it's time to REALLY challenge yourselves. Can you come up with one that looks like the Blackbird? Go!

FASTEST ON LAND

Mankind has always been fascinated with travelling at terrific speeds. When it comes to land-speed records, engineers would often bring out the big boys... Rocket engines!

	VEHICLE	TYPE	DRIVER	DATE	LOCATION	TOP SPEED (KPH)	(MPH)
1	ThrustSSC	Rocket car	Andy Green	Oct 15, 1997	Black Rock Desert (USA)	1,223.66	760.34
2	Thrust2	Rocket car	Richard Noble	Oct 4, 1983	Black Rock Desert (USA)	1,020.41	634.05
3	Blue Flame	Rocket car	Gary Gabelich	Oct 28, 1970	Bonneville Salt Flats (USA)	1,014.66	630.48
4	Spirit Of America: Sonic 1	Rocket car	Craig Breedlove	Nov 15, 1965	Bonneville Salt Flats (USA)	955.95	594
5	Green Monster	Rocket car	Art Arfons	Oct 5, 1964	Bonneville Salt Flats (USA)	927	576
6	Spirit Of America	Rocket car	Craig Breedlove	Aug 5, 1963	Bonneville Salt Flats (USA)	846.96	526.28
7	Bluebird CN7	Car	Donald Campbell	Jul 17, 1964	Lake Eyre (Aus)	690	429
8	Wingfoot Express	Car	Tom Green	Oct 2, 1964	Bonneville Salt Flats (USA)	664.66	413
9	Railton Mobil Special	Car	John Cobb	Sep 16, 1947	Bonneville Salt Flats (USA)	634.40	394.20
10	Top 1 Oil-Ack Attack	Motorcycle	Rocky Robinson	Sep 25, 2010	Bonneville Salt Flats (USA)	605.7	376.36

FACT FLASH!
SPEED
760
MPH

THRUSTSSC

XTREME FACT
If you ever find yourself visiting Coventry in the UK, make sure you take a trip to the Coventry Transport Museum, because the ThrustSSC and Thrust2 (the fastest two cars, ever) are on display there, along with 640 other vehicles! You can even ride a simulator which gives you the ThrustSSC driver's perspective on the record.

CHECK IT OUT!
The Bluebird CN7 is a great example of how futuristic cars were envisaged back in the 1960s. Quirky design aside, its shell was incredibly streamlined, and an explosive 4,000-horsepower turboprop engine under its hood made it the fastest non-rocket-assisted car, ever!

FASTEST PRODUCTION CARS

Did you know that the expressways in Germany don't have speed limits? However, it would be madness to try to reach THESE speeds anywhere other than a race track...

	MODEL	YEAR BUILT	TOP SPEED (KPH)	(MPH)
1	Bugatti Veyron 16.4 Super Sport	2010	415.21	258
2	Bugatti Veyron 16.4	2005	408.5	253.8
3	McLaren F1	1993	372	231
4	Jaguar XJ220	1992	343	213
5	Bugatti EB110 GT	1991	336	209
6	Ferrari F40	1987	326.2	202.7
7	Porsche 959	1986	314	195
8	Ferrari 288 GTO	1984	303	188
9	Ferrari 365 GTB/4 Daytona	1968	280	174
10	Lamborghini Miura P400	1967	275	171

YOU RATE!

1 to 100

OFF THE CHART

NOBLE M600

The Veyron smashes the Noble M600 when it comes to top speed BUT the Noble has a higher brake horsepower of 650 bhp. Techy gobbledygook aside, this means its engine can handle cornering and inclines better than its nemesis the Veyron. Want one? Got a spare $320,000? It's yours!

BUGATTI VEYRON 16.4 SUPER SPORT

XTREME FACT

Its technology may be the cutting edge of driving technology now, but this car came from humble beginnings. Way back in 1909, Bugatti was founded. But it wasn't until 96 years later, in 2005, that the first version of the Veyron 16.4 was launched...

ANOTHER THING!

Wanna sit next to someone driving the fastest production car at top speed? Be warned, you will go through the same kind of physical stresses as an astronaut experiences during launch!

OUR TOP 10 UNOFFICIAL
MOVIE VEHICLES

	VEHICLE	MOVIE(S)
1	The Tumbler	The Dark Knight movies
2	Speeder Biker	Star Wars Episode VI: Return Of The Jedi
3	DeLorean DMC-12	Back To The Future trilogy
4	Serenity	Serenity
5	SHIELD Helicarrier	The Avengers
6	Ecto-1	Ghostbusters
7	The Batpod	The Dark Knight movies
8	Aston Martin DB5	James Bond movies
9	X-Jet	X-Men movies
10	Nautilus	20,000 Leagues Under The Sea

THE TUMBLER
XTREME FACT
Don't be fooled into thinking Batman's car was simply movie magic... The Tumbler was built from scratch and was a 2.5-tonne working beast of a machine! It could go 110 mph (177 kph) and jump distances of up to 30 ft (9 m)!

Check out the Top 10 biggest movies of all time on p230!

CHECK IT OUT!
It's not only made it into the Top 10 for speed, but the BMW S1000RR has been given numerous awards, including 2010 Motorcycle Of The Year from both *Motorcyclist* magazine and motorcycle.com.

YOU RATE!

1 to 100

SHOEI

TOP 10 FASTEST PRODUCTION MOTORBIKES

Street Hawk, the fictional super-bike from the 1985 TV series, could reach 300 mph (483 kph). But until that becomes a reality, these are the quickest...

	MODEL	MODEL YEARS	TOP SPEED (KPH)	(MPH)
1	Suzuki Hayabusa GSX1300R	1999-2000	312	194
2	Ducati Desmosedici RR	2007-08	307.3	191
3	BMW S1000RR	2010-present	303	188
=	MV Agusta F4 R 312	2007-present	303	188
5	Kawasaki ZX-14	2006-present	299.3	186
6	Kawasaki ZX-12R	2000-05	299.2	185.8
7	Honda CBR1100XX Super Blackbird	1996-2007	290	180
8	Kawasaki Ninja ZX-11	1990-2001	282	175
9	Bimota YB6 EXUP	1989-90	270	168
10	Kawasaki GPZ900R Ninja	1984-96	254	158

BIGGER THE BETTER

From building a goliath machine to micro-managing a project to create the tiniest vehicle ever, in this zone it's all about size leading the way...

TOP 10 HEAVIEST LAND TRANSPORTERS

The bulkiest brutes of the tarmac are here, and you really won't believe just how big these transportation devices can get...

	VEHICLE	USAGE	WEIGHT (TONNES)
1	Krupp Bagger 288	Power shovel excavator	45,500
2	Marion 5960-M aka Big Digger	Power shovel excavator	17,825
3	Marion 6360 aka The Captain	Power shovel excavator	15,000
4	TAKRAF Bagger 293	Power shovel excavator	14,200
=	Tenova TAKRAF SRs 8000	Power shovel excavator	14,200
6	F60 Overburden Conveyor Bridge	Moving bridges	13,600
7	4250-W aka Big Muskie	Power shovel excavator	13,500
8	SRs(H) 1050	Bucket wheel excavator	6,000
9	Herrenknecht EPB Shield S-300	Tunnel maker	4,364
10	Crawler-transporter	NASA shuttle transport	2,400

YOU RATE!
1 to 100

CHECK IT OUT!

If you're going to build something as massive and heavy as a space shuttle, you'll also have to find a vehicle powerful enough to move it! Here is the crawler-transporter using its 16 motors to deliver Discovery into place on August 4, 2009, at the Kennedy Space Center, Cape Canaveral, Florida, USA.

FACT FLASH!
WEIGHT
2,400 TONNES

3 SIDE

BIGGEST PASSENGER CARRIERS

1	**Airship**
2	Cruise liner
3	Hydrofoil
4	TGV train
5	Airbus A380
6	Seaplane
7	Taipei Metro (MRT)
8	Underground train
9	Tour coach
10	Double-decker bus

AIRBUS A380

STAT ATTACK

AIRBUS A380

Engines	4
Passengers	853
Active planes	89
Max speed	634 mph (1,020 kph)
Debut flight	April 27, 2005

XTREME FACT

Although 89 Airbus A380s are currently in operation, there have been 257 orders placed for the aircraft. Airbus is continuously innovating its specifications, too. A special reinforced adhesive called GLARE (glass laminate aluminium reinforced epoxy) is used to make the plane. This amazing material reduces the weight of the plane, as well as protecting the A380 against structural fatigue and damage.

GIANT MACHINE DISASTERS

	EVENT	DATE	WHAT HAPPENED
1	**Space Shuttle Challenger**	Jan 28, 1986	Exploded shortly after take-off, killing all on board
2	Deepwater Horizon spill	Apr 20, 2010	Oil leak caused huge damage to the environment
3	R101 airship crash	Oct 5, 1930	Crashed during a storm killing all on board
4	RMS Titanic	Apr 15, 1912	Hit an iceberg and sank killing more than 1,500 people
5	Harrow & Wealdstone rail crash	Oct 8, 1952	Three-train pileup that killed hundreds in the UK
6	Los Rodeos airport disaster	Mar 27, 1977	Two Boeing 747s collided on the runway
7	Costa Concordia	Jan 13, 2012	Struck rocks and partially sank
8	Belle Harbour crash	Nov 12, 2001	Flight 587 crashed shortly after take- off
9	Morrell airship crash	May 23, 1908	Crash-lands in Berkeley, California, USA
10	Shanghai rail disaster	Sep 27, 2011	Signal failure caused two trains to collide

BIGGER THE BETTER

PLANES WITH THE LARGEST WINGSPAN

If the notion of a big, heavy, metal plane actually getting off the ground has always impressed you, check out these giants for size...

YOU RATE!
1 to 100

	NAME	COUNTRY	DATE OF DEBUT FLIGHT	WINGSPAN (M)	(FT)
1	Hughes H-4 Spruce Goose	USA	Nov 2, 1947	97.5	319.8
2	An-225 Mriya	USSR (Russia)	Nov 21, 1988	88.4	290
3	Airbus A380-800	Europe (various)	Apr 21, 2005	79.8	261.8
4	Antonov An-124	USSR (Russia)	Dec 26, 1982	73.3	240.5
5	Convair B-36J-III	USA	Aug 8, 1946	70.1	230
=	Convair XC-99	USA	Nov 23, 1947	70.1	230
7	Boeing 747-8F	USA	Feb 8, 2010	68.5	224.7
8	Lockheed C-5B	USA	Jun 30, 1968	67.9	222.7
9	Boeing 747-400	USA	Feb 9, 1969	64.4	211.3
=	Antonov An-22	USSR (Russia)	Feb 27, 1965	64.4	211.3

ANTONOV AN-124

XTREME FACT

Costing up to $100 million to make, the Russian giant of the skies Antonov An-124 is still in use today. It holds the world record for the longest distance covered without the need for a refuel. In one flight taking 25.5 hours, the plane clocked 12,521 mi (20,151 km)!

OFF THE CHART

BOEING 747-100B/200B/300

This is no camera trickery, it actually happened! Here's a NASA-modified Boeing 747 carrying the Space Shuttle Endeavour on a very special "retirement flight" on September 21, 2012. The commemorative five-hour flight was part of 2012's celebrations of the Space Shuttle being taken out of service from space exploration.

FACT FLASH!
WINGSPAN
240
FT

SMALLEST MAN-DRIVEN MACHINES

PEEL P50

XTREME FACT

You might think an added advantage to owning a car this small would be easier parking, but the Peel P50 doesn't have a reverse gear! However, it's still a mighty mini-car and can reach a top speed of 38 mph (61 kph).

	VEHICLE NAME	TYPE
1	Bumblebee II	Plane
2	GEN H-4	Helicopter
3	BIG	Submarine
4	The Turtle	Combat submersible
5	Peel P50	Car
6	Smalltoe	Motorcycle
7	Rhino ATV	All-terrain vehicle
8	Superwedge	Hovercraft
9	The Badger	Tank
10	Micro Monsters	Mini Monster Truck

CHECK IT OUT!

Goose by name and goose by nature... The Hughes H-4 Spruce Goose was a heavy transport flying "boat". It regularly shipped allied munitions and vehicles (including 750 tanks at once). It's also one of a kind, as no more were ever crafted beyond the first model!

FACT FLASH!
WINGSPAN
320 FT

HIGH PERFORMANCE

When someone laid down the challenge: "Okay...
I want a really powerful car that is also superbly
streamlined," these car designers were all over it!

TOP 10 MOST POWERFUL CAR ENGINES

For gearheads who only care about their car having the power of
over 1,000 horses under the hood, these are the cars for you...

	MODEL	HORSEPOWER
1	SSC Ultimate Aero	1,287
2	2010 Hennessey Venom GT	1,200
=	Bugatti Grand Sport Vitesse Veyron	1,200
=	Bugatti's Super Sport	1,200
=	2004 Lotec Sirius	1,200
6	Koenigsegg Agera R	1,140
7	Zenvo ST1	1,100
8	Koenigsegg Trevita CCXR	1,018
9	2006 Bristol Fighter T	1,012
10	2005 Bugatti Veyron 16.4	1,001

YOU RATE!

1 to 100

ZENVO ST1

XTREME FACT

Car names often come
from marketing
brainstorms, but the
Danish Zenvo's origins are
much simpler: apparently
it's a combination of
the owners' names,
Jesper Jensen and
Troels Vollertsen...

ZENVO

CHECK IT OUT!

The Koenigsegg CCXR packs an acceleration punch, aided by its six gears and a supercharged 4.7L engine. For the über-extravagant, the limited-edition Trevita model comes with a diamond-weave carbon fibre bodywork. But even for those who love to collect expensive cars, the $4.85 million Trevita is not being mass-produced... Only three have been made!

EXTRA! Horsepower (hp) is exactly as it sounds. A power of 1 hp relates to the approximate power of a horse. Drag relates to how aerodynamic something is: the higher the value of drag, the slower and less aerodynamic the design.

FACT FLASH! HORSEPOWER 1,018

TOP 10 MOST STREAMLINED CARS

None of these makes are a drag as they are the 10 most aerodynamic cars around!

YOU RATE! 1 to 100

	MODEL	ORIGIN	YEAR BUILT	DRAG AREA (SQ FT)
1	GM EV1	USA	1996	3.95
2	Honda Insight	Japan	1999	5.10
3	Opel Calibra	Germany	1989	5.40
4	Ferrari 308 GTB	Italy	1980	5.54
5	Mazda RX-7	Japan	1993	5.61
=	McLaren F1	UK	1993	5.61
7	Bugatti EB110	France	1990	5.64
8	Honda CRX	Japan	1990	5.71
9	Honda NSX	Japan	2002	5.74
10	Toyota 2000GT	Japan	1968	5.76

GIVE IT A TRY... CAR DESIGN

Love cars? Have these designs got some creative ideas firing in your mind? Grab some pens and start sketching out what your ultimate drive would look like. Sleek? Like a tank? Monster truck? Get drawing!

TOP 10 HIGHEST PASSENGER NUMBERS

The cost of taking a trip to anywhere in the world is cheaper than ever before, so engineers have had to come up with craft that can carry thousands of people...

	NAME	MAIDEN VOYAGE	MAXIMUM CAPACITY
1	**Allure Of The Seas**	**Dec 1, 2010**	**6,400**
2	Oasis Of The Seas	Dec 5, 2009	6,296
3	Norwegian Epic	Jun 24, 2010	5,183
4	Freedom Of The Seas	Jun 4, 2006	4,375
=	Liberty Of The Seas	May 19, 2007	4,375
=	Independence Of The Seas	May 2, 2008	4,375
7	MSC Divina	May 27, 2012	3,900
8	Navigator Of The Seas	Dec 14, 2002	3,807
9	Mariner Of The Seas	Nov 16, 2003	3,807
10	RMS Queen Mary 2	Jan 12, 2004	3,090

YOU RATE! 1 to 100

STAT ATTACK

ALLURE OF THE SEAS

Maiden voyage .... December 1, 2010
Construction cost .... $1.2 billion
Weight.................. 225,282 gross tonnage
Number of decks 16
Crew 2,384

ALLURE OF THE SEAS

XTREME FACT

This vast floating fortress of luxury and entertainment is totally colossal in length, measuring a staggering 1,187 ft (362 m)!

FACT FLASH! CAPACITY 6,400 PASSENGERS

ALLURE the SEAS

COOLEST AMPHIBIOUS VEHICLES

Prefer to be driven down a road to cruising through the waves? These amazing machines can do BOTH...

	NAME	USAGE
1	**BHC SRN4 Mk III**	**Hovercraft**
2	BTR-80	Armoured personnel carrier (APC)
3	Land Tamer 8x8	All-terrain vehicle (ATV)
4	Hydra Spyder	Open-top amphibious sports car
5	AmphiCoach GTS-1	Passenger coach
6	SBK Engineering Shuttle-Bike	Floating mountain bike
7	Landing Craft Air Cushion (LCAC)	US Navy hovercraft
8	Orukter Amphibolos	1840s steam-powered barge with wheels
9	Sherman DD (Duplex drive)	World War II tank
10	Amphicar	Car and boat

BTR-80

XTREME FACT

Since 1986, the BTR-80 has been used by the Russian military. Built at the Arzamas Machinery Construction Plant, Nizhny Novgorod, Russia, it can carry up to 10 people and provides vital support to a variety of missions, including peacekeeping operations. As bulky as it is, it can achieve speeds of 50 mph (80 kph) on land and 5.5 mph (9 kph) in water.

CHECK IT OUT!

As extravagant as an amphibious car sounds, the Amphicar is surprisingly affordable at $15,000. As many as 4,500 were produced in the mid-1960s. It can achieve 70 mph (113 kph) on the road and 9 mph (15 kph) on water.

ANOTHER THING

What would you least expect to find on a cruise ship? A skating rink? Well, the Allure Of The Seas has one!

CASH MACHINES

Whether it's the development of a pricey transport system or an extravagant purchase by a flashy celebrity, the cost of these vehicles takes things up several gears...

TOP 10 MOST EXPENSIVE RAILWAY SYSTEMS

From the days of the humble steam train, technology has transformed the railways into high-speed wonders, with tunnels under oceans and even magnetic hover-trains!

	TRAIN	TYPE	PLACE(S)	COST ($ BILLION)	YOU RATE!
1	**CRH Beijing-Shanghai**	**High-speed railway**	**China**	**33.1**	1 to 100
2	CRH Beijing-Guangzhou-Shenzhen-Hong Kong	High-speed railway	China	18.46	
3	Toei Ōedo Line	Subway	Japan	18.4	
4	Channel Tunnel	High-speed railway	UK, France	15.4	
5	Barcelona Metro: Line 9	Metro rail system	Spain	8.9	
6	Channel Tunnel Rail Link	High-speed railway	UK	8.4	
7	Øresund Bridge	Railway and road bridge	Sweden, Denmark	5.7	
8	CRH Beijing-Tianjin Intercity	High-speed railway	China	3.2	
9	SMT (Shanghai Maglev Train)	High-speed magnetic levitation railway	China	1.33	
=	Transrapid	High-speed magnetic levitation railway	Germany	1.33	

CHECK IT OUT!

The CRH Beijing-Shanghai train can carry around 1,050 passengers. And it certainly is a high-speed service as it's capable of achieving 236 mph (380 kph)!

ANOTHER THING!

The CRH Beijing-Shanghai high-speed railway takes a route across the longest bridge in the world, China's Danyang-Kunshan Grand Bridge!

CRH₂-061C

XTREME FACT

This photo was taken just before Christmas 2009 in Beijing, China, and shows the construction process of the city's section of the high-speed railway line. At 818 mi (1,318 km) long, the railway provides an essential connection between Beijing and Shanghai, China's most important economic areas.

YOU RATE!
1 to 100

TOP 10 MOST EXPENSIVE PRIVATE BOATS

When money is no object, some people just spend, spend, spend... Even on something like a boat! Check out the insane cost of these...

	NAME	OWNER(S)	COST ($)
1	History Supreme	Anonymous Malaysian businessman	4.8 billion
2	Streets Of Monaco	Unknown	1.1 billion
3	Eclipse	Roman Abramovich	1 billion
4	Dubai	Sheikh Mohammed bin Rashid Al Maktoum	350 million
5	Superyacht A	Andrey Melnichenko	323 million
6	Al Said	Sultan Qaboos bin Said Al Said	300 million
7	Dilbar	Alisher Usmanov	263 million
8	Al Mirqab	Sheikh Hamad bin Jassim bin Jaber al-Thani	250 million
9	Lady Moura	Nasser Al-Rashid	210 million
10	Rising Sun	David Geffen	200 million

FACT FLASH!
COST
33.1 BILLION DOLLARS

FACT FLASH!
COST
1 BILLION DOLLARS

CHECK IT OUT!

Mini-submarine? Check. Armoured plating and a missile defence system? Absolutely. When you're making a 533 ft (163 m) luxury yacht with helipads, like the Eclipse, you may as well not hold back!

OFF THE CHART

OCTOPUS

Allegedly costing over $200 million, the super-yacht Octopus is owned by Paul Allen, who you may not know, but you'll certainly know his products... He's the co-founder of Microsoft.

CASH MACHINES

 TOP 10

MOST EXPENSIVE PLANES TO BUILD

The days of planes being exclusively propeller-driven are long gone. These days, they've almost got artificial intelligence level computer systems. Here are the costliest...

	NAME	PRODUCTION COST ($)
1	B-2 Spirit	2.4 billion
2	F-22 Raptor	350 million
3	C17A Globemaster III	328 million
4	P-8A Poseidon	290 million
5	VH-71 Kestrel	241 million
6	E-2D Advanced Hawkeye	232 million
7	F-35 Lightning II	122 million
8	V-22 Osprey	118 million
9	EA-18G Growler	102 million
10	F/A-18 Hornet	94 million

YOU RATE! 1 to 100

F-22 RAPTOR

XTREME FACT

When it comes to "stealth mode", planes like this F-22 Raptor are amazing. The radar signature, or signal, that the F-22 gives off is as tiny as a bee, meaning that even the most advanced radar systems can't see it!

FACT FLASH! COST **2.4 BILLION DOLLARS**

TOP 10

MOST EXPENSIVE PRODUCTION CARS

There are bank-breaking cars and then, way up the charts of bling, there are these extravagant ways of getting around...

	NAME	PURCHASE COST ($)
1	Bugatti Veyron Super Sports	2,400,000
2	Aston Martin One-77	1,850,000
=	Pagani Zonda Clinque Roadster	1,850,000
4	Lamborghini Reventón	1,600,000
=	Koenigsegg Agera R	1,600,000
6	Maybach Landaulet	1,380,000
7	Zenvo ST1	1,225,000
8	Hennessey Venom GT Spyder	1,100,000
9	McLaren F1	970,000
10	Ferrari Enzo	670,000

YOU RATE! 1 to 100

 **FACT FLASH!** COST **1.6 MILLION DOLLARS**

ANOTHER THING!

The B-2 can fly at a maximum height of 50,000 ft (15,240 m). That's more than 9 mi (15 km) up!

B-2 SPIRIT

XTREME FACT

This haunting-looking stealth bomber was first shown to the public on November 22, 1988. It is equipped with both nuclear and standard bombing capabilities, with the added advantage of being virtually invisible to radar. Many UFO sightings around the time of this plane's first test flights turned out to be none other than the B-2.

OUR TOP 10 UNOFFICIAL

BILLIONAIRE OWNERS & THEIR HARDWARE

	NAME	EXPENDITURE(S)
1	Sultan of Brunei	1,900 cars
2	Bill Gates	Classic Porsches
3	Richard Branson	Galactic plane: the SpaceShipTwo
4	Samuel Truett Cathy	Original Batmobile from the 1989 Batman movie
5	Roman Abramovich	Submarines
6	Donald Trump	Private Boeing 747
7	Frits Goldschmeding	Three-mast tall ship
8	Sultan of Brunei	Star Of India Rolls-Royce
9	Steven Spielberg	The sled from the 1941 movie Citizen Kane
10	Vijay Mallya	State-of-the-art yacht

CHECK IT OUT!

Once you've splashed out $1.6 million on the Lamborghini Reventón, make sure you look after your precious purchase as only 21 have been built.

ARMED AND DANGEROUS

Military organizations around the world develop an array of fearsome vehicles and cutting-edge weaponry to protect their countries against dangerous assailants...

TOP 10 BIGGEST TANKS

There have been many kinds of tanks created for the military, but these 10 are the largest that man has conjured up...

	TANK	COUNTRY	YEAR	LENGTH (M)	(FT)
1	**Landkreuzer P 1500 Monster**	**Germany**	1942 (concept)	**42**	**137.8**
2	Landkreuzer P 1000 Ratte	Germany	1942 (concept)	35	114.8
3	K-Wagen	Germany	1917 (concept)	13	42.7
4	T-28	USA	1933 (503 built)	11	36.1
=	FCM F1	France	1940 (concept)	11	36.1
6	Panzer VIII Maus	Germany	1944 (two prototypes)	10	32.8
=	E-100 Tiger-Maus	Germany	1944 (concept)	10	32.8
=	O-I	Japan	1944 (one built)	10	32.8
=	TOG2	UK	1940 (one prototype)	10	32.8
=	A39 Tortoise	UK	1945 (six built)	10	32.8

YOU RATE!
1 to 100

FACT FLASH!
LENGTH
36 FT

T-28

XTREME FACT

Here's the fourth biggest tank in the world, the mighty 100-tonne T-28 super heavy tank (not to be confused with the 1930s Russian tank, the T28). Unlike most tanks, the T-28 didn't have a movable turret and cannon. Instead, the 4 in (10 cm) caliber gun barrel was fixed onto the front of the tank.

OFF THE CHART

LEOPARD II BATTLE TANK

The German Leopard II tank narrowly misses out on a place in the Top 10 by just a few centimetres, with a length of 32.7 ft (9.97 m). This model of tank first appeared for duty in 1979 and is still in operation today. It's not a slowcoach, either, with a speed of 45 mph (72 kph)!

Y·902 065

OUR  UNOFFICIAL

BATTLING MOVIE ROBOTS

When it comes to Team T-10's love of the movies, we adore all things robotic! Here are the 'bot fights that we have watched over and over again, MANY times...

	ROBOT WAR	MOVIE	DATE
1	**Rodimus Prime vs Unicron**	**Transformers: The Movie**	**1986**
2	Sentinel Prime vs Optimus Prime	Transformers: Dark Of The Moon	2011
3	Atom vs Zeus	Real Steel	2011
4	Megatron vs Optimus Prime	Transformers: The Movie	1986
5	T-X vs T-800	Terminator 3: Rise Of The Machines	2003
6	EVE & WALL·E vs Axiom's Robots	WALL·E	2008
7	T-800 vs Marcus Wright	Terminator Salvation	2009
8	R2-D2 vs Battle Droids	Star Wars Episode III: Revenge Of The Sith	2005
9	Good vs Evil Bill and Ted Robots	Bill & Ted's Bogus Journey	1991
10	V.I.N.Cent vs Maximillian	The Black Hole	1979

CHECK IT OUT!

This is the terrifying metallic endoskeleton, technically known as Cyberdyne Systems Model 101. But, to the casual observer, it's simply The Terminator. In the 2009 movie *Terminator Salvation*, a combination of full-scale puppets and visual effects created the cyber-creature.

ATOM VS ZEUS

XTREME FACT

To make the robot boxing fights in *Real Steel* look as realistic as possible, a lot of the action was based on motion captured from actual boxers' moves.

SHUFFLE UP

Did we get the robot wars in the right order? Do you think that Atom vs Zeus should be Number One? Shuffle them into the list you like the most!

1 ....
2 ....
3 ....
4 ....
5 ....
6 ....
7 ....
8 ....
9 ....
10 ....

Not a big fan of some of them? Add any movie robo-battles you like... It's YOUR list!

TOP 10 MISSILES WITH THE LONGEST RANGE

Nations around the world have developed some mighty missiles capable of travelling extraordinary distances as part of their defence systems...

	NAME	COUNTRY	RANGE (KM)	(MI)
1	Taepo Dong-2	North Korea	15,000	9,320.6
2	DF-5A	China	13,000	8,077.8
=	Minuteman III	USA	13,000	8,077.8
4	DF-5	China	12,000	7,456.5
5	DF-31A	China	11,270	7,002.9
6	SS-27	Russia	11,000	6,835.1
7	SS-25	Russia	10,500	6,524.4
8	SS-18 / 19	Russia	10,000	6,213.7
9	M51	France	8,000	4,971
=	SS-N-18	Russia	8,000	4,971

YOU RATE! 1 to 100

MINUTEMAN III

XTREME FACT

This epic shot shows the might of the Minuteman III inside a silo (an underground missile launch facility). There are 450 of these rockets dotted around US airbases...

FACT FLASH! RANGE 8,077.8 MI

CHECK IT OUT!

It's very important that missiles are tested, but these are done with unarmed versions. Here is an M51 being tested over the Bay of Biscay (French Atlantic coast) on November 9, 2006.

TOP 10 LARGEST BATTLESHIPS

YOU RATE! 1 to 100

These floating fortresses are astounding examples of engineering. Check out the weight of these oceanic titans...

	NAME(S)	COUNTRY	WEIGHT (TONNES)
1	Yamato	Japan	72,809
=	Musashi	Japan	72,809
3	BB-61 to BB-64	USA	55,710
4	Bismarck	Germany	50,153
=	Tirpitz	Germany	50,153
6	Richelieu	France	47,500
=	Jean Bart	France	47,500
8	HMS Hood	UK	46,200
9	B-55, BB-56	USA	44,800
10	King George V	UK	44,780

YAMATO

XTREME FACT

Although this photo shows the Yamato receiving direct hits from US bombers (during the Battle of the Philippine Sea in June 1944), the Japanese battleship never actually fired any of her armaments. This image was taken during her retreat from the fight.

STAT ATTACK

YAMATO

Length ....862.9 ft (263 m)
Speed ....31.1 mph (50 kph)
Aircraft capabilities 7
Maiden voyage .... August 8, 1940
Sank.................................... April 7, 1945

FACT FLASH!
WEIGHT
72,809
TONNES

CHECK IT OUT!

Pictured in this epic photo (below) is the French battleship Richelieu, shortly after her maiden voyage on January 14, 1939. And, as big as she was, she could still cut through the waves at a speed of 34.8 mph (56 kph).

When it comes to classified designs and hi-tech capabilities, these are the machines that serve the most secret of operations...

TOP 10 WORST NUCLEAR SUBMARINE DISASTERS

There are always risks when technology advances into weaponized areas. These are the submarine accidents that had the most fatalities...

	SUBMARINE	COUNTRY	DISASTER	DATE	INJURED	FATALITIES
1	USS Thresher (SSN-593)	USA	Sank	Apr 10, 1963	-	129
2	K-141 Kursk	Russia	Sank	Aug 12, 2000	-	118
3	USS Scorpion (SSN-589)	USA	Sank	May 22, 1968		99
4	K-8	Russia (USSR)	Fire	Apr 11, 1970	-	88
5	Eurydice	France	Sank	Mar 4, 1970	-	57
6	K-278 Komsomolets	Russia (USSR)	Sank	Apr 7, 1989		42
7	K-152 Nerpa	Russia	Unknown	Nov 8, 2008	21	20
8	K-431	Russia (USSR)	Explosion	Aug 10, 1985	-	10
9	K-27	Russia (USSR)	Reactor damaged	May 24, 1968	-	9
=	Greenville	USA	Collision	Feb 9, 2001	-	9

K-141 KURSK

XTREME FACT

Although the K-141 Kursk had the ability to fire cruise missiles that were nuclear powered, the explosion that sank it was the result of a malfunction during practice fires with "blanks". The accident occured when hydrogen peroxide leaked out of one of the torpedoes.

FACT FLASH!
FATALITIES
118

CHECK IT OUT!

Here is the K-141 Kursk being brought to the surface on October 23, 2001. It took 26 reinforced steel cables to hoist the submarine off the ocean bed!

CHECK IT OUT!

The Northrup Grumman X-47B is a top-secret, future-shock machine, which is all very exciting, but it's also incredibly costly. For example, Smiths Aerospace, the company that scored the contract to supply JUST the landing gear for the X-47B, got itself a deal worth a casino-happy $150 million! If that's just for the wheels and struts, the fuel caps must be worth about $7 million!

GIVE IT A TRY...
SCIENCE TIME

Check out your nearest science museum where you'll be able to learn all about how submarines operate. Discover how their sonar radar and nuclear armaments work... You might even be able to pick up a submarine model-making kit!

BOEING X-45A
XTREME FACT

This bizarre craft may look like something out of an *X-Men* movie, but this drone is the real deal! The X-45A can carry "smart" bombs that can be programmed as to where and when they detonate.

FACT FLASH!
SPEED
207
MPH

TOP 10 FASTEST UNMANNED STEALTH AIRCRAFT

No pilot required here... These super-advanced planes take off, fly, carry out classified missions and land, all remotely!

	AIRCRAFT	COUNTRY	SPEED (KPH)	(MPH)
1	**Barracuda**	Spain/Germany	1,041.3	647
2	Dassault nEUROn	France	980	608.9
3	Boeing X-45A	USA	919	571
4	MiG Skat	Russia	800	497.1
5	RQ-3 Dark Star	USA	464	288.3
6	Northrop Grumman X-47B	USA	333	206.9
7	Rheinmetall KZO	Germany	220	136.7
8	Armstechno NITI	Bulgaria	120	74.6
9	RQ-170 Sentinel	USA	Classified	Classified
10	BAE Systems Taranis	UK	Classified	Classified

YOU RATE!
1 to 100

X-45A

OUR TOP 10 UNOFFICIAL

ALIEN CRAFT DISCOVERY CLAIMS

	LOCATION OF ALLEGED CRASH	REPORTED INCIDENTS	DATE
1	Aurora, Texas (USA)	Crashed craft and the burial of an alien	Apr 17, 1897
2	Tunguska, Siberia (Russia)	Gigantic explosion that some believe was a UFO	Jun 30, 1908
3	Roswell, New Mexico (USA)	Crashed UFO and aliens recovered by the Army	Jul 2, 1947
4	Gdynia (Poland)	Aliens recovered from harbour crash	Jan 21, 1959
5	Praia Grande, São Paulo (Brazil)	UFOs attacked Brazilian military	Nov 4, 1957
6	Primorsky Krai (Russia)	Mothership craft filmed in the sky	Aug 26, 2012
7	Ely, Nevada (USA)	16 alien bodies retrieved from a crash site	Aug 14, 1952
8	Padcaya (Bolivia)	UFO crashed into a mountain but left no trace	May 6, 1978
9	Llandrillo, Wales (UK)	Roads sealed off after a UFO crashed	Jan 23, 1974
10	Los Angeles (USA)	Military opened fire at a UFO in the sky	Feb 24, 1942

PRIMORSKY KRAI

XTREME FACT

Galliya Zheneveskaya was the witness who captured the unexplained video footage of a huge UFO over Primorsky Krai in 2012.

OUR TOP 10 UNOFFICIAL

SECRET MILITARY INTELLIGENCE PROJECTS

	PROJECT NAME	DETAILS
1	Area 51	Alleged development of new technologies from alien craft
2	Majestic 12	Alleged 1947 recovery of the crashed UFO in Roswell, New Mexico
3	Hughes Mining Barge	CIA allegedly stole secrets from an enemy submarine
4	Operation Morning Light	Russian cleanup of crashed radioactive satellite
5	MKUltra	Controversial CIA experiments on humans for mind control
6	Project Sign	Official 1948 investigation into UFOs by US Air Force
7	Project Grudge	Continued 1949 UFO studies by US Military
8	Project Blue Book	Further US Air Force studies into UFO phenomena
9	Project Nutmeg	Nuclear armament tests by US in Nevada desert
10	B-2 Stealth Bomber	Previously classified aircraft project

CHECK IT OUT!

We wanted to show you a closer picture of this facility, but then again, it is highly classified! Here's a glimpse of Area 51 in Rachel, Nevada, USA. Signs that warn "Deadly force is authorized", mean you can be legally killed if you trespass!

TOP 10 MOVIE SECRET AGENT/ DETECTIVE VEHICLES

Government agents and detectives often have a mechanical sidekick. These cars definitely play a key supporting role in their owners' adventures on the big screen...

	VEHICLE	CHARACTER(S)	MOVIE(S)	NUMBER OF MOVIES	BOX OFFICE ($ WORLDWIDE)
1	**Aston Martin DB5**	**James Bond**	**The Bond movies**	**6**	**2,197,325,582**
2	Agent K's Modified 1987 Ford LTD Crown Victoria	Agent K	Men In Black trilogy	3	1,655,236,118
3	The Tumbler	Batman	The Dark Knight movies	2	1,278,777,117
4	1972 Corvette Convertible	Det James Carter	Rush Hour trilogy	3	854,603,131
5	VW Beetle and Cadillac for time travel	Austin Powers	The Austin Powers movies	2	608,672,289
6	Chrysler Voyager	John and Jane Smith	Mr. & Mrs. Smith	1	478,207,520
7	Mystery Machine	Mystery Inc gang	Scooby-Doo movies	2	457,117,536
8	Futuristic Lexus	Chief John Anderton	Minority Report	1	374,218,673
9	1967 Pontiac GTO Custom Hardtop	Xander Cage	xXx	1	277,448,382
10	Black Beauty (Modified 1965 Chrysler Imperial)	The Green Hornet	The Green Hornet	1	227,817,248

Source: IMDB.com

YOU RATE! 1 to 100

ASTON MARTIN DB5
XTREME FACT

The Aston Martin DB5 starred in *Skyfall* (2012), the biggest UK movie of all time! In its first 40 days in UK cinemas, *Skyfall* made $151,914,626, beating *Avatar*'s $151,494,552, which took 11 months!

FACT FLASH! APPEARED IN **6** MOVIES

NASSAU 56526 BAHAMAS

STAT ATTACK

BOND'S ASTON MARTIN DB5

Weapons............Machine guns, overriders, wheel slashers

Protection..........Bullet-proof rear window shield, ejector seat

Stealth ....Rotating number plates

Speed ....142 mph (229 kph)

First time in a Bond movie ....Goldfinger (1964)

HIGH-OCTANE MACHINES

YOUR SHOUT!

Check out these questions. Can you answer them without looking back through the book?

Welcome to the first "Your Shout" zone of this book! You'll find one of these activity sections after each and every T-10 zone. It's your chance to test your knowledge AND get creative...

YOU RATE!

T-10 MACHINES

Gather up all of the "You Rate" scores that you gave the machines and put them in order here, to see which one has triumphed...

	NAME	"YOU RATE" SCORE
1		
2		
3		
4		
5		
6		
7		
8		
9		
10		

EXTREME SPEED

TRUE OR FALSE...

1. The 10th fastest aircraft is slower than the fastest land vehicle. T ☐ F ☐

2. An aircraft has not broken into the Top 10 Fastest In The Air since 1976. T ☐ F ☐

3. Ferrari occupy five spots in the Top 10 Fastest Production Cars list. T ☐ F ☐

Can you name the car manufacturer that has this bull as its logo?

NAME:

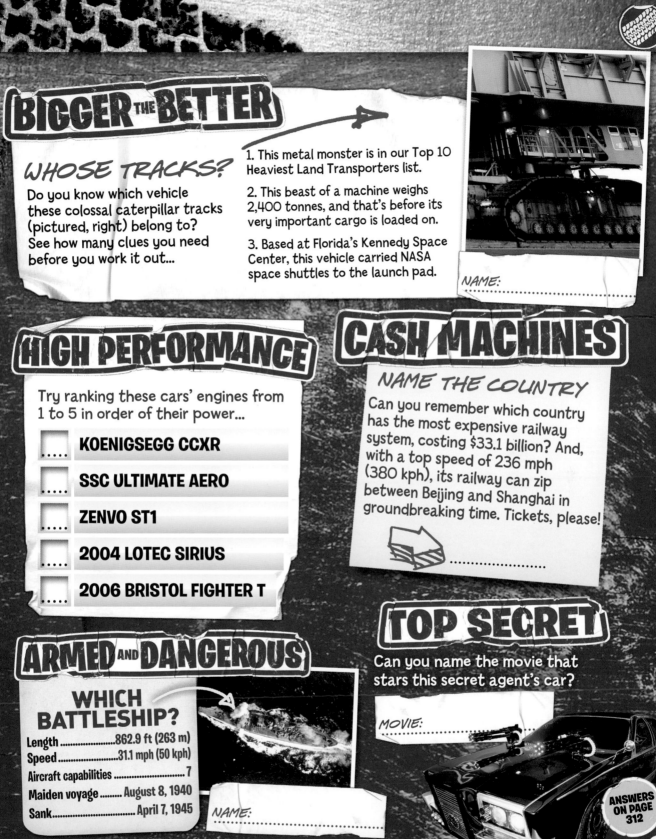

BIGGER THE BETTER

WHOSE TRACKS?

Do you know which vehicle these colossal caterpillar tracks (pictured, right) belong to? See how many clues you need before you work it out...

1. This metal monster is in our Top 10 Heaviest Land Transporters list.

2. This beast of a machine weighs 2,400 tonnes, and that's before its very important cargo is loaded on.

3. Based at Florida's Kennedy Space Center, this vehicle carried NASA space shuttles to the launch pad.

NAME:
....

HIGH PERFORMANCE

Try ranking these cars' engines from 1 to 5 in order of their power...

.....	KOENIGSEGG CCXR
.....	SSC ULTIMATE AERO
.....	ZENVO ST1
.....	2004 LOTEC SIRIUS
.....	2006 BRISTOL FIGHTER T

CASH MACHINES

NAME THE COUNTRY

Can you remember which country has the most expensive railway system, costing $33.1 billion? And, with a top speed of 236 mph (380 kph), its railway can zip between Beijing and Shanghai in groundbreaking time. Tickets, please!

....

ARMED AND DANGEROUS

WHICH BATTLESHIP?

Length	862.9 ft (263 m)
Speed	31.1 mph (50 kph)
Aircraft capabilities	7
Maiden voyage	August 8, 1940
Sank	April 7, 1945

NAME:
....

TOP SECRET

Can you name the movie that stars this secret agent's car?

MOVIE:
....

ANSWERS ON PAGE 312

35

ANIMAL KINGDOM

Us humans think that we're pretty cool, what with our internet, skateboard parks and MP3 players. However, can we fly? Can we breathe underwater? Do we have massive claws? Okay, some girls do head to crazy-town with super-long nail extensions! But what we're addressing here is that the animal kingdom is WAY cooler than you could ever have imagined it to be...

OUT FOR BLOOD

Planet Earth is pretty awesome, right? It's beautiful but it's also home to some very dangerous creatures! We're kicking things off by saluting the kings of all things deadly, from the safety of these pages...

TOP 10 MOST DEADLY

There are many ways that animals can be dangerous to us, but these guys cause more human deaths every year than any other...

	CREATURE	HUMAN DEATHS PER YEAR
1	Mosquito	2,000,000
2	Tsetse Fly	300,000
3	Indian Cobra	50,000
4	Buthidae Family of Scorpions	3,250
5	Saltwater Crocodile	1,000+
6	Hippopotamus	500+
7	Elephant	500
8	Cape Buffalo	200+
9	African Lion	150
10	Australian Box Jellyfish	90

AFRICAN LION

XTREME FACT

Heard of a "pride" of lions? It means "family". The mums do most of the hunting, leaving the dads (with the cool hairdos) to protect their land. Plus, those huge claws? Like X-Men's Wolverine, lions can retract them so they're always razor-sharp!

ANOTHER THING!

These powerful predators are pretty lazy. A-hunting they may go, but male lions are said to spend up to 20 hours of each day just lounging about!

YOU RATE! 1 to 100

MOSQUITO

XTREME FACT

It's actually the diseases spread through the bites of mosquitoes and tsetse flies that cause so many deaths. Another crazy fact: that squealing noise mosquitoes make? It comes from their wings. Unbelievably, they flap at a mind-blowing 300-600 times per second!

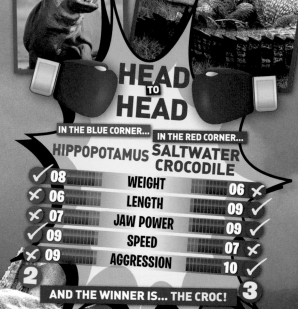

HEAD TO HEAD

IN THE BLUE CORNER...		IN THE RED CORNER...
HIPPOPOTAMUS		**SALTWATER CROCODILE**
✓ 08	WEIGHT	06 ✗
✗ 06	LENGTH	09 ✓
✗ 07	JAW POWER	09 ✓
✓ 09	SPEED	07 ✗
✗ 09	AGGRESSION	10 ✓
2		**3**

AND THE WINNER IS... THE CROC!

ANOTHER THING!

Also called Sasquatch and Yeti, there have been thousands of reported sightings but no scientific proof that Bigfoot really exists.

BEEN & SEEN

Tick the boxes of the predators you've seen with your own eyes, in the wild or at a zoo!

- ☐ LION
- ☐ OWL
- ☐ BEAR
- ☐ HAWK
- ☐ CROCODILE
- ☐ TIGER
- ☐ BAT
- ☐ SNAKE
- ☐ WOLF
- ☐ SHARK

OUR TOP 10 UNOFFICIAL

MYTHICAL MONSTERS

	*CRYPTOZOOLOGICAL BEAST	DESCRIBED AS
1	Loch Ness Monster	Plesiosaur
2	Bigfoot	Giant hairy beast
3	Mokele-mbembe	Looks like a Brontosaurus
4	Cadborosaurus	Huge sea serpent
5	Beast of Bodmin Moor	Large wildcat
6	Chupacabra	Hairless dog/wolf
7	Mothman	Man-sized, with wings
8	Jersey Devil	Like a horse with wings
9	Kappa	Turtle-like amphibian
10	Batsquatch	Giant reptile bat

EXTRA!

*CRYPTOZOOLOGY is the study of "*cryptids*" (from the Greek for "hidden") - creatures/plants that may exist because of many reported events, but no scientific evidence has been found to back these reports up. There are actually hundreds of examples of strange animal sightings in lakes and on land all over the world!

TOP 10 MOST POISONOUS

It's not just size, claws and jaws that makes them deadly.
These guys use some seriously killer toxins...

YOU RATE!
1 to 100

GOLDEN POISON DART FROG

XTREME FACT

These little guys are only 5 cm (2 in) long, but they're SO toxic! The poison secreted from ONE could kill 10 people! Colombia's Emberá (the indigenous people) wipe the toxins on darts: the ammo for the blowpipes they hunt with.

	ANIMAL	HOW MANY HUMANS COULD ITS POISON KILL?
1	Box Jellyfish	3,600
2	Sea Snake	1,000
3	Inland Taipan Snake	100
4	Blowfish	30
5	Blue-ringed Octopus	26
6	Fat Tailed Scorpion	20
=	Marbled Cone Snail	20
8	Stonefish	18
9	Brazilian Wandering Spider	12
10	Golden Poison Dart Frog	10

TOP 10 LONGEST SNAKES

Slithering and sneaky, snakes are amazing assassins of the animal kingdom. Check out how big these tubular titans can get...

YOU RATE!
1 to 100

FACT FLASH!
LENGTH
49
FT

	SNAKE	LONGEST FOUND (M)	(FT)
1	Reticulated Python	14.94	49
2	Green Anaconda	11.28	37
3	Scrub Python	7.92	26
4	African Rock Python	6.1	20
5	King Cobra	5.64	18.5
6	Boa Constrictor	3.96	13
7	Bushmaster	3.05	10
8	Indian Python	2.99	9.8
9	Diamondback Rattlesnake	2.74	8.9
10	Western Rat Snake	2.44	8

CHECK IT OUT!

Funny word "python", isn't it? Any fans of mythological monsters out there? You'll like this: in ancient Greek culture Python was a dragon, shown as a serpent. Apollo, the Greek god of music, slayed the "dragons". He obviously hated croc 'n' roll...

VAMPIRE BAT

XTREME FACT

These little suckers really ARE vampires! They are the only mammals that feed exclusively on blood. On the dining list are: large birds, cattle, horses, pigs, dogs and, yes, humans. Garlic bread doesn't ward them off, either...

NIGHT HUNTERS

The dead of night is a time when nocturnal predators thrive. We think these ones rule...

	PREDATOR	DESCRIPTION
1	**Vampire Bat**	**This bat survives on blood**
2	Anglerfish	Deep-sea fish with a lure on its head
3	Sugar Glider	Australian possum that can glide
4	Gila Monster	Big lizard with venomous saliva
5	Caiman	Related to crocs and alligators
6	Great Horned Owl	Tufts of feathers that look like horns
7	Aye-aye	Lemur with big eyes and long fingers
8	Vinegarroon	Resembles but is not a true scorpion
9	Tasmanian Devil	Meat-eating marsupial
10	Zorilla (Striped Polecat)	Skunk-like African mammal

STAT ATTACK

HUNTSMAN

Eats......................... Insects & invertebrates

Venomous...................... Yes, but not fatal

Home countries.......................... Australia, the Caribbean, Florida, Hawaii, New Zealand, South Africa & Southeast Asia

Lifespan........................ Approx two years

Parent skills.................. Can lay 200 eggs

TOP 10 LARGEST SPIDERS

Are you, or is someone you know, scared of spiders? Best look away... This list features some massive eight-legged freaks!

	SPIDER	LEG SPAN (CM)	(IN)
1	**Huntsman**	30	11.8
2	Brazilian Salmon Pink	27	10.6
3	Goliath Birdeater	25.4	10
=	Wolf Spider	25.4	10
5	Purple Bloom Bird-eating Spider	23	9
6	Hercules Baboon	20.3	8
7	Hysterocrates Spellenbergi	17.8	7
8	Brazilian Wandering Spider	15	5.9
=	Cerbalus Aravensis	15	5.9
10	Tegenaria Parietina	14	5.5

YOU RATE!
1 to 100

A Huntsman spider devouring a helpless Praying Mantis

41

OUT FOR BLOOD

TOP 10 POWERFUL JAWS

Us humans have a bite pressure of around 120 psi, but check out these beastly bites!

YOU RATE! 1 to 100

	ANIMAL	BITE FORCE PSI
1	**Nile Crocodile**	5,000
2	Great White Shark	4,000
3	Alligator	2,000
4	Hippopotamus	1,800
5	Gorilla	1,300
6	Hyena	1,100
7	Tiger	1,000
=	Alligator Snapping Turtle	1,000
9	Harpy Eagle	910
10	Bear	750

NILE CROCODILE

XTREME FACT

This incredible predator takes on any sized prey in the water or on land. Water buffalo, kangaroos, sharks, humans, these crocs have got the power, armour and the attitude to kill them all. Never smile at a crocodile...

COMPARE-O-METER

Here's how the impact of our actions measures up...

HUMAN BITE
84.4 t
120 psi

MARTIAL ARTS ROUNDHOUSE KICK
984 t
1,400 psi

HEAVYWEIGHT BOXER'S PUNCH
998 t
1,420 psi

TOP 10 MOST SHARK ATTACKS

2,463 unprovoked shark attacks have been recorded, ever. If you think that figure is low, check out our Xtreme Fact over on the right...

	LOCATION	TOTAL ATTACKS	FATAL ATTACKS
1	USA (exc. Hawaii)	980	37
2	Australia	488	144
3	Africa	314	85
4	Asia	124	51
=	Oceania/Pacific Islands (exc. Hawaii)	124	50
6	Hawaii	105	8
=	South America	105	23
8	Antilles and Bahamas	67	15
9	Middle America	56	27
10	New Zealand	47	8

Source: Florida Museum Of Natural History

GREAT WHITE

XTREME FACT

The Great White strikes fear into many of us, but it's a myth that this amazing creature loves to eat people. Surfers and swimmers simply resemble one of its favourite foods, seals. So shark attacks on humans are simply a case of mistaken identity!

MOST BIZARRE WAYS TO KILL

	ANIMAL	METHOD USED
1	**Electric Eel**	**Electric shock**
2	Python	Swallows huge prey alive & whole
3	Crocodile	The death roll
4	Praying Mantis	Eats her husband after mating
5	Boa Constrictor	Crushes and suffocates
6	Viperfish	Dislocates jaw to eat
7	Amazonian Tree Ant	Builds traps & dismembers prey
8	Hagfish	Burrows into creatures/eats it inside-out
9	Assassin Bug	Injects toxin via mouth tube
10	Football Fish	Lit branches on head attract prey

CROC DEATH ROLL

XTREME FACT

Although crocs have mind-blowingly powerful jaws, they cannot chew from side to side at all! This is why they have to kill their prey with a "death roll". They clamp on and, with ferocious force, drown their victim and tear it limb from limb. Terrifying, but utterly amazing.

EXTRA! Recent studies have discovered that the ancient Tyrannosaurus Rex could bite down with a staggering force of 13,489 psi (9,480 t), that's almost three times more powerful than the mighty reptilian bite of the Nile Crocodile!

CHECK IT OUT!

Going fishing off the coast of Australia? You might need to get a bigger boat... Statistically, if you want to avoid the chance of a shark bite, be careful swimming there, too, as one-third of all fatal shark attacks have occurred here!

FACT FLASH! BITE 4,000 PSI

SHUFFLE UP

What would you have as your Number One? Now you've seen our Top 10, why not list them in the order that creeps you and your friends out the most!

1
2
3
4
5
6
7
8
9
10

Know of any other bizarre animal killing methods? Add them in, it's YOUR list!

OUT FOR BLOOD

FACT FLASH!
UP TO
100
IN A PACK

ANOTHER THING!

The hyena has a large heart, which means it is built for stamina! This powerful predator can track its prey over great distances.

HYENA PACK

XTREME FACT

These carnivores are very social, and it often sounds like they're laughing! Hyenas use a wide range of different howls, cackles and calls to communicate and these often warn other pack members of nearby trouble.

TOP 10

PACK HUNTERS

Some of the planet's best hunters kill as a team. With these guys, there's a lot more than "double trouble" for their prey...

CHECK IT OUT!

Army Ants are the ultimate pack hunter. Their queen can lay up to 120,000 eggs, and an ant colony can feature a staggering TWO MILLION adults! No wonder they're such busy creatures. That's a lot of mouths to feed...

YOU RATE!
1 to 100

	ANIMAL	GROUP SIZE
1	**Army Ants**	**100,000+**
2	Piranha	100+
3	Hyena	up to 100
4	Chimpanzee	36
5	Dolphin	15
6	Wolf	10
=	African Wild Dog	10
8	Killer Whale	8
9	African Lion	6
10	Harris Hawk	2-6

BLACK MAMBA

XTREME FACT

This snake gets its name from the striking blue-black colour inside its mouth. Don't get too close as it has the most rapid-acting venom of any snake! It's also the fastest snake in the world, slithering up to 12.4 mph (20 kph).

HEAD TO HEAD

IN THE BLUE CORNER... IN THE RED CORNER...

BLACK MAMBA		PHILIPPINE EAGLE
✗ 01	WEIGHT	02 ✓
✗ 02	SIZE	03 ✓
✗ 04	SPEED	05 ✓
✗ 05	JAW POWER	06 ✓
✗ 06	ATTACK	07 ✓
0		5

AND THE WINNER IS... THE EAGLE!

CHECK IT OUT!

The Philippine Eagle is arguably one of the kings of the clouds. This impressive raptor (bird of prey) will happily attack larger animals such as young pigs, big lizards, other birds, and even deadly snakes.

TOP 10 LARGEST BIG CATS

Of all the predatory felines out there, these are the cats that carry the most muscle...

YOU RATE!
1 to 100

	CAT	WEIGHT (KG)	(LBS)
1	Tiger	420	925.9
2	Lion	270	595.3
3	Jaguar	140	308.6
4	Cougar	120	264.6
5	Snow Leopard	73	160.9
6	Leopard	64	141.1
7	Cheetah	55	121.3
8	Lynx	35	77.2
9	Clouded Leopard	25	55.1
10	Caracal	20	44.1

OUR TOP 10 UNOFFICIAL KILLER BATTLES

Believe it or not, all of these beastly battles actually do occur in nature!

1	Alligator vs. Python
2	Black Mamba vs. Crowned Hawk-eagle
3	Moray Eel vs. Octopus
4	Tiger vs. Crocodile
5	Sea Snake vs. Tiger Shark
6	Puma vs. Brown Bear
7	Walrus vs. Polar Bear
8	Wasp vs. Tarantula
9	Lion vs. King Cobra
10	Hyena vs. Lion

MOST HUNTED

The petrified prey that is to become victim of the food chain can often pack a punch of its own. Here, we look at the animals that have the best means to protect themselves, and species that have sadly become endangered...

TOP 10 LARGEST DEFENCE WEAPONS

It's not about being the biggest, it's about how effective their defensive element is compared to their body size. These guys have the tools and the talents...

FACT FLASH!
HORNS
59
IN

	ANIMAL	WEAPON (IN COMPARISON TO SIZE OF ANIMAL)
1	Fiddler Crab	Massive claws
2	Stag Beetle	Armour plating and pincers
3	Pistol Shrimp	Shock-wave claw
4	Mantis Shrimp	Boxing fists
5	Lobster	Pincers
6	Crested Porcupine	Barbed quills
7	Caribou	Antlers
8	Elk	Antlers
9	Elephant	Tusks
10	Rhinoceros	Horns

YOU RATE!
1 to 100

CHECK IT OUT!
The Pistol Shrimp is dangerously weaponized! When it snaps its claw shut, the 60 mph (97 kph) shock wave sends bubbles that collapse, creating for a brief moment the temperature of the sun! Prey has no chance...

OFF THE CHART

CAPE BUFFALO
Cape Buffalo are not to be messed with. They maim and kill over 200 people every year! So it will come as no surprise that Africans also call them the "Black Death". As for those horns? They can grow to an insane 59 in (150 cm) long, so even their predators like lions and crocodiles have to be wary...

TOP 10

FASTEST LAND PREY

If you're the chosen target of one of these, you better run fast because these guys are SPEEDY...

YOU RATE!

1 to 100

	ANIMAL	SPEED (KPH)	(MPH)
1	**Pronghorn Antelope**	98	61
2	Wildebeest	80	49.7
=	Thomson's Gazelle	80	49.7
4	Elk	72	44.7
=	Cape Hunting Dog	72	44.7
6	Coyote	69	42.9
7	Gray Fox	67	41.6
8	Hyena	64	39.8
=	Zebra	64	39.8
=	Mongolian Wild Ass	64	39.8

CHECK IT OUT!

The Pronghorn Antelope rightfully earns the number one spot here. While the Cheetah may achieve faster speeds, that's only for accelerated bursts. This means that when the hungry Cheetah slows down to catch its breath, the Pronghorn Antelope can maintain that 61 mph (98 kph) speed and often escapes!

COMPARE-O-METER

Here's how some human speeds measure up

FASTEST RUN

FASTEST TENNIS SERVE

FASTEST RUN

FASTEST TENNIS SERVE

44.7 kph
27.8 mph

263 kph
163.4 mph

BLOWFISH

XTREME FACT

The poisonous liver from these spiny dudes may only give a bigger fish munching on them a bad tummy ache, but to us humans, it can be fatal. Can you believe that specialized chefs actually train for years to learn how to prepare this toxic fishy for dinner?! We'll just have the fish sticks, thanks...

OUR TOP 10 UNOFFICIAL

BEST DEFENCE METHODS

	ANIMAL	WEAPON
1	**Vampire Squid**	**Inverts itself & lights up**
2	Hairy Frog	Breaks its limbs to reveal claws
3	Horned Lizard	Squirts blood from its eyes
4	Pygmy Sperm Whale	Emits a dark red cloud
5	Blowfish	Puffs up with deadly spines
6	Veined Octopus	Equips itself with shells & coconuts
7	Three-Banded Armadillo	Rolls into a protective ball
8	Stingray	Poisonous barb in its tail
9	Hognose Snake	Pretends it's dead
10	Malaysian Ant	Explodes itself

TOP 10 PRIORITY SPECIES

The World Wildlife Fund (WWF) has a list of animals that help focus conservation awareness. These are the most endangered...

TIGER
XTREME FACT

Tigers are an endangered species because logging and deforestation destroys their homes, and there's also the horrible act of poaching. The tiger's fur is sold at illegal trade shows, and their body parts are highly prized for use in traditional medicines, mostly because of the tiger's physical strength and its roots being in ancient mystical folklore.

CROSS RIVER GORILLA
XTREME FACT

The numbers of this great ape are at a staggering low. This is due to the mix of ongoing destruction of where they live, disease and poaching. Conservationists are working hard to save this amazing animal.

	ANIMAL	EST. NUMBER REMAINING
1	Chinese Paddlefish	Possibly extinct
=	Wondiwoi Tree Kangaroo	Possibly extinct
3	Northern White Rhinoceros	4
4	Amur Leopard	37
5	Javan Rhinoceros	Less than 50
6	Amsterdan Albatross	100
7	Sumatran Rhinoceros	Less than 200
8	Cross River Gorilla	300
9	Mountain Gorilla	786
10	Kemp's Ridley Turtle	1,000

Source: WWF

GIVE IT A TRY... CONSERVATION

There are many wildlife conservation groups out there that you can join to help protect the natural world, especially endangered species. Check out WWF (www.gowild.wwf.org.uk) and National Geographic (www.kids.nationalgeographic.co.uk) for fun activities!

ANOTHER THING!

Longline fishing has a devastating effect on all marine life, including Leatherback Turtles, who get tangled up in the lines and drown.

TOP 10 ENDANGERED MAMMALS

Although not as terrifyingly low in numbers, these mammals are still classified as being in danger of becoming extinct...

	ANIMAL	EST. NUMBER REMAINING
1	**Panda**	**1,600**
2	Greater One-Horned Rhino	2,913
3	Tiger	3,200
4	Black Rhinoceros	4,838
5	Snow Leopard	6,500
=	Nigeria-Cameroon Chimpanzee	6,500
7	Sumatran Orangutan	7,500
8	Clouded Leopard	10,000
9	Southern White Rhinoceros	20,000
10	Polar Bear	25,000

Source: WWF

BEEN & SEEN

These animals are all dying out in many parts of the world. If you've seen one in the last year, tick the box!

- [ ] TORTOISE
- [ ] SHARK
- [ ] BUMBLEBEE
- [ ] CORAL REEF
- [ ] TOAD
- [ ] EAGLE
- [ ] OTTER
- [ ] DEER
- [ ] SQUIRREL
- [ ] BEAR

CHECK IT OUT!

Conservation workers in Africa are doing an amazing job of helping the population of Black Rhinos. Although there are now 90 per cent less Black Rhinos than three generations ago, happily numbers are on the increase. But the battle against the illegal trade of rhino horns continues...

ANOTHER THING!

Want to find out more about ways you can help put a stop to poaching? Check out the World Wildlife Fund at worldwildlife.org

RAPID MOVEMENT

Blink your eyes... Did you miss it? Some of the weird and wonderful animals out there can do things at speeds so fast they make us lumbering humans look like complete slowpokes!

FACT FLASH!
SPEED
202
MPH

PEREGRINE FALCON

XTREME FACT

There isn't just one kind of this super-bird, there are 19 different species of Peregrine Falcon all over the world! In fact, it's only Iceland, Antarctica and New Zealand that they don't hang out in so, chances are, you'll find these fast falcons in the skies above your head. Your local bird reserve will almost definitely have one as well.

North American Peregrine Falcon

TOP 10

FASTEST OF ALL

When you compare the speeds of animals from the land, sea and air, which come out as the most lightning-quick? These 10 speed-demons...

YOU RATE! 1 to 100

	ANIMAL	SPEED (KPH)	(MPH)
1	**Peregrine Falcon**	**325**	**202**
2	Spine-tailed Swift	171	106.2
3	Magnificent Frigatebird	153	95.1
4	Spur-winged Goose	142	88.2
5	Cheetah	113	70.2
6	Sailfish	110	68.3
7	Pronghorn Antelope	98	61
8	Springbok	97	60.3
9	Mako Shark	95	59
10	American Quarter Horse	86	53.4

COMPARE-O-METER

The Peregrine Falcon is almost as fast as a sports car!

FREEFALL PARACHUTE JUMP	BUGATTI VEYRON 16.4 SUPER SPORT	PASSENGER JET
192 kph	**415.2** kph	**885** kph
119.3 mph	**258** mph	**550** mph

CHECK IT OUT!

Magnificent by name and magnificent by nature! Speed aside, the Magnificent Frigatebird knows how to make the most of its wingspan (over two metres) and the thermal updrafts, rising to a staggering 8,202 ft (2,500 m). It is also happy to spend rather a long time up there, often travelling for more than 124 mi (200 km) before it decides to land and have a breather. Legend!

OFF THE CHART

GRAY FOX

Only just missing out on being one of our T-10 Fastest Of All, the Gray Fox is still a very quick quadruped (four-footed animal) at 42 mph (67 kph). This breed is thought to be one of the most primitive of its kind.

OUR TOP 10 UNOFFICIAL

SPEEDY REACTIONS

	ANIMAL
1	**Trap-jaw Ant**
2	Star-nosed Mole
3	Frogfish
4	Giant Palm Salamander
5	Wood Stork
6	Housefly
7	Hummingbird
8	Chameleon
9	Shortfin Mako Shark
10	Asian Cobra

CHECK IT OUT!

Have you ever seen a snake charmer? The species they use is the Asian Cobra, because its hood and threatening swaying looks like it is dancing. Sensibly, the venom from this cobra is "milked" out first to prevent any nasty accidents...

TOP 10 FASTEST OCEAN CREATURES

With a little help from things like speedboats and Jet Skis, we can reach pretty fast speeds on the water, but these guys take all the prizes for underwater travel...

	FISH	SPEED (KPH)	(MPH)
1	**Sailfish**	**110**	**68.3**
2	Mako Shark	95	59
3	Marlin	80	49.7
4	Wahoo	78	48.5
5	Bluefin Tuna	70	43.5
6	Great Blue Shark	69	42.9
7	Bonefish	64	39.8
=	Swordfish	64	39.8
9	Four-winged Flying Fish	56	34.8
10	Tiger Shark	53	33

YOU RATE!
1 to 100

FACT FLASH! SPEED **68** MPH

GREAT BLUE SHARK

XTREME FACT

Also known simply as the Blue Shark, this is one of the fastest sharks in the world and we're giving it the full respect of its GREAT name! Huge fins and built like a torpedo, this shark loves to eat fast-moving small fish and squid.

CHECK IT OUT!

So that it doesn't cause any drag to slow it down, the Sailfish's magnificent sail is often kept down during swimming. The exact reason behind this amazing fin is still unknown, but raising it can aid sharp turns as well as act like a defensive weapon to shock predators.

SAILFISH

XTREME FACT

Check out the speed again of this incredible animal. No engine required! The Sailfish can reach almost the same speed that you've experienced in a grown-up's car on the highway. That's all down to its design. This oceanic race leader has a very muscular body, a massive powerful tail, all paring down to that sleek barb of a nose. It really is designed like a fishy rocket, and the Sailfish is also famous for its eye-popping leaps out of the water.

ANOTHER THING!

Even this shark's babies are efficient! The mums give birth to live young, and there can be more than 100 shark pups!

COMPARE-O-METER

Even an ocean liner like Titanic looks slow!

RMS TITANIC
43 *kph*
26.7 *mph*

JET SKI
113 *kph*
70.2 *mph*

CHECK IT OUT!

If any sea animal should earn the name "Flipper" it is the Humpback Whale. With pectoral fins (the ones on its sides) being a massive 16.4 ft (5 m) long, that's nearly one-third of its entire body length! These are gentle giants who migrate together to tropical waters to breed every year.

TOP 10 LONGEST JOURNEYS

You may think you travel far for your summer vacation, but check out the distances these animals clock up!

STAT ATTACK

ARCTIC TERN

Length .... Up to 15.4 in (39 cm)
Wingspan .... Up to 33.5 in (85 cm)
Lifespan .... Up to 30 years
Diet .... Insects, invertebrates, marine worms, small fish

YOU RATE!
1 to 100

ANOTHER THING!

No prizes for guessing where this seal gets its name from! Its elephant-like trunk makes VERY loud honking noises for communication.

	ANIMAL	DISTANCE (KM)	(MI)
1	**Arctic Tern**	**71,000**	**44,117**
2	Sooty Shearwater	64,000	39,768
3	Elephant Seal	32,200	20,008
4	Pectoral Sandpiper Bird	28,000	17,398
5	Humpback Whale	25,700	15,969
6	Grey Whale	22,500	13,981
7	Leatherback Turtle	19,300	11,992
8	Pied Wheatear Bird	18,000	11,185
9	Short-tailed Shearwater	17,000	10,563
10	Bar-tailed Godwit Bird	11,500	7,146

TOP 10 FASTEST ANIMALS ON FOUR LEGS

What's the fastest vehicle on land you've ever been in? Check out the speeds these animals achieve just with their legs...

YOU RATE!
1 to 100

	ANIMAL	SPEED (KPH)	(MPH)
1	**Cheetah**	113	70.2
2	Pronghorn Antelope	98	60.9
3	Springbok	97	60.3
4	American Quarter Horse	86	53.4
5	Lion	80	49.7
6	African Wild Dog	72	44.7
=	Elk	72	44.7
8	Coyote	69	43
9	Thomson's Gazelle	64	39.8
=	Wildebeest	64	39.8

FACT FLASH!
SPEED
70
MPH

CHEETAH

XTREME FACT

The Cheetah really is built to be an acceleration machine. Its spine is very flexible with a body that is elongated, narrow and packed with muscles. The paws' semi-retractable claws are perfect for traction and dragging its prey to the ground.

OFF THE CHART

GREYHOUND

Our trusty four-legged friend the Greyhound may not have made it into the Top 10, but it's still the fastest dog in the world, reaching speeds of around 42.3 mph (68 kph)! Greyhound racing is hugely popular all over the world, and sees the dogs competing by chasing a fluffy lure (made to look like a rabbit/hare). However, even as a pet, these dogs love to exercise by sprinting in the park.

EXTRA! Greyhounds may be fast but they also love to be lazy. If you know a greyhound, you'll know how much they love sleeping.

GIVE IT A TRY...
PETS & PALS RACE

Get together with your friends, their families and their dogs! Yes, it's time for a cross-species sprint race. Put you and your pals (and your FURRY four-legged friends) to the test in a local park and see who is the fastest!

CHECK IT OUT!

The Ostrich is a bird and it does have wings, but it cannot fly! Good thing it can run so fast to avoid predators...

FACT FLASH! SPEED 44.7 MPH

FASTEST ANIMALS ON TWO LEGS

TOP 10

We humans can run at an average speed of 8 mph (13 kph), but most of these animals make a mockery of that when they run two-footed...

YOU RATE! 1 to 100

	ANIMAL	SPEED (KPH)	(MPH)
1	Ostrich	72	44.7
2	Eastern Grey Kangaroo	70	43.5
3	Red Kangaroo	69	42.9
4	Western Grey Kangaroo	50	31.1
5	Antilopine Kangaroo	60	37.3
6	Black Spiny-tailed Iguana	35	21.7
7	Roadrunner Bird	32	20
8	Black Wallaroo	25	15.5
9	Swamp Wallaby	15	9.3
10	Basilisk Lizard	8	5

COMPARE-O-METER

These human skills are pretty speedy, too...

SPEED ICE SKATING

SKATEBOARDING

ICE SPEED SKATING
59 kph
36.6 mph

SKATEBOARD SPEED RECORD
129 kph
80.7 mph

OUR TOP 10 UNOFFICIAL

DANGEROUS JOURNEYS

	ANIMAL	ENCOUNTERS
1	Atlantic Salmon	Waterfalls, rapids, thousands of miles
2	Leatherback Turtle	To tropical waters over 9,300 mi away
3	Monarch Butterfly	3,100 mi trip: North America to Mexico
4	Humpback Whale	Avoiding whale poachers for 6,200 mi
5	Wildebeest	Crocodiles, lions, drowning, 1,900 mi trip
6	Common Toad	Roads, cars, predators, pesticides
7	Zebra	Huge river crossings, lions, crocodiles
8	Narwhal Whale	Fishermen, ice entrapment, polar bears
9	Hummingbird Hawk-moth	Weather and predators from Africa to UK
10	Osprey	Planes and weather changes on its long trip

ATLANTIC SALMON

XTREME FACT

The Salmon's migration journey is like an Iron Man Challenge, times a million! It travels thousands of miles, battles waterfalls, has rapids to swim against and then there are the predators to escape: eagles, bears, seals, sea lions, otters, sharks and, of course, humans.

SIZING THINGS UP

Let's cut to the chase: when it comes to focusing on the animal kingdom we love to look in awe at the biggest, don't we? As most of the prehistoric giants are no longer living (but we WILL cover them), these are our planet's medal-winners for their size...

TOP 10 HEAVIEST ON LAND

Of all the creatures that roam the land, these 10 dwarf all the others with their magnificent mass. Check them out...

ANIMAL	WEIGHT (KG)	(LB)
1 African Bush Elephant	12,000	26,455
2 Asian Elephant	5,200	11,464
3 Southern Elephant Seal	4,000	8,818
= Southern White Rhinoceros	4,000	8,818
5 Hippopotamus	3,200	7,054
6 Pacific Walrus	2,000	4,409
= Saltwater Crocodile	2,000	4,409
8 Black Rhinoceros	1,400	3,086
9 Giraffe	1,360	2,998
10 Wild Water Buffalo	1,200	2,645

YOU RATE! 1 to 100

AFRICAN BUSH ELEPHANT

XTREME FACT

Along with its chart-winning weight, this elephant is a towering 13+ ft (4 m) tall! And the gentle vegetarian giant uses its tusks as defensive weapons, but mainly to dig and scrape the ground and trees looking for food.

FACT FLASH!
WEIGHT
26,455
LB

CHECK IT OUT!

If we had based our "Heaviest" chart on ALL life on Earth, all 10 entries would have been types of whales. They are unbelievably MASSIVE! The heaviest living animal is the Blue Whale, at a colossal 146 tonnes. That's as much as 30 elephants!

HEAD TO HEAD

IN THE BLUE CORNER...   IN THE RED CORNER...

	PACIFIC WALRUS		POLAR BEAR	
✓	06	WEIGHT	05	✗
✓	06	SIZE	05	✗
✗	04	SPEED	05	✓
✗	05	JAW POWER	06	✓
✗	05	ATTACK	07	✓
2				**3**

AND THE WINNER IS... POLAR BEAR!

OUR TOP 10 UNOFFICIAL

BIGGEST MOVIE BEASTS

	BEASTS	MOVIE
1	Unknown Creature	Cloverfield
2	Godzilla	Godzilla
3	Mothra	Mothra
4	Chitauri's Space Eel	The Avengers
5	Kraken	Clash Of The Titans
6	Mountain Dragon	How To Train Your Dragon
7	Exogorth	Star Wars: Episode V
8	Jabberwocky	Alice In Wonderland
9	Kong	King Kong
10	Spinosaurus	Jurassic Park III

TOP 10 TALLEST OF ALL

Have you got any really tall friends? So have we, but these towering titans make them look like little toy figures...

	ANIMAL	HEIGHT (M)	(FT)
1	Giraffe	5.5	18
2	African Bush Elephant	4	13
3	Polar Bear	3.4	11.1
4	Asian Elephant	3	9.8
5	Ostrich	2.8	9.2
6	Grizzly Bear	2.7	9
7	Moose	2.3	7.6
8	Shire Horse	2.1	6.9
=	Red Kangaroo	2.1	6.9
10	Sarus Crane	1.8	6

YOU RATE! 1 to 100

ANOTHER THING!

The giraffe reaches the acacia tree to eat its leaves with its long neck (6.6 ft) and impressive tongue (17.7 in)!

SIZING THINGS UP

TOP 10 WIDEST WINGSPANS

Wouldn't it be cool to be able to fly? And if you had a wingspan like these graceful giants of the sky, it would be amazing!

YOU RATE! 1 to 100

	BIRD	WINGSPAN (M)	(FT)
1	**Wandering Albatross**	3.6	11.8
=	**Great White Pelican**	3.6	11.8
3	Marabou Stork	3.4	11.2
=	Andean Condor	3.4	11.2
5	Mute Swan	3.1	10.17
6	Bearded Vulture	3	9.8
7	Griffin Vulture	2.8	9.2
=	California Condor	2.8	9.2
9	Grey Crowned Crane	2.5	8.2
=	Golden Eagle	2.5	8.2

GREAT WHITE PELICAN

XTREME FACT

They may have one of the largest wingspans, but the Great White Pelican also has one of the slowest wing-beats at just over one flap per second. Are these sky giants solitary animals? No. As many as 75,000 pairs have been known to hang out together in breeding colonies. That's a lot of big wings!

CHECK IT OUT!

The majestic wings of the Golden Eagle are a key component to its success as a predator. This bird of prey can reach a speed of 149 mph (240 kph) during a dive, meaning its unsuspecting target, which amazingly can include young deer, goats and sheep, rarely sees it coming...

TOP 10 LARGEST INSECTS

If you don't like normal-sized creepy crawlies, you might want to hold someone's hand while you read these measurements... These are all absolutely GIGANTIC critters!

YOU RATE! 1 to 100

	INSECT	MEASUREMENT	(CM)	(IN)
1	**Giant Stick Insect**	Length	61	24
2	Giant African Millipede	Length	38.5	15.2
3	Amazonian Giant Centipede	Length	33	13
4	Atlas Moth	Wingspan	32	12.6
5	Queen Alexandra's Birdwing Butterfly	Wingspan	31	12.2
6	Titan Beetle	Length	16.7	6.6
7	Giant Weta	Length	15	5.9
8	Giant Dragonfly	Wingspan	12.5	4.9
9	Actaeon Beetle	Length	12	4.7
10	Goliath Beetle	Length	11	4.3

CHECK IT OUT!

Not just huge but poisonous, too. Although not usually fatal to humans, the Giant Centipede's venom can cause great pain and make you very ill.

GIVE IT A TRY... BUTTERFLY HOUSE

Ever been to a Butterfly House? They don't just house all manner of amazing butterflies, they often have a huge range of whacky insects, too. Ask a grown-up to help you find out where your local "insect zoo" is and take your T-10 book along to see how many you can recognize and name.

TALLEST DOGS KEPT AS PETS

Do you have a dog or do you know someone who does? Check out these big barkers and see how they compare in size...

YOU RATE!
1 to 100

	DOG	HEIGHT (CM)	(IN)
1	**Irish Wolfhound**	86.4	34
2	Great Pyrenees	81.3	32
3	Leonberger	80	31.5
4	Neapolitan Mastiff	78.7	31
5	Great Dane	76.2	30
6	Newfoundland	71.1	28
7	Saint Bernard	69.9	27.5
=	Bernese Mountain Dog	69.9	27.5
9	Bullmastiff	68.6	27
=	Dogue De Bordeux	68.6	27

BEEN & SEEN

There are more animals and insects on your doorstep than you'd think! Tick the ones you've spotted:

- ☐ **DRAGONFLY**
- ☐ **WASP**
- ☐ **CATERPILLAR**
- ☐ **PIKE**
- ☐ **ALBATROSS**
- ☐ **WOODLOUSE**
- ☐ **NEWT**
- ☐ **FOX**
- ☐ **HAWK**
- ☐ **CENTIPEDE**

IRISH WOLFHOUND

XTREME FACT

In Ancient Rome, the Wolfhound was a beast to be feared. Nowadays, it's a lovable four-legged friend. The modern Irish Wolfhound is known for its loyalty and quiet temperament, and reflects the "pack mentality" of its wolf heritage by enjoying being with its family.

TOP 10 LARGEST TEETH

They don't have the luxury of electric toothbrushes, but that doesn't stop these animals' chompers from growing to monstrous sizes...

FACT FLASH!
TEETH
3
IN

YOU RATE!
1 to 100

	ANIMAL	LENGTH (CM)	(IN)
1	African Elephant	300	118.1
2	Walrus	100	39.4
3	Hippopotamus	91	35.8
4	Warthog	23	9.1
5	Sperm Whale	18	7.1
6	Lion	9	3.5
7	Great White Shark	7.5	3
8	Goliath Tigerfish	7	2.8
9	Alligator	4	1.6
10	Vampire Fish	3.5	1.4

GREAT WHITE SHARK
XTREME FACT

When it comes to teeth, this guy has MORE than got it covered. Not only are the teeth serrated and big, but the shark replaces any damaged or lost teeth regularly. In fact, it can go through 1,000 each year, as new teeth are in multiple rows, ready to rotate into place when one is broken away. No wonder this is such a formidable flesh-tearing fish.

STAT ATTACK

WARTHOG

Diet ...Berries, dead animals, grass, insects
Protection ....Fast sprinting, tusks
Lifestyle..............Live in groups in Africa
Weight.....................Up to 250 lb (113 kg)
Enemies .. Big cats, crocodiles, humans

CHECK IT OUT!

The Walrus's tusks are used to carve holes in the ice and also to help it get out of the water, but they are also perfect for fighting. When it comes to choosing girlfriends, the male walrus is not shy about getting physical to prove who is the toughest and the coolest potential mate. This takes place with the clash of tusks to prove which one is "the man" in the walrus herd.

FACT FLASH!
TEETH
39.4
IN

OUR TOP 10 UNOFFICIAL

STRONGEST ANIMALS
(RELATIVE TO SIZE)

	ANIMAL
1	**Rhinoceros Beetle**
2	Elephant
3	Leafcutter Ant
4	Gorilla
5	Golden Eagle
6	Tiger
7	Ox
8	Anaconda
9	Mussels
10	Grizzly Bear

ANOTHER THING!

The Anaconda is an incredibly powerful beast and happily takes on wild pigs, jaguars and caimans, which it crushes then swallows whole!

CHECK IT OUT!

It may be a beetle but don't underestimate this little guy - it's the strongest creature on the planet. The Rhinoceros Beetle can lift not 50 times, not 500 times, but a staggering 850 times its body weight! Imagine carrying 850 people on your back...

TOP 10 BIGGEST BEARS

With their powerful jaws, claws and body mass, if you go down to the woods today, you wouldn't want to come face-to-face with these guys...

YOU RATE!
1 to 100

	ANIMAL	WEIGHT (KG)	(LBS)
1	**Polar Bear**	1,002	2,209
2	Kodiak Brown Bear	967	2,131.9
3	Grizzly Bear/North American Brown Bear	680	1,499
4	Brown Bear	635	1,399.9
5	Black Bear	250	551.2
6	Moon Bear	200	440.9
7	Spectacled Bear	175	385.8
8	Giant Panda Bear	150	330.7
9	Sloth Bear	124	273.4
10	Sun Bear	70	154.3

FACT FLASH!
WEIGHT
1,499 LB

GRIZZLY BEAR

XTREME FACT

With 8 in (15 cm) claws, it's no wonder the Grizzly Bear is a predator we should be wary of. Don't worry, though, because it actually eats fish, and those claws come in handy for tearing off bark to find bugs, too. This bear is also more likely to stand up tall, often over 10 ft (3 m), and roar as a warning, before using its paws as a means of defending itself.

HIGHLY EVOLVED

In the animal kingdom, you need a lot more than big teeth and claws to survive. These incredible life forms have been around longer than dinosaurs, and they're still goin' strong...

TOP 10 OLDEST SURVIVING SPECIES

We often think "living dinosaurs" are things like crocodiles. However, there are life forms that have remained unchanged for much, much longer...

FACT FLASH!
TIME EXISTED
505
MILLION YEARS

	SPECIES	TIME EXISTED (YEARS)
1	Cyanobacteria	2.8 billion
2	Nautilus	500 million
3	Jellyfish	505 million
4	Sponge	580 million
5	Horseshoe Crab	445 million
6	Coelacanth	360 million
7	Ginkgo Biloba Tree	270 million
8	Horseshoe Shrimp	200 million
9	Sturgeon	200 million
10	Martialis Heureka Ant	120 million

YOU RATE!
1 to 100

JELLYFISH

XTREME FACT
The oldest fossilized evidence of prehistoric jellyfish (505 million years ago) was found by the University of Utah's Richard D. Jarrard and Susan Halgedahl. What's mind-blowing is that the fossil is incredibly similar to the jellyfish that we see in our oceans today.

CHECK IT OUT!

If we're being specific, technically, the Horseshoe Crab isn't a crab at all, it is more closely related to the likes of the scorpion and spider. It looks like a stingray tank, doesn't it? But that spiny-looking tail isn't a poisonous barb at all, it's just used to help move the Horseshoe Crab along. The tail is also handy to help right the crab if it gets stuck on its back. When it comes to swimming, this crab can happily travel upside-down, using its legs and claws to propel it as well.

HARDEST TO DESTROY

CHECK IT OUT!

The Cockroach, yuck! It scavenges and feeds on most things and can live for ages without food or water. Nuclear radiation isn't much of a problem, either. It also adapts to pesticides so quickly that humans have trouble staying ahead of the battle.

	SPECIES
1	**Immortal Jellyfish**
2	Tardigrade
3	Haemaphysalis Flava (Tick)
4	Cockroach
5	Giant Weta
6	Giant Tube Worm
7	Bedbug
8	Ocean Quahog
9	Barbus Thermalis Fish
10	Lungfish

TOP 10 BACK FROM THE DEAD

Many species that were thought extinct have been found alive & kicking! These "resurrected" creatures made their comeback on our chart...

YOU RATE!
1 to 100

CHECK IT OUT!

Since these cute little Furby-like primates have been rediscovered, there's been a boom of interest in the mouse-sized animal. You can even find Pygmy Tarsier fan clubs online, which have been set up for supporters of this struggling species to get together and help spread the Pygmy Tarsier word.

	LIFE FORM	EXTINCT?	REDISCOVERED
1	**La Palma Giant Lizard**	1500s	2007
2	New Zealand Storm Petrel	1850s	2003
3	Terror Skink	1870s	2003
4	Banggai Crow	1885	2009
5	Nelson Small-eared Shrew	1894	2009
6	Dwarf Cloud Rat	1896	1960
7	Pygmy Tarsier	1921	2000
8	Lord Howe Island Stick Insect	1930	2001
9	Black Kokanee Salmon	1940	2010
10	Bavarian Pine Vole	1962	2001

HIGHLY EVOLVED

TOP 10 SONIC SUPER-ANIMALS

One of the amazing talents some animals have is "echolocation": using their sound to "see" other animals and obstacles. Here are the most talented sonic-searchers...

	ANIMAL	SOUND FREQUENCY	RANGE
1	**Bottlenose Dolphin**	**Varied**	**Exceptional**
=	Killer Whale	Varied	Exceptional
3	Greater Horseshoe Bat (Microbat)	Varied	Broad to detailed
=	Egyptian Fruit Bat (Megabat)	Varied	Broad to detailed
5	Porpoise	Narrowband	Directional/exact
=	Pygmy Sperm Whale	Narrowband	Directional/exact
7	Oilbird	Limited	Basic
=	Swiftlet Bird	Limited	Basic
9	Tenrec	Low	Very basic
=	Shrew	Low	Very basic

YOU RATE! 1 to 100

CHECK IT OUT!

Think that ALL bats use echolocation? They don't! There are two kinds of bats: microbats and megabats. All microbats echolocate but of the megabats, just the Egyptian Fruit Bat has this amazing skill. It only eats fruit, but does use the skill for navigation and communication.

HEAD TO HEAD

IN THE BLUE CORNER... **IN THE RED CORNER...**

KILLER WHALE		GREAT WHITE SHARK
✓ 08	WEIGHT	06 ✓
✓ 08	SIZE	07 ✗
✓ 07	SPEED	07 ✓
✓ 08	JAW POWER	07 ✗
✗ 07	ATTACK	08 ✓
4		**3**

AND THE WINNER IS... KILLER WHALE!

BOTTLE-NOSE DOLPHIN

XTREME FACT

Dolphins and whales use echolocation (their biological sonar) to find food and chat with one another. You'll have heard them on nature documentaries with their series of whistles and clicks. When they make a sound, it bounces back through their surroundings and is analyzed by the their brain. How cool is that?!

XTREME FACT

Monarchs migrate across thousands of miles, but this ISN'T the amazing thing about it. What is? Well, it only lives for a few months. This means that after a bunch of miles, it lays eggs, dies, then its young continues the migration route! How do they know where to go?!

CHECK IT OUT!

Mystique is one of our favourite comic book characters, and she's played brilliantly by Rebecca Romijn and Jennifer Lawrence in the *X-Men* films. She is the most evolved as she is a shapeshifter: taking on the appearance and voice of anyone! Not only that, she has kick-ass agility and fighting skills. She's one lethal lady...

OUR TOP 10 UNOFFICIAL

UNBELIEVABLE SENSES

	ANIMAL	SENSE
1	**Grizzly Bear**	**Can smell prey 19 mi (30 km) away**
2	Jumping Spider	Sees in four primary colours & 360° views
3	Pigeon	GPS/navigation system
4	Monarch Butterfly	Telepathic/psychic with dead relatives
5	Shark	Detects electrical impulses
6	Jewel Beetle	Senses fire from 9 mi (15 km) away
7	Mantis Shrimp	Can see different bands of light
8	Bat	Echolocation
9	Cat	Sees in almost complete darkness
10	Moth	Smells a potential mate 6 mi (10 km) away

OUR TOP 10 UNOFFICIAL

MOST EVOLVED SCI-FI CHARACTERS

Here are the awesomely evolved movie characters we love the most...

	CHARACTER(S)	MOVIE(S)	SPECIAL QUALITIES
1	**Mystique**	**The X-Men movies**	**Can shape-shift into anything**
2	Mogwai	Gremlins 1 & 2	Furball eggs change to reptilian beasts
3	Wolverine	The X-Men movies	Super-fast healer & razor claws
4	Triffid	The Day Of The Triffids	Intelligent, walking, attacking plant
5	Crusoe	The Water Horse	Mystical plesiosaur-type monster
6	Sleestak	Land Of The Lost	Bug-eyed, intelligent lizard men
7	Dark Phoenix	X-Men: The Last Stand	Jean Grey's unstoppable mutation
8	Howl	Howl's Moving Castle	Can turn into a dragon-like creature
9	Balrog	The Lord Of The Rings	Towering fire demon
10	Catbus	My Neighbour Totoro	A cat that is also a functioning bus

MILLIONS OF YEARS AGO...

We've shown you how amazing our animal kingdom is, but what about millions of years ago, when the biggest EVER beasts ruled the Earth? Let's step back in time to when massive teeth and claws got you a long way in the prehistoric ecosystem...

TOP 10 LARGEST CARNIVORES OF THEM ALL

Who doesn't think that the T-Rex rules? We LOVE him! But did you know that Mr. Rex was NOT the biggest meat-eater?

	DINOSAUR	LENGTH (M)	(FT)
1	**Spinosaurus**	18	59
2	Carcharodontosaurus	13.2	43.3
=	Giganotosaurus	13.2	43.3
4	Chilantaisaurus	13	42.7
5	Tyrannosaurus Rex	12.3	40.4
6	Tyrannotitan	12.2	40
7	Torvosaurus	12	39.4
=	Allosaurus	12	39.4
9	Acrocanthosaurus	11.5	37.7
10	Deltadromeus	11	36.1

Source: David Martill, Palaeobiologist

YOU RATE! 1 to 100

SPINOSAURUS

XTREME FACT

The name Spinosaurus means "spine lizard", and it is likely you've seen this ferocious-looking dino as the star "villain" in the movie *Jurassic Park III*. Its long, narrow skull and jaws have led scientists to believe that, like a crocodile, it could have lived and hunted near rivers. The first remains of this dino fan-fave were found in Egypt 101 years ago in 1912.

VELOCIRAPTOR

We think *Jurassic Park* is an awesome movie, and the Velociraptor was one of the coolest things in it. But did you know that the Velociraptor was really about 6.9 ft (2.1 m) long? The ones in the movie were based more on its cousin, Deinonychus, which was over 9.8 ft (3 m) in length!

OFF THE CHART

COMPARE-O-METER

Here are some modern day sizes to compare these extinct giants to:

BUS

LENGTH OF A BUS
15 m
49.2 ft

SOCCER FIELD

LENGTH OF A SOCCER FIELD
100 m
328.1 ft

ANOTHER THING!

The "sail" is made of neural spines that grew to more than 4.9 ft (1.5 m) long, and it is believed it was used to regulate body temperature.

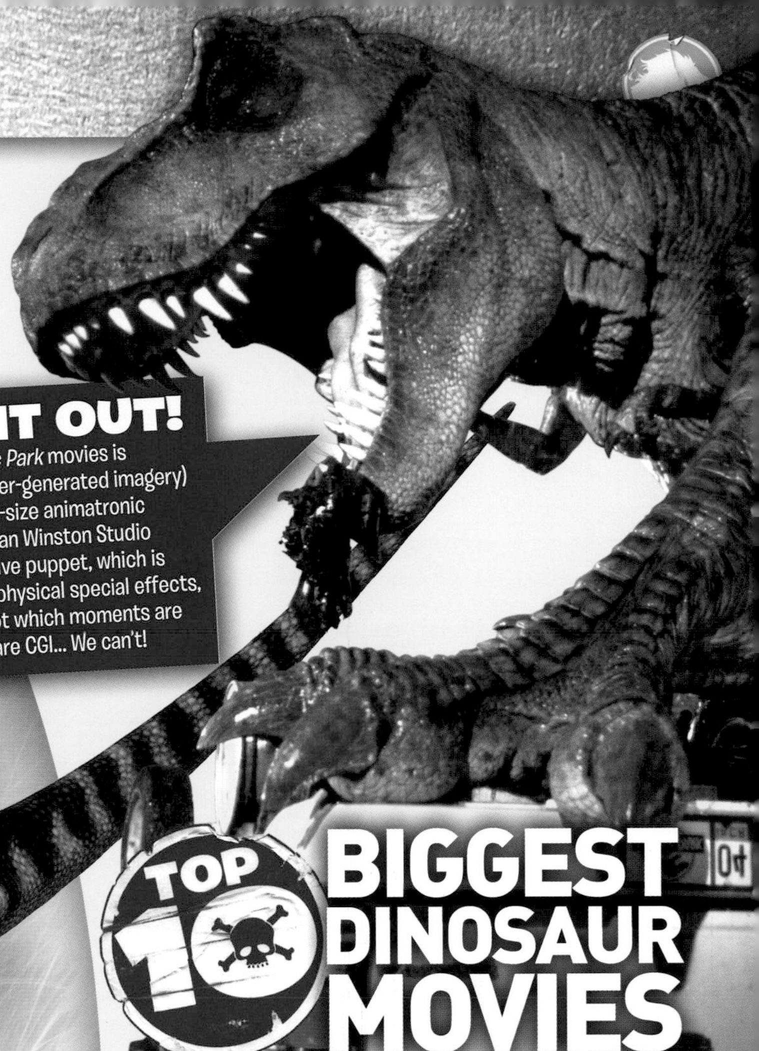

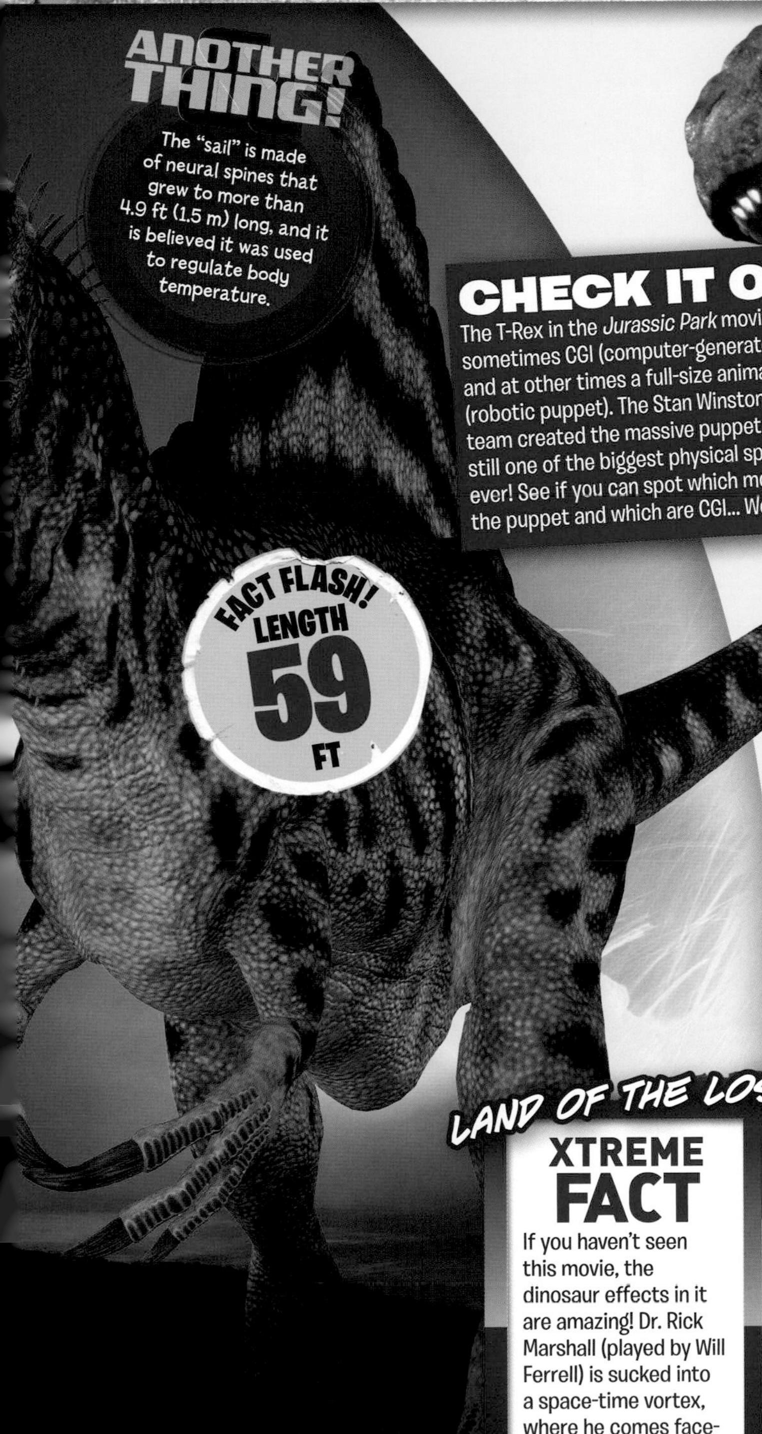

CHECK IT OUT!

The T-Rex in the *Jurassic Park* movies is sometimes CGI (computer-generated imagery) and at other times a full-size animatronic (robotic puppet). The Stan Winston Studio team created the massive puppet, which is still one of the biggest physical special effects, ever! See if you can spot which moments are the puppet and which are CGI... We can't!

FACT FLASH!
LENGTH
59
FT

TOP 10 BIGGEST DINOSAUR MOVIES

To say we love dinosaurs at Team T-10 is a HUGE understatement, so here are the most successful dino movies of all time...

	MOVIE	BOX OFFICE TAKINGS ($)
1	**Jurassic Park**	**914,691,118**
2	Ice Age: Dawn Of The Dinosaurs	886,686,817
3	The Lost World: Jurassic Park	618,638,999
4	Jurassic Park III	368,780,809
5	Dinosaur	349,822,765
6	The Land Before Time	84,460,846
7	Land Of The Lost	68,777,554
8	Baby: Secret Of The Lost Legend	14,972,297
9	Barney's Great Adventure	12,218,638
10	We're Back! A Dinosaur's Story	9,317,021

Source: IMDB.com

LAND OF THE LOST

XTREME FACT

If you haven't seen this movie, the dinosaur effects in it are amazing! Dr. Rick Marshall (played by Will Ferrell) is sucked into a space-time vortex, where he comes face-to-face with all manner of weird creatures and dino-sized monsters.

BIGGEST IN THE AIR

Swooping through the air armed with awe-inspiring wingspans and colossal beaks, these monsterous flying reptiles (pterosaurs) conquered the skies in prehistoric times...

	PTEROSAUR	WINGSPAN (M)	(FT)
1	**Hatzegopteryx**	13	42.7
2	Arambourgiania	11	36.1
3	Quetzalcoatlus	9	29.5
4	Pteranodon	8	26.2
5	Coloborhynchus	7	23
=	Moganopterus	7	23
7	Tupuxuara	6	19.7
=	Ornithocheirus	6	19.7
9	Cearadactylus	5.5	18
10	Thalassodromeus	4.5	14.8

YOU RATE! 1 to 100

Source: David Martill, Palaeobiologist

CHECK IT OUT!
Ornithocheirus had an absolutely HUGE beak in relation to the size of the rest of its body. Those teeth would've been perfect for snapping up fish from the choppy waves. This beast looks a bit like a mutant reptilian pelican, doesn't it?!

LARGEST OCEAN REPTILES

Everyone at Team T-10 is a pretty good swimmer, but millions of years ago THESE guys were the absolute masters of the oceans...

	REPTILE	LENGTH (M)	(FT)
1	**Mauisaurus**	20.1	66
2	Liopleurodon	18	59
3	Mosasaurus	15.2	49.9
=	Hainosaurus	15.2	49.9
5	Elasmosaurus	14	46
6	Pliosaurus	12.2	40
=	Megalneusaurus	12.2	40
=	Plotosaurus	12.2	40
9	Tylosaurus	10.7	35.1
=	Libonectes	10.7	35.1

YOU RATE! 1 to 100

LIOPLEURODON

XTREME FACT
One of prehistory's most formidable marine carnivores, Liopleurodon was part of the plesiosaur family. Its four huge flippers would have provided incredible acceleration to hunt prey.

Source: David Martill, Palaeobiologist

ARGENTINOSAURUS

XTREME FACT

If your family ever takes you to visit the natural history museum in Frankfurt, Germany, you will come face to face with the biggest reconstruction of an Argentinosaurus. There's also a model of one on display in the United States, at Fernbank Museum of Natural History in Atlanta, Georgia.

STAT ATTACK

DIPLODOCUS

Diet ....Vegetation (herbivore)
Teeth .... Small, peg-like
Features................. Hugely long neck & tail
Fossils found ....Loads! It's one of the most studied dinosaurs
In museums?........ Yes, full-size skeletons

HEAD TO HEAD

IN THE BLUE CORNER...   IN THE RED CORNER...

ORNITHOCHEIRUS   ARGENTINOSAURUS

	ORNITHOCHEIRUS			ARGENTINOSAURUS	
✗	05	WEIGHT	10	✓
✗	07	SIZE	10	✓
✓	07	SPEED	05	✗
✓	07	JAW POWER	05	✗
✗	04	ATTACK	07	✓
2			**3**	

AND THE WINNER IS... ARGENTINOSAURUS!

YOU RATE!
1 to 100

TOP 10 LONGEST HERBIVORES ON LAND

We gave you the rundown of the 10 biggest meat-eaters earlier, but let's not forget those vegetarian dinos...

	DINOSAUR	LENGTH (M)	(FT)
1	**Amphicoelias**	**60**	**196.8**
2	Argentinosaurus	36	118.1
3	Supersaurus	34	111.5
=	Futalognkosaurus	34	111.5
=	Sauroposeidon	34	111.5
6	Diplodocus	33.5	109.9
7	Antarctosaurus	33	108.3
8	Paralititan	32	105
9	Turiasaurus	30	98.4
=	Puertasaurus	30	98.4

Source: David Martill, Palaeobiologist

OUR TOP 10 UNOFFICIAL

DEADLIEST WEAPONS

It's not always the size of the weapon that makes it lethal, as these dangerous horns, teeth and claws show...

OFF THE CHART

NEDOCERATOPS

Bet you thought this dude was a Triceratops... Nope! Ned (as we like to call him) is related, hence the intimidating horns, big beak and the armour-plating. But all of the 'tops family were actually vegetarian. They grazed on low ground-based plants, using that beak (and jaws lined with hundreds of grinding molars) to mash ferns and leaves to a pulp.

TRICERATOPS

XTREME FACT

Paleontologist (a scientist who studies prehistoric life) Othniel Charles Marsh made a bit of an embarrassing mistake in 1887 when he first thought a Triceratops' skull was a kind of bison!

DEINONYCHUS

XTREME FACT

Deinonychus means "terrible claw", and with its 5 in (13 cm) central sickle-like claw on its foot, that's a perfect description! Recent studies on its jaws suggest it had a similar bite force to a modern-day crocodile, too.

	PREHISTORIC ANIMAL	WEAPON
1	**Triceratops**	**39 in (100 cm) long horns**
2	Liopleurodon	16 in (40 cm) teeth
3	Therizonosaurus	39 in (100 cm) long claws
4	Giganotosaurus	9 in (30 cm) teeth
5	Utahraptor	15 in (38 cm) claws
6	T-Rex	9 in (30 cm) teeth
7	Megaraptor	14 in (35 cm) claws
8	Carcharodontosaurus	8 in (20.3 cm) teeth
9	Deinonychus	5 in (13 cm) middle sickle-like claw
10	Spinosaurus	4.5 in (11.4 cm) claws

TOP 10 BIGGEST FISH

Millions of years ago, if you weren't big, bony or tooled up with dental weaponry, you had no chance in the ocean. These 10 were MONSTROUS fish...

	FISH	LENGTH (M)	(FT)
1	**Megalodon**	20	65.6
2	Leedsichthys	16	52.5
3	Dunkleosteus	10	32.8
4	Onchopristis	8	26.2
5	Rhizodus	7	23
6	Cretoxyrhina	6.1	20
7	Isurus	6	19.7
=	Xiphactinus	6	19.7
9	Hyneria	5	16.4
10	Mawsonia	4	13.1

Source: Luke Hauser, Palaeobiologist

YOU RATE! 1 to 100

MEGALODON

XTREME FACT

The tooth on the left is from the jaws of a Great White Shark. On the right? A fossil replica of a Megalodon's tooth. This is the world's largest EVER carnivorous shark. Makes the Great White look like a goldfish...

CHECK IT OUT!

Dunkleosteus is from the beastly fish species called Placoderm. These guys didn't have teeth, they had jagged, shearing bony plates, instead. Imagine a mouth with a guillotine inside it...

⬆⬇ SHUFFLE UP

Teeth and claws are one thing, but which are YOUR favourite beasts from our chart? Here you can make a definitive list of which ones YOU think rock the most!

1 ....
2 ....
3 ....
4 ....
5 ....
6 ....
7 ....
8 ....
9 ....
10 ....

Not a big fan of some of them? Add any cool dinos you prefer... It's your list!

OUR TOP 10 UNOFFICIAL

COOLEST BEASTS UNEARTHED

1	**Titanoboa** (15.2 m/50 ft long, 1 m/3.3 ft wide prehistoric snake's remains were discovered in Columbia in 2004)
2	Woolly Mammoth (preserved in ice in Siberia)
3	Giant Penguin (as big as 6.5 ft/2 m)
4	Mummified Hadrosaur (skin and tissue intact)
5	Arthropleura Millipede (8.5 ft/2.59 m in length)
6	Gigantic Ground Sloth/Megatherium (17,600 lb/8,000 kg sloth as big as an elephant)
7	Moa (12 ft/3.66 m flightless bird)
8	Giant Sea Scorpion (the size of a crocodile)
9	Helicoprion/Spiral Saw Shark (serrated teeth)
10	Microraptor (feathered, four-winged glider)

The Titanoboa, the largest snake to ever live, swallowing a whole crocodile!

ANIMAL KINGDOM

YOUR SHOUT!

You've witnessed the many, MANY, wonders of the natural world, and now it's time to dedicate some activity pages to YOU, our awesome T-10 fans!

Check out these questions. Can you answer them without looking back through the book?

YOU RATE!

TOP 10

T-10 CREATURES

Go back through the Animal Kingdom section and find the 10 creatures that you scored the highest in the "You Rate" buttons. Now list them in order below for YOUR ultimate T-10 animals!

	NAME OF CREATURE	"YOU RATE" SCORE
1		
2		
3		
4		
5		
6		
7		
8		
9		
10		

OUT FOR BLOOD

WHOSE JAW?

This beast features on two T-10 Out For Blood lists. See how many clues you need below before you work out what carnivore we are talking about...

1. It has a bite pressure more powerful than that of a tiger...
2. A pack can bring down an adult male Wildebeest...
3. It is famous for sounding like it's laughing...

ANIMAL:
....

TRUE OR FALSE...

1. The Tsetse Fly kills thousands of people by spreading diseases. ☐T ☐F

2. The Golden Poison Dart Frog fires toxic darts from its mouth. ☐T ☐F

3. Australia has the most fatal shark attacks of anywhere in the world. ☐T ☐F

MOST HUNTED

The Polar Bear is featured on the T-10 chart of Endangered Mammals, but can you remember three others that are also named on that list?

1 ....

2 ....

3 ....

RAPID MOVEMENT

With the fastest as Number One, can you place these speed demons in order?

.....	**Cheetah**
.....	**Peregrine Falcon**
.....	**Swordfish**
.....	**Sailfish**
.....	**Ostrich**

BONUS POINT!
....
IS THE TOP SPEED OF A SAILFISH

HIGHLY EVOLVED

GIVE IT A TRY...

Have you heard of a bat box? It is just like a bird box but for bats, and is a fantastic way to help care for our furry flying friends. Ask a grown-up to put one up outside your home to give the little guys somewhere to hang out. Then you can watch them come and go!

SIZING THINGS UP

This tooth is the actual size of the real thing! Grab a ruler, measure it and see if you can identify its flesh-tearing beastly owner!

WHICH ANIMAL?

Diet ...Berries, dead animals, grass, insects

Protection ....Fast sprinting, tusks

Lifestyle..............Live in groups in Africa

Weight................... Up to 113.4 kg/250 lb

Enemies .. Big cats, crocodiles, humans

THESE STATS BELONG TO A...

....

THIS IS THE TOOTH OF A

MILLIONS OF YEARS AGO...

Can you work out which reptile this immense 59-foot long skeleton belonged to?

REPTILE:

....

ANSWERS ON PAGE 312

GAMING GALAXY

When it comes to experiencing adventures that are out of this world, there is nothing quite like an immersive video game. Alien realms, high-speed race tracks, motion-detection party games... The options are endless! Prepare for T-10 to take gaming data up a level...

DEVELOPMENT

The more complex video games become, the more money it takes to make them. With budgets as big as movies, check out these pricey productions...

TOP 10 MOST EXPENSIVE GAMES TO DEVELOP

It used to be the movie business where the REALLY big bucks were spent but, nowadays, just as much money is put into developing a hit video game. Check out these big spenders...

GRAN TURISMO 5

XTREME FACT

Talk about detailed development... *GT5* features amazing additions to the virtual car-racing experience, taking realism to crazy heights. The cars can be damaged by dirt, scratches and the weather... Even the strain on the car's engine can be recorded to your profile!

FACT FLASH!
PRODUCTION COST
80 MILLION DOLLARS

YOU RATE!
1 to 100

	GAME	PRODUCTION COST ($ MILLION)
1	Gran Turismo 5	80,000,000
2	Shenmue	70,000,000
3	Final Fantasy XII	52,300,000
4	Final Fantasy VII	45,000,000
5	Final Fantasy IX	40,000,000
6	Final Fantasy X	32,300,000
7	Ghostbusters	20,000,000
8	Psychonauts	12,000,000
9	Grim Fandango	3,000,000
10	Dragon's Lair	1,300,000

GIVE IT A TRY...
GAMES DESIGNER

Dreaming of becoming a game designer? Why not flick through all of the pages of your T-10 book to look for inspiration? Could it be an ancient beast that becomes your game's star? Or sprawling, high-tech buildings with sports stars of the future? Get your brain fired up and grab a sketchbook, fast!

CHECK IT OUT!

This lady is from *Shenmue*. You might not have heard of this game, but upon its release in 1999 for Sega's Dreamcast, it was one of the most expensive video games ever developed. This is because it featured details such as real-time weather changes, fully voiced non-player characters, sleep patterns for the main characters... Crazy stuff! This open-world adventure inspired many "sandbox" games that followed.

DEVELOPMENT BREAKTHROUGH

	TECHNOLOGY	COMPANY	BREAKTHROUGH
1	Periscope	Sega	1966 electro-mechanical arcade machine
2	PS3	Sony	First full HD console + Blu-ray player
3	Game & Watch	Nintendo	First handheld LCD gaming
4	Wii	Nintendo	Motion-sensor board & controllers
5	Kinect	Microsoft	Full-body motion-sensor game play
6	Game Boy	Nintendo	First global hit handheld console
7	Virtual Reality	Various	Interactive VR helmet and glove
8	PlayStation 2	Sony	First-ever CD-ROM based console
9	Amiga	Commodore	Advanced home computer gaming
10	Game Gear	Sega	First colour handheld console

FACT FLASH!
FULL-BODY MOTION SENSOR

KINECT
XTREME FACT
The technology behind Kinect is highly impressive. The system uses special depth sensors, microphones, cameras and even voice-recognition software. With sales exceeding 20 million units, fans voted with their wallets to show that full-motion gaming is the future... And no wonder, as it feels like technology from a sci-fi movie!

TOP 10 LARGEST VIDEO-GAME DEVELOPING COUNTRIES

If you were ever in any doubt about how big the video game industry is, check out the amount of developers there are in these territories...

	COUNTRY	NUMBER OF COMPANIES
1	**USA**	640
2	Japan	339
3	UK	272
4	Canada	83
5	France	63
6	Germany	60
7	South Korea	37
8	Sweden	36
9	Australia	31
10	Russia	23

YOU RATE!

1 to 100

CHECK IT OUT!

Tablet technology is zooming into the future with, appropriately, Sonic the Hedgehog in play! Yes, *Sonic CD* will already be installed on NEC's Medias Tab UL N-08D, as shown in this photo from its grand unveiling in Tokyo (September 2012). The tablet's innovations include a large-but-portable 7 in (18 cm) touch-screen. Fingers crossed it will be released outside of Japan!

USA

XTREME FACT

The Wii U has already taken the gaming world by storm, showing that Nintendo is never short of ideas. This new console has a unique controller with an integrated second screen, and this photo shows it being played by President of Nintendo of America's Reggie Fils-Aime, at 2012's E3 (Electronic Entertainment Expo) video game conference in Los Angeles, USA.

NEW ZEALAND

There are only five active companies that develop games in New Zealand. This includes Sidhe, the makers of *GripShift*, which has sold 90,000 copies worldwide.

OFF THE CHART

SONIC

XTREME FACT

It's not just the world of video games that this feisty, spiky dude has conquered, he's also been the star of his own cartoon series, comic, and movie! Disney's 2012 movie *Wreck-It Ralph* featured Sonic, including the guy who voices him, Roger Craig Smith!

STAT ATTACK

SONIC THE HEDGEHOG

Created by.............................. Yuji Naka

Sonic's fave food ....Hot dogs with hot sauce

First-ever game ......Sonic The Hedgehog (June 23, 1991)

Games featuring Sonic 78

CHECK IT OUT!

The superbly designed duo of Ratchet & Clank have starred in no less than 13 video game adventures... Not bad for a mechanic and his robot sidekick! And, if you're a manga fan, there's a collected comic starring the dudes called *Ratchet & Clank: Bang Bang Bang! Critical Danger Of The Galaxy Legend...*

OUR TOP 10 UNOFFICIAL

BEST CHARACTER DESIGNS

	CHARACTER	GAME(S)
1	Lammy	UmJammer Lammy
2	Yoshi	Various Super Mario, Yoshi and Nintendo titles
3	GLaDOS	Portal 2, Portal
4	Disco Zombie	Plants Vs Zombies
5	Sonic The Hedgehog	Various Sonic The Hedgehog titles
6	Chop Chop Master Onion	PaRappa The Rapper titles, UmJammer Lammy
7	Ratchet	Various Ratchet & Clank titles
=	Clank	Various Ratchet & Clank titles
9	Drippy	Ni no Kuni
10	Dirk The Daring	Dragon's Lair

GOLD COINS

The video-game industry is now the most successful entertainment business in the world, bigger than movies and music! It's definitely not just Mario who's raking in those magic coins...

TOP 10

BIGGEST SELLING CONSOLE GAMES

It's time to finally settle all those arguments... And, look, it's a one-horse race! The most successful 10 games of all time are ALL from platforms created by the mighty Nintendo...

FACT FLASH! SOLD 40 MILLION

YOU RATE! 1 to 100

	GAME(S)	GENRE	RELEASED	PLATFORM	SALES (MILLIONS)
1	Wii Sports	Sports	2006	Wii	80.55
2	Super Mario Bros	Platform	1985	NES*	40.24
3	Pokémon Red/Blue/Green	RPG	1996	Game Boy	33.11
4	Mario Kart Wii	Racing	2008	Wii	32.36
5	Wii Sports Resort	Sports	2009	Wii	30.97
6	Tetris	Puzzle	1989	Game Boy	30.26
7	New Super Mario Bros	Platform	2006	DS	28.90
8	Wii Play	Party	2006	Wii	28.68
9	Duck Hunt	Shooter	1984	NES*	28.31
10	New Super Mario Bros Wii	Platform	2009	Wii	26.33

Nintendo Entertainment System
Source: VGChartz

SUPER MARIO BROS

XTREME FACT

Plumber, brother to Luigi and all-round adventurer, Mario first made his gaming appearance in 1981 as "Jumpman" in the arcade game *Donkey Kong*! It was the first (of many) times that he would rescue the Princess. He was renamed "Mario" in 1982 in *Donkey Kong Junior*...

DONKEY KONG

XTREME FACT

Many gaming fans believed that the original name for Donkey Kong was Monkey Kong, and that an error in translation created the name. However, creator Shigeru Miyamoto has said he intentionally used "Donkey Kong" to express "a stupid ape".

CHECK IT OUT!

Street Fighter II is the most influential fighting game ever, with dozens of imitators. Capcom's classic combat game has had success on every system, and is still their most successful game of all time.

HEAD TO HEAD

IN THE BLUE CORNER... SUPER MARIO			IN THE RED CORNER... DONKEY KONG
✗ 03	WEIGHT	08 ✓	
✗ 04	SIZE	08 ✓	
✓ 09	SPEED	04 ✗	
✓ 10	JUMP POWER	06 ✗	
✓ 10	MAGIC POWER	02 ✗	
3		**2**	

AND THE WINNER IS... SUPER MARIO!

GIVE IT A TRY... FIGHTING TALK

Get your paws on a copy of *Street Fighter II* for your gaming system, and then gather your friends and family for a day of the ultimate fighting challenge! Who has the best combo moves? But be warned, if the adults played this when they were younger, they might still be awesome at it now...

TOP 10 BIGGEST ARCADE GAMES

You may have played updated versions of these games on your current system, but look out for them on a classic machine at an arcade near you...

YOU RATE! 1 to 100

	GAME(S)	RELEASED	SALES OF ARCADE MACHINES
1	Pac-Man	1980	400,000
2	Space Invaders	1978	360,000
3	Street Fighter II (all versions)	1991	200,000
4	Donkey Kong	1981	132,000
5	Ms. Pac-Man	1981	125,000
6	Asteroids	1979	100,000
7	Defender	1981	60,000
8	Centipede	1981	55,988
9	Galaxian	1979	40,000
10	Donkey Kong Jr.	1982	30,000

TOP 10

BIGGEST SELLING PS3 GAMES

The results are in for all you PS3 owners... And, wow, you guys really love the soccer and racing games on this system!

	GAME	GENRE	RELEASED	SALES (MILLIONS)
1	**Gran Turismo 5**	**Racing**	2010	7.81
2	FIFA Soccer 12	Sports	2011	6.13
3	LittleBigPlanet	Platform	2008	4.96
4	FIFA Soccer 11	Sports	2010	4.87
5	Gran Turismo 5 Prologue	Racing	2007	4.10
6	MotorStorm	Racing	2006	3.47
7	FIFA Soccer 10	Sports	2009	3.51
8	Sports Champions	Sports	2010	3.34
9	LittleBigPlanet2	Platform	2011	2.61
10	Need For Speed: Shift	Racing	2009	2.52

Source: VGChartz

YOU RATE!
1 to 100

GRAN TURISMO 5

XTREME FACT

Racing games have come and gone, but the *Gran Turismo* series has constantly raised the bar (well, the starting flag!) of excellence. *GT5* has an eye-popping 81 different tracks to choose from, with 31 different locations to race in! Then, of course, there are the cars... How does a choice of 1,083 sound?! Too. Many. Choices!

FIFA SOCCER 13

As the 20th FIFA game, *FIFA Soccer 13* continues Electronic Arts' reign of the soccer video game. The demo version was downloaded just short of TWO MILLION times in only three days!

OFF THE CHART

FACT FLASH! SOLD 7.81 MILLION

BIGGEST SELLING Wii GAMES

It's no surprise to see the games that take advantage of the Wii's movement-detection system are overcrowding the 10 bestsellers here...

YOU RATE! *1 to 100*

	GAME	GENRE	RELEASED	SALES (MILLIONS)
1	**Wii Sports**	**Sports**	2006	79.30
2	Mario Kart Wii	Racing	2008	33.11
3	Wii Sports Resort	Sports	2009	30.97
4	Wii Play	Party	2006	28.68
5	New Super Mario Bros. Wiii	Platform	2009	26.33
6	Wii Fit	Sports	2007	22.72
7	Wii Fit Plus	Sports	2009	20.68
8	Super Smash Bros. Brawl	Combat	2008	11.15
9	Super Mario Galaxy	Platform	2007	10.24
10	Just Dance 3	Party	2011	9.36

Source: VGChartz

WII SPORTS RESORT

XTREME FACT

With over 30 MILLION sales worldwide, it's clear that Nintendo nailed it with this Wii game. The sports on offer really show off the motion-sensor controller's abilities, and gaming fans picked up over a million copies in its first week on sale in Japan and the US, combined.

GIVE IT A TRY... BATTLE YOUR BUDDIES

With so many party games available, there's no excuse not to arrange a championship battle between you and your friends. Decide on a game and then let the competition commence! Make sure you keep a log of all the highest scores, and see how long the tournament lasts before you end with the "champion of champions". Maybe let the grown-ups get involved, too, but only if they're not terrible at your chosen game!

BIGGEST SELLING XBOX 360 GAMES

The Kinect system has completely revolutionized the gaming appeal of the Xbox, with two out of the top three entries here combining to over 20 million sales...

YOU RATE! *1 to 100*

	GAME	GENRE	RELEASED	SALES (MILLIONS)
1	**Kinect Adventures!**	**Party**	2010	16.85
2	Forza Motorsport 3	Racing	2009	5.09
3	Kinect Sports	Sports	2010	4.42
4	Guitar Hero III: Legends Of Rock	Party	2007	4.36
5	FIFA Soccer 12	Sports	2011	3.99
6	Forza Motorsport 2	Racing	2007	3.98
7	LEGO Indiana Jones: The Original Adventures	Adventure	2008	3.60
8	FIFA Soccer 11	Sports	2010	3.46
9	Kung Fu Panda	Platform	2008	3
10	Sega Superstars Tennis	Sports	2008	2.83

Source: VGChartz

CHECK IT OUT!

T-10 LOVES *Guitar Hero*! However, we're not as good as the world record holder Danny Johnson, who can play DragonForce's *Through The Fire And The Flames* perfectly on Expert level!

TOP 10

BIGGEST SELLING GAME BRANDS

Games prices are pretty varied across the consoles, so the best way to judge a successful gaming brand is on units sold. Here are the winners, with some huge sales figures...

YOU RATE!
1 to 100

	BRAND	TOTAL UNITS SOLD (MILLIONS)
1	**Mario**	450.2
2	Pokémon	275.3
3	Wii Series	219.3
4	The Sims	150
5	Tetris	125
6	Wii Sports	109.7
7	Final Fantasy	102
8	FIFA	100
=	Need For Speed	100
10	Madden NFL	90

CHECK IT OUT!

You'd think with a name like *Final Fantasy* that this epic saga, featuring Serah Farron, would be the ending of an adventure. Not with this franchise, which has had more than 50 releases and spin-offs since it made its debut back in 1987.

FACT FLASH!
AGE OF GAME
26 YEARS

HEAD TO HEAD

IN THE BLUE CORNER... | IN THE RED CORNER...

SERAH FARRON | **ZELDA**

SERAH FARRON		ZELDA	
✓	08	HEIGHT	06 ✗
✓	07	SPEED	07 ✓
✓	07	INTELLIGENCE	06 ✗
✓	09	BEAUTY	07 ✗
✗	06	FIGHT SKILLS	08 ✓
4			**2**

AND THE WINNER IS... SERAH FARRON!

TOP 10 LONGEST-RUNNING GAME BRANDS

You can't keep a good frog down: *Frogger* hops on!

Think that some of your best games have been going for a long time?
You're in for a shock when you see who the REAL legends of gaming are...

	BRAND	FIRST APPEARANCE	LATEST APPEARANCE	TOTAL GAMING YEARS
1	Pong	Pong (1972)	Atari iOS Pong (2013)	41
2	Space Invaders	Space Invaders (1978)	Space Invaders 2012 (2012)	34
3	Mario	Donkey Kong (1981)	New Super Mario Bros U (2013)	32
=	Asteroids	Asteroids (1979)	Asteroids Gunner (2011)	32
5	Galaxian	Galaxian (1979)	Namco Museum Megamix (2010)	31
=	Frogger	Frogger (1981)	Frogger: Hyper Arcade Edition (2012)	31
7	Star Wars	The Empire Strikes Back (1982)	Kinect Star Wars (2012)	30
8	Donkey Kong	Donkey Kong (1981)	Donkey Kong Country Returns (2010)	29
9	Tetris	Tetris (1984)	Tetris Stars (2011)	27
10	The Legend Of Zelda	The Legend Of Zelda (1986)	The Legend Of Zelda: Skyward Sword (2012)	26

THE LEGEND OF ZELDA

XTREME FACT

We adore the *Zelda* video games, which have been testing our puzzle-solving and adventurous minds since 1986! And guess who helped create *Zelda*? The man behind Mario, of course, Shigeru Miyamoto!

OUR TOP 10 UNOFFICIAL

COOLEST GAME BRANDS

You've seen the official lists, so now you can check out the brands that Team T-10 likes to play and is crazy about!

1	Skylanders
2	Rock Band
3	Guitar Hero
4	Myst
5	Professor Layton
6	Plants vs Zombies
7	SingStar
8	Kirby
9	LEGO Adventures
10	Yoshi

SKYLANDERS

XTREME FACT

Team T-10 has a pretty impressive collection of *Skylanders*. How about you? We love how this game took the awesome Spyro The Dragon character from his own game series and made him a star among so many new, kick-ass creatures and characters! In fact, *Skylanders* was originally going to be called *Spyro's Kingdom*. All hail that cool, purple dragon!

DOWNLOAD FOCUS

The world of gaming on mobile devices is huge! Here's where we dip into that universe...

DOWNLOADED MOBILE GAMES

TOP 10

The smartphones are taking over the planet, and we love it! In this section we celebrate the greatest mobile phone app games out there...

	GAME	DOWNLOADED
1	**Angry Birds**	**1 billion+**
2	Tetris	100 million+
=	The Sims FreePlay	100 million+
4	Smurfs' Village	56 million+
5	Bejeweled	50 million+
=	Draw Something	50 million+
=	Angry Birds Space	50 million+
8	Pac-Man	30 million+
9	Fruit Ninja	20 million+
10	Block Breaker Deluxe	8 million+

YOU RATE!
1 to 100

FACT FLASH! UNITS SOLD 1 BILLION+

ANGRY BIRDS
XTREME FACT

Aside from being one of the most addictive games ever made, around the world the *Angry Birds* machine has rolled out the likes of *Angry Birds* soda drinks, special Hot Wheels track and cars, and even an official logo for the 2012 Ice Hockey World Championships!

CHECK IT OUT!

Since their first flight in 2009, the *Angry Birds* phenomenon has exploded the world over. Late 2012 saw the release of the spin-off *Bad Piggies*. Unlike the flinging antics of the birds, *Bad Piggies* needs the player to build a device to get the pigs from A to B. Will it be another massive hit? Let's just say it went to the Number One spot in three hours after its release...

THE SIMS FREEPLAY
XTREME FACT

The first ever *Sims* game was for the PC in 2000, and since then there have been eight sequels, spin-offs and extension packs released.

BEST-SELLING MODERN MOBILE GAMING DEVICES

Since the dawn of the iPhone in 2008, mobile phone gaming has never been the same again. Here are the kings of cell phone gaming...

	MOBILE	MADE BY	FIRST RELEASED	UNITS SOLD (MILLIONS)
1	Nokia 701	Nokia	2011	180
2	Nokia 5230	Nokia	2009	150
3	iPhone 4S	Apple	2011	70+
4	Samsung Galaxy S II	Samsung	2011	63+
5	iPhone 3GS	Apple	2009	35
=	iPhone 3G	Apple	2008	35
=	Nokia 1680 classic	Nokia	2008	35
8	Samsung Galaxy S III	Samsung	2012	31
9	iPhone 4	Apple	2010	28+
10	Nokia 2700 classic	Nokia	2009	20

NOKIA XTREME FACT

Nokia wasn't always in the communications business... Its origins at the turn of the 19th century was in paper manufacturing!

ANOTHER THING!

Nokia has a massive 22.5 percent share of the global mobile phone market, with staff in 120 countries!

FACT FLASH!
UNITS SOLD
28 MILLION+

CHECK IT OUT!

Smartphones seem to be able to do pretty much anything. We're convinced that somewhere, someone is creating an app so we won't have to make the bed or do the dishes. And did you know, in 2011, two iPhone 4Ss were sent into space by NASA and used on the International Space Station?!

TOP 10

BIGGEST FREE iPHONE APPS

Need to find something? There's an app for that. Want to learn about anything? You'll find one for that, too! Here are the apps iPhone users love the most...

YOU RATE!
1 to 100

	APP
1	Google Maps
2	Facebook
3	Pandora Radio
4	Words With Friends Free
5	Skype
6	The Weather Channel
7	Google Search
8	Google Earth
9	Angry Birds Free
10	Shazam

FRUIT NINJA LITE

XTREME FACT

The developers of the massively popular *Fruit Ninja* game are Halfbrick Studios, based in Queensland, Australia. And they are also the geniuses behind *Jetpack Joyride*. The well-respected magazine *Time* loves the fruity game, too, and in 2011, they praised it by naming it as one of the 50 Best iPhone Apps.

SHUFFLE UP

What would you have at Number One? Now you've seen the Top 10 apps of all time, why not list them in order of YOUR all-time faves?

1 ....
2 ....
3 ....
4 ....
5 ....
6 ....
7 ....
8 ....
9 ....
10 ....

Not a big fan of some of these? Add any apps you like... It's YOUR list!

CHECK IT OUT!

At T-10, we love sending and receiving photos on our phones, so is it any surprise that Facebook is high on the chart? No! Especially when you consider that there are now over one BILLION users of the social networking site. To put that into context, there are just over seven billion people on Earth... How long before the whole planet has signed up?!

BIGGEST FREE iPAD APPS

Touch-screen tablets are fast becoming the norm for our daily lives, with the iPad leading the way. Here are its most popular downloads...

YOU RATE! 1 to 100

	APP
1	Skype
2	Angry Birds HD
3	Angry Birds Rio HD
4	Fruit Ninja HD Lite
5	Talking Tom Cat 2
6	Angry Birds Seasons HD
7	Calculator for iPad
8	MyPad For Facebook & Twitter
9	Smurfs' Village
10	Talking Tom Cat

STAT ATTACK

ANGRY BIRDS HD

Genre .... Skill/Puzzle
Objective .... Smash the piggies by launching the angry birds
Bonuses .... 24 exclusive levels set in eight mini episodes

CHECK IT OUT!

Never underestimate the power of *The Smurfs*... In late 2010, Capcom's *Smurfs' Village* smashed *Angry Birds* off the app charts and became the best-selling iPhone game for a while. Since these little blue creatures smurfed their way onto the Android system, too, this game has sky rocketed in sales, exceeding 10 million units on Android alone. There's life in old Papa Smurf, yet!

SKYPE
XTREME FACT

Since Skype's release in 2003, it has truly revolutionized how we communicate with our loved ones around the world. By simply using the internet to connect calls, we can video chat or just talk as though we're on the phone, often for FREE! It's not surprising that this application is on the chart here, as over 600 million people use it regularly!

BEYOND THE CONSOLE

Video gaming is one of the most profitable creative industries in the world, with the games' characters often cropping up outside of the small screen...

TOP 10 BIGGEST MOVIES BASED ON VIDEO GAMES

Sometimes a video game you love ends up taking big bucks at the box office as a movie...

	MOVIE	YEAR OF RELEASE	GAME	BOX OFFICE ($ WORLDWIDE)
1	Prince Of Persia: The Sands Of Time	2010	Prince Of Persia	335,154,643
2	Lara Croft: Tomb Raider	2001	Tomb Raider	274,703,340
3	Lara Croft Tomb Raider: The Cradle of Life	2003	Tomb Raider	156,505,388
4	Mortal Kombat	1995	Mortal Kombat	122,195,920
5	Street Fighter	1994	Street Fighter	99,423,521
6	Final Fantasy: The Spirits Within	2001	Final Fantasy	85,131,830
7	Mortal Kombat: Annihilation	1997	Mortal Kombat	51,376,861
8	Super Mario Bros	1993	Super Mario Bros	20,915,465
9	In The Name Of The King: A Dungeon Siege Tale	2007	Dungeon Siege	13,097,915
10	Street Fighter: The Legend Of Chun-Li	2009	Street Fighter	12,764,201

Source: IMDB.com

YOU RATE! 1 to 100

FACT FLASH! BOX OFFICE **335** MILLION DOLLARS

CHECK IT OUT!

The first *Mortal Kombat* movie was made with a budget of $18 million, which is pretty tiny when you compare it to the *Pirates Of The Caribbean* movies. The cost of each one of those alone was around $300 million!

PRINCE OF PERSIA: THE SANDS OF TIME

XTREME FACT

The blockbuster movie starring actor Jake Gyllenhaal may have been released in 2010, but the video game it was based on came out seven years earlier, in 2003. The *Prince Of Persia: The Sands Of Time* game was a significant release because it reinvented the franchise from being a slow-paced puzzle/platform adventure into a high-octane epic tale of heroic battles.

OUR TOP 10 UNOFFICIAL

COMIC BOOKS BASED ON GAMES

	NAME	PUBLISHER	FIRST PUBLISHED	BASED ON THE GAME OR GAME FRANCHISE
1	Sam & Max: Surfin' The Highway	Marlowe & Co	1995	Sam & Max
2	Sonic The Hedgehog	Archie/Egmont	1993	Sonic The Hedgehog
3	The Legend Of Zelda: A Link To The Past	Future	1992	The Legend Of Zelda
4	Indiana Jones And The Fate Of Atlantis	Dark Horse	1991	Indiana Jones And The Fate Of Atlantis
5	Ratchet & Clank	DC Comics	2010	Ratchet & Clank
6	Prince Of Persia	Magic Press	2008	Prince Of Persia
7	Street Fighter	Malibu Comics	1993	Street Fighter II
8	Pokémon Adventures	Shogakukan	1997	Pokémon
9	Atari Force	DC Comics	1982	Came with Atari classics like Defender & Galaxian
10	Double Dragon	Marvel	1991	Double Dragon

SAM & MAX: SURFIN' THE HIGHWAY

XTREME FACT

Sam & Max fans were rewarded for their love and dedication to these video game legends when a special anniversary edition of all their comic-based stories was published in 2007! It features exclusive artwork and lots of cool bonuses. And, you're in for a real video gaming treat if you can get hold of the rare game *Sam & Max Hit The Road*.

GIVE IT A TRY... COMIC CREATION

If you like drawing and creative writing, why not come up with a comic based on your favourite video game? You could craft a comic adaptation of a level that you really love or write an extension to the game's original story. If you're feeling really inspired, maybe you could try to plan out an entire trilogy...

CHECK IT OUT!

The amazing movie adventurer Indiana Jones has also starred in a string of massively successful gaming sagas that are not simply movie adaptations, including *Indiana Jones And The Staff Of Kings*!

TOP 10 BIGGEST GAMING CONVENTIONS

Playing video games by yourself or with friends is always awesome, but imagine if there were huge annual events for gaming... Wait a sec, there ARE!

	NAME	LOCATION (2012)	ATTENDANCE
1	**G-Star**	**Busan (South Korea)**	**296,169**
2	Gamescom	Cologne (Germany)	275,000+
3	Tokyo Game Show (TGS)	Tokyo (Japan)	223,753
4	Gen Con	Indiana (USA)	134,775
5	IgroMir	Moscow (Russia)	105,000
6	Brasil Game Show	São Paulo (Brazil)	100,000+
7	PAX Prime	Seattle (USA)	70,000+
8	PAX East	Boston (USA)	52,290
9	Eurogamer Expo	London (UK)	50,000
10	E3	Los Angeles (USA)	45,700

YOU RATE! 1 to 100

FACT FLASH! ATTENDANCE 45,700

GAMESCOM

XTREME FACT

The 2012 Gamescom trade fair in Germany's Cologne was a huge success, and allowed gamers to get hands-on with all the latest video games and classics like as *Gran Turismo*.

ANOTHER THING!

Gamescom was first held in 2009, so it's still a young gaming convention, but it is growing in popularity every year.

CHECK IT OUT!

E3 (Electronic Entertainment Expo), held annually in Los Angeles, California, doesn't just attract thousands of video game journalists and mega fans... The biggest stars in music perform there, too! At the event in 2012, Usher took to the stage and showed off his moves to promote the *Dance Central 3* game.

CHECK IT OUT!

Portal's Companion Cube Cookie Jar may sound like a bizarre game tie-in, but if you love the *Portal* series you'll know there's nothing cooler to munch snacks out of!

MOST BIZARRE GAMES MERCHANDISE EVER CREATED

Once a game is on the shelf, it's time for the merchandising machine to kick in to help promote it. Here are some very weird tie-ins...

	GAME/FRANCHISE	MERCHANDISE
1	**Super Mario Bros**	"Shower Power" shower head
2	Pokémon	Curry
3	Portal	Companion Cube Cookie Jar
4	Street Fighter: The World Warrior	Toy Chopper Bike
5	Final Fantasy	Makeup Bag
6	LittleBigPlanet	Espresso Set
7	Minecraft	Necklace
8	Sonic The Hedgehog	Soda drink
9	Ms. Pac-Man	Air Freshener
10	Asteroids	Costume: dress up as Asteroids

LITTLE BIG PLANET

XTREME FACT

We love Sack Boy. Look how cool he is! The cloth star of the puzzling platformer *LittleBigPlanet* (the original video game featuring him) has sold over five million copies.

GIVE IT A TRY...
CREATE YOUR OWN STUFF!

Is there a video game franchise that you love more than any other? Why not come up with some ideas for fun "merchandise"? You could design and create posters or stickers of your fave characters!

TOTAL PLATFORMS

The gloves are off, the controllers are on the ground and it's time to pitch all of the gaming platforms against each other in a battle royale of consoles!

TOP 10 BESTSELLING GAMING PLATFORMS

To put an end to all of those arguments you and your friends have about which are the most popular consoles, the results are in...

	PLATFORM	MADE BY	RELEASED	SALES WORLDWIDE (MILLIONS)
1	**PlayStation 2**	**Sony**	**2000**	**153.6**
2	Nintendo DS	Nintendo	2004	152.5
3	Game Boy/Game Boy Color	Nintendo	1989/1998	118.7
4	PlayStation	Sony	1994	102.5
5	Wii	Nintendo	2006	97.2
6	Game Boy Advance	Nintendo	2001	81.5
7	PlayStation Portable (PSP)	Sony	2004	73.9
8	Xbox 360	Microsoft	2005	70
9	PlayStation 3	Sony	2006	63.9
10	Nintendo Entertainment System	Nintendo	1983	61.9

Source: VGChartz

YOU RATE! 1 to 100

FACT FLASH! WORLDWIDE SALES **153.6 MILLION**

NINTENDO'S Wii U

OFF THE CHART

Although the Wii is still selling strong, in November 2012 Nintendo released its successor, the Wii U, featuring a controller with a high-definition touch-screen!

CHECK IT OUT!

In summer 2001, Sony decided to celebrate selling 20 million units of its PlayStation 2 by releasing this cool range of limited editions. Sadly, for Western gaming fans, these were only available in Japan.

FIRST EVER GAMING CONSOLES

The PS3 and Xbox 360 may boast the best graphics and sound, but they both grew from these earlier technological gaming breakthroughs...

YOU RATE!
1 to 100

FACT FLASH!
RELEASED
1977

	CONSOLE	MADE BY	RELEASED
1	**Telstar**	**Coleco**	**1976**
2	Atari 2600	Atari	1977
=	Color TV Game	Nintendo	1977
4	Intellivision	Mattel	1980
5	Nintendo Entertainment System	Nintendo	1983
6	Master System	Sega	1985
7	Atari 7800 ProSystem	Atari	1986
8	TurboGrafx-16	NEC	1987
9	Mega Drive/Genesis	Sega	1988
10	Game Boy	Nintendo	1989

SHUFFLE UP

What would you have at Number One? Now you've seen the Top 10 bestselling consoles of all time, why not list the platforms in order of YOUR top systems?

1 ....
2 ....
3 ....
4 ....
5 ....
6 ....
7 ....
8 ....
9 ....
10 ....

Not a big fan of some of them? Add any gaming platform you like... It's YOUR list!

XBOX 360

XTREME FACT

The 360's Kinect sensor has been a runaway success, with 18 million purchasers agreeing that the full-body motion control is an amazing experience!

CHECK IT OUT!

Pac-Man, one of the most successful video games of all time, found fame outside of the arcades on the Atari 2600 in 1981. Although this system's manufacturing ceased in 1992, video games fans still seek out used copies of it to complete their retro gaming collection.

TOP 10 BESTSELLING HOME CONSOLES

As far as sales go, this bunch is way ahead of the game! So the current kings of home entertainment, Xbox 360 and PS3, are not the overall champions here...

	CONSOLE	MADE BY	RELEASED	UNIT SALES (MILLIONS)
1	**PlayStation 2**	**Sony**	**2000**	**153.6**
2	PlayStation	Sony	1994	102.5
3	Wii	Nintendo	2006	97.2
4	Xbox 360	Microsoft	2005	70
5	PlayStation 3	Sony	2006	63.9
6	NES (Nintendo Entertainment System)	Nintendo	1983	61.9
7	SNES (Super Nintendo Entertainment System)	Nintendo	1990	49.1
8	Genesis/Megadrive	Sega	1988	40
9	N64	Nintendo	1996	32.9
10	Atari 2600	Atari	1977	30

Source: VGChartz

YOU RATE! 1 to 100

STAT ATTACK

SNES

Made by .... Nintendo
Game style .... Top-loaded cartridge
First released .... Nov 1990
Last issued .... Sep 2003
Rival console ...... Sega Megadrive/Genesis

PLAYSTATION 3

FACT FLASH! WORLDWIDE SALES **63.9** MILLION

PLAYSTATION 3

XTREME FACT

Unlike its rival, the Xbox 360, the PlayStation 3 has a Blu-ray player. This means that not only can it be used to play full HD (High Definition) Blu-ray movie discs, PS3 games can also be coded to be full HD in both visuals and sound.

TOP 10 BESTSELLING HANDHELD PLATFORMS

The handheld video game market is stronger than ever and these are the most successful portable ones...

	PLATFORM	MADE BY	RELEASED	SALES WORLDWIDE (MILLIONS)
1	Nintendo DS	Nintendo	2004	152.50
2	Game Boy/Game Boy Color	Nintendo	1989/1998	118.7
3	Game Boy Advance	Nintendo	2001	81.5
4	PlayStation Portable (PSP)	Sony	2004	73.9
5	Nintendo 3DS	Nintendo	2011	22.2
6	Game Gear	Sega	1990	11
7	N-Gage	Nokia	2003	3
8	PlayStation Vita	Sony	2011	2.2
9	Neo Geo Pocket/Pocket Color	SNK	1998/1999	2
10	TurboExpress	NEC	1990	1.5

Source: VGChartz

YOU RATE!
1 to 100

NINTENDO DS

XTREME FACT

It's hard to be believe that the DS was first released back in 2004! Its successors were the DS Lite, DSi, the huge screen of the DSi XL, the magical 3DS and its big brother the 3DS XL. The latest 3DS XL has already sold more than two million copies since its July 2012 release!

GIVE IT A TRY... COMPETITION TIME!

With so many handhelds and even more games available for them, why not set up a kind of Olympics of handheld games! You could draw up a chart of different styles of games (platform, racing, puzzle, etc), and throughout the tournament against your friends, see who is the ultimate portable gamer!

CHECK IT OUT!

Nokia dipped its toe into the world of handheld gaming with the N-Gage (see what Nokia did there?!) in 2003. Although it sold three million copies, key territories such as Japan weren't particularly "N-Gaged", so it was never released there... This must have N-raged Nokia, somewhat!

GAMING GALAXY

YOUR SHOUT!

Check out these questions. Can you answer them without looking back through the book?

That's the T-10 world of gaming completed! Well, not quite... Here is your very own extra bit of "downloadable content" for YOU to interact with...

YOU RATE!

T-10 GAME STUFF

Remember all those places where you got to "rate" something? Add your scores to this list and show your friends YOUR decisions!

	NAME	"YOU RATE" SCORE
1		
2		
3		
4		
5		
6		
7		
8		
9		
10		

DIGITAL DEVELOPMENT

You've seen some of the most famous and recognizable characters in gaming in the past few pages and, in many cases, the tens of millions of dollars it costs to produce the games they are in! Have a try at creating your own video game character here...

Divide 1,000 points between these 10 stats. How you spread them out is up to you! Your character might be a wiry villain or a super-buff hero. Let's play!

HEROIC FACTOR	
EVIL FACTOR	
SIZE	
HEIGHT	
SPEED	
MENTAL STRENGTH	
PHYSICAL STRENGTH	
WEAPONS	
SKILLS	
ARMOUR	

NOW, GET DRAWING AND BRING THIS PIXEL CREATION TO LIFE!

TOTAL: 1,000

GOLD COINS

These screenshots are from a game that features on two Top 10 lists: biggest selling PS3 games and biggest selling XBox 360 games. Can you name the game?

GAME: ....

BONUS POINT!
....
MILLION COPIES
SOLD ON THE PS3

DOWNLOAD FOCUS

Here are the five biggest download games but not necessarily in the right order! Can you rank them, 1 to 5, in order of the biggest to the smallest...

☐ ..... **TETRIS**

☐ ..... **THE SIMS FREEPLAY**

☐ ..... **ANGRY BIRDS**

☐ ..... **BEJEWELED**

☐ ..... **SMURFS' VILLAGE**

BEYOND THE CONSOLE

THE MOVIE TREATMENT

Why not come up with a movie idea based around YOUR Number One video game? Take the characters and their world to come up with a brand new story that would make the biggest blockbuster movies look boring!

TOTAL PLATFORMS

The logos may have been stripped from these gaming devices, but can you name each one and its manufacturer?

A

DEVICE: ....

MADE BY: ....

B

DEVICE: ....

MADE BY: ....

C

DEVICE: ....

MADE BY: ....

ANSWERS ON PAGE 312

99

SPORT ZONE

The range of skills on display in the world of sport is so vast. Hand-eye coordination, powerful muscles, intense concentration and, often, the ability to work as a team, are all essential. You may think you can name all of the sports, but Team T-10 can guarantee we've found loads you've never heard of. On your marks... Get set... GO!

JUST FOR KICKS

Some of the most popular sports of all time heavily feature the use of legs to score winning points. Let's look at the ball punters, as well as the combat kickers...

TOP 10

LARGEST ATTENDENCE TO SPORTS THAT KICK

As you can see from the crowd numbers that turned up below, kicking sports are incredibly popular, with soccer easily taking the Number One slot...

YOU RATE!
1 to 100

PRO WRESTLING

XTREME FACT

We thought Dwayne "The Rock" Johnson had hung up his wrestling tights for his movie acting. But he returned to fight at Florida's WrestleMania XXVIII in April 2012 and battled for the WWE title at the epic Royal Rumble in January 2013!

	SPORT	MATCH(ES)	YEAR	ATTENDANCE RECORD
1	**Soccer**	**Brazil vs Uruguay**	**1950**	**199,854**
2	Australian football	Carlton vs Collingwood	1970	121,696
3	American football	Dallas Cowboys vs Houston Oilers	1994	112,376
4	Rugby Union	Australia vs New Zealand	2000	109,874
5	Rugby League	Melbourne vs St George-Illawarra	1999	107,558
6	Pro Wrestling	WrestleMania III	1987	93,173
7	Women's soccer	USA vs Japan	2012	83,000
8	Mixed martial arts	Mirko Filipovic vs Kazushi Sakuraba	2002	71,000
9	USA Sevens Rugby	International tournament*	2012	30,323
10	Indoor swimming	Sydney Olympics*	2000	17,595

Multiple matches/races

CHECK IT OUT!

Women's soccer at the London 2012 Olympics was a blistering tournament. Check out Japan's Saki Kumagai taking on three US defenders on her own! Japan took the silver in the end, with USA claiming the gold with a 2-1 win.

SCOTT NORWOOD

XTREME FACT

Not all kicks go according to plan... Buffalo Bills' kicker Scott Norwood actually missed this field goal attempt at Super Bowl XXV on January 27, 1991. It meant his team lost against the New York Giants, by ONE point, 19-20.

Maradona dances around a group of defenders

OUR TOP 10 UNOFFICIAL

MOST IMPORTANT KICKS IN SPORT

	THE SWING	THE RESULT
1	Diego Maradona's goal against England in 1986	Considered by many to be the greatest soccer goal of all time
2	Scott Norwood's missed field goal at Super Bowl XXV	Blew the last chance for the Buffalo Bills to win in the dying seconds
3	Jonny Wilkinson's drop goal at the 2003 Rugby World Cup	With just 26 seconds left he completed the goal that won England the final
4	Soccer's Xabi Alonso's 2005 goal against AC Milan	Final match-time goal in a fight back from 3-0 down. Liverpool won on pens
5	Buakaw Por Pramuk's kicks at the K-1 World MAX 2004	Beat Masato with four rounds of Muay Thai kicks to win the title
6	Paul McCallum's 62-yard Canadian Football League field goal	Made 30 successful consecutive field goals attempts in 2001. A CFL record
7	Spencer Fisher's flying knee kick at UFC 60 in 2006	An epic knockout blow to Matt Wiman in a lightweight bout
8	Tony Lockett's 1,300th Aussie Rules goal in 1999	Broke the 62-year record to have the most goals of any player in the AFL/VFL
9	Andrés Iniesta's winning World Cup goal against Holland	The 116th minute goal won Spain the soccer World Cup 2010
10	Soccer's Eric Cantona's "kung-fu" kick of a supporter in 1995	Convicted for assault and served 120 hours of community service

JUST FOR KICKS

OUR TOP 10 UNOFFICIAL

MOST DAMAGING KICK SPORTS

1	**Muay Thai**
2	Krav Maga
3	Keysi Fighting Method
4	Taekwondo
5	Kung Fu
6	Tang Soo Do
7	Savate
8	Kick-boxing
9	Taekkyeon
10	Karate

CHECK IT OUT!

Here is Krav Maga being taught. This form of combat is a self-defence system with the intention of bringing a fight to an end swiftly. With roots in street-fighting, founder Imi Lichtenfeld developed it by combining elements of his boxing and wrestling experience. Krav Maga is a deadly skill that is taught to the armed forces, and it is often used in movie fights.

MUAY THAI

XTREME FACT

This is Italy's Alan Saitta (below, right) super-kicking Slovakia's Marcel Jager during their Muay Thai meet on May 28, 2011. There is no "one" set of rules, each country involved has a different approach to what is legal and allowed.

ANOTHER THING!

The Keysi Fighting Method was used to design the fights in *Batman Begins* and *The Dark Knight*!

STAT ATTACK
MUAY THAI

Origin..Thailand
Description.........Mixed martial arts/kick-boxing
Earliest battles...............................1257 AD
The first world Amateur Championships........1995
Popular culture...........Features in video games like Street Fighter II and Mortal Kombat

TOP 10 FASTEST SHOTS IN SOCCER

When you're a goalkeeper staring into the eyes of a soccer player who is preparing to take a shot, these are the 10 players that would've blasted that ball at you like a rocket...

YOU RATE!

1 to 100

	PLAYER	CLUB	DATE	SPEED (KPH)	(MPH)
1	Ronny Heberson	Sporting Clube de Portugal	Nov 26, 2006	210.9	131.82
2	David Hirst	Sheffield Wednesday	Sep 16, 1996	183.5	114
3	David Beckham	Manchester United	Feb 22, 1997	157.6	97.9
4	David Trézéguet	Monaco	Mar 19, 1998	154.5	96
5	Ritchie Humphreys	Sheffield Wednesday	Aug 17, 1996	154.3	95.9
6	Matt Le Tissier	Southampton	Jan 18, 1997	139.7	86.8
7	Alan Shearer	Newcastle United	Feb 2, 1997	138.1	85.8
8	Roberto Carlos	Brazil	Jun, 3 1997	137.1	85.2
9	Tugay Kerimoğlu	Blackburn Rovers	Nov 3, 2001	135.5	84.2
10	Obafemi Martins	Newcastle United	Jan 14, 2007	135.2	84

DAVID BECKHAM

XTREME FACT

He's not just a soccer megastar (for Manchester United, LA Galaxy and Paris Saint-Germain), David Beckham also has his own line of aftershaves! We're not sure what his "Instinct" smells like, but it can't be too unpleasant as he has more than 23 million fans on Facebook! He's also connected to several sports video games including *EA Sports Active 2*.

GIVE IT A TRY...
ON THE SPOT

Next time you're with your friends and family in the park, set up some kicking challenges to see who has the most accuracy. A great way to do this is with a penalty shoot-out.

ANOTHER THING!

Aside from his club matches, David Beckham has captained the England soccer team 59 times.

CHECK IT OUT!

This is Roberto Carlos doing one of his well-known power shots for Brazil. He's represented his country 125 times, with an impressive 11 goals scored. That's not bad at all when you consider he's a defender!

TOP 10 MOST ACCURATE NFL KICKERS

Striking that ball with a good percentage of accuracy is crucial to being a successful NFL superstar, and these 10 are the kings of the kick...

	NAME	YEARS ACTIVE	ACCURACY (PERCENT)
1	Nate Kaeding	2004-12	86.957
2	Mike Vanderjagt	1998-2006	86.466
3	Robbie Gould	2005-12	86.161
4	Shayne Graham	2001-12	85.938
5	Rob Bironas	2005-12	85.903
6	Garrett Hartley	2008-12	85.185
7	Connor Barth	2008-12	84.946
8	Stephen Gostkowski	2006-12	84.746
9	Matt Bryant	2002-12	84.426
10	Matt Stover	1991-2009	83.659

YOU RATE! [ ] 1 to 100

ANOTHER THING!

There are lots of rules to do with NFL kicking, including, if a punt or missed field goal makes contact with any part of a goalpost, it's a dead ball.

NATE KAEDING

XTREME FACT

Here is the man himself, Nate Kaeding of the San Diego Chargers, the most accurate American Football kicker in the world! And his longest-ever successful field goal? A massive 57 yards!

EXTRA! Nate Kaeding's not just got NFL skills... During his time at high school, he played soccer and basketball, too. He had a skill level that meant he played those sports, along with American Football, to state championship level. In his adult years, he has remained multitalented: he reviews movies for a website and is co-owner of a restaurant called Short's Burger & Shine! Bet he's not allowed to eat many of those when he's training...

ILLEGAL KICKS IN SPORT

	KICK	DESCRIPTION/EXAMPLE
1	Dolphin	A kick in swimming that is not allowed in the breaststroke
2	Up-kick	Use of this in UFC results in immediate disqualification
3	Two-footed "tackle"	Jumping at a player with two feet in a soccer match can result in a red card
4	Knee	A blow to your opponent's knee in kick-boxing is banned
5	Kicking a loose ball	No player can deliberately kick a loose ball, according to NFL rules
6	Raking	A rugby player deliberately scrapes an opponent with the studs of his boots
7	Drop	Illegal in Canadian football if the ball bounces multiple times before it's kicked
8	Head	MMA rules state kicks to the head of a grounded opponent are forbidden
9	Tackle the "keeper"	In soccer, it's illegal for an opponent to kick the ball while the goalkeeper holds it
10	Brogue	The WWE Superstar Sheamus' infamous kick is banned from the division

FACT FLASH!
KICK ACCURACY
85.185 PERCENT

CHECK IT OUT!

This is Garrett Hartley, and he has such an amazing kick percentage that the big bosses at the New Orleans Saints are reportedly paying him $822,000 for the 2014 season! With possibly up to half a million in bonuses on top of that...

DOLPHIN KICK

XTREME FACT

South African Cameron van der Burgh (left) holds the world record for the 100 m breaststroke in 58.46 secs, from the 2012 Olympics. However, he later admitted he'd used the illegal dolphin kick.

TOP 10 GREATEST UFC HALL OF FAMERS

Hard men don't come much tougher than the guys in UFC. Since the Hall Of Fame was set up, these legends have been inducted...

CHUCK LIDDELL

XTREME FACT

As title reigns go, Chuck "The Iceman" Liddell holds one of the longest ever in UFC: a whopping 771 days!

EXTRA! Since the UFC was founded in 1993 only NINE guys have ever been inducted into its Hall Of Fame (set up in 2003). And, get this, Charles Lewis Jr. was not even a fighter! He got in by being a promoter and one of the biggest MMA fans ever...

YOU RATE! 1 to 100

	NAME	INDUCTION	FIGHTS WON	LOST	WINS (PERCENTAGE)
1	Royce Gracie	November 21, 2003	13	2	86.7
2	Matt Hughes	May 29, 2010	45	7	86.5
3	Dan Severn	April 16, 2005	70	13	84.3
4	Chuck Liddell	July 11, 2009	28	8	77.8
5	Ken Shamrock	November 21, 2003	26	11	70.3
6	Randy Couture	June 24, 2006	19	11	63.3
7	Mark Coleman	March 1, 2008	16	10	61.5
8	Tito Ortiz	July 7, 2012	17	11	60.7
9	Charles Lewis Jr.	July 11, 2009	0	0	0
10	-	-	-	-	-

LEAP OF FAITH

By honing their physiques, some athletes can achieve insane distances using jumping skills, alone...

TOP 10

SPORTS WITH THE HIGHEST JUMPS

If you train hard, you could end up being able to reach some amazing heights like these guys...

HIGH JUMP

XTREME FACT

Javier Sotomayor's record-breaking jump hasn't been beaten since 1993. It's the equivalent of jumping straight over a full-grown man's head with lots of room to spare!

YOU RATE!
1 to 100

GERALD SENSABAUGH

XTREME FACT

Played by some of the biggest and fastest athletes, a typical player will weigh around 220 lbs (100 kg) and be able to sprint 40 yd (36.6 m) in around five seconds!

	SPORT	ATHLETE	COUNTRY	HEIGHT JUMPED (CM)	(IN)
1	Acrobatics	Yan Zhi Cheng	China	246	97
2	High jump	Javier Sotomayor	Cuba	245	96.5
3	Martial arts	Tony Jaa	Thailand	200	78.7
4	Basketball	Kadour Ziani	France	142.2	56
5	Parkour	Hanuman	Mumbai	137.2	54
6	Volleyball	Leonel Marshall	Cuba	127	50
7	American football	Gerald Sensabaugh	USA	117	46
8	Australian football	Jared Brennan	Australia	102	40.2
9	Ice hockey	Mac Bennett	USA	86	34
10	Soccer	Cristiano Ronaldo	Portugal	78	30.7

TOP 10 SPORTS WITH THE LONGEST JUMPS

From the giddy lengths achieved by ski and skateboard jumps to the impressive, gravity-defying leaps from the ground, these are sports' finest jumpers...

YOU RATE!
1 to 100

	SPORT	ATHLETE	COUNTRY	DATE	DISTANCE JUMPED (M)	(FT)
1	Ski jump	Johan Remen Evensen	Norway	Feb 11, 2011	246.5	809
2	Stunt bike	Robbie Maddison	Australia	Dec 31, 2011	115.5	378.9
3	Snowboard	Mads Jonsson	Norway	May 9, 2005	57	187
4	BMX bike	Colin Winkelmann	USA	Dec 21, 2000	35.6	116.9
5	Skateboard	Danny Way	USA	Aug 8, 2004	24.1	79
6	Triple jump	Jonathan Edwards	UK	Aug 7, 1995	18.29	60
7	Long jump	Mike Powell	USA	Aug 30, 1991	8.95	29.4
8	Parkour	Richard Barnes	USA	Jul 18, 2010	5.8	19.03
9	Basketball	Michael Jordan	USA	1988	4.57	15
10	Standing long jump	Arne Tvervaag	Norway	Nov 11, 1968	3.71	12.2

CHECK IT OUT!

Danny Way started skateboarding when he was six years old, and won his first competition at 11. As well as breaking records for the longest jump, fastest land speed and highest air off a ramp, in 2005 he also jumped over the Great Wall Of China!

OUR TOP 10 UNOFFICIAL

MOST IMPORTANT LEAPS IN SPORTING HISTORY

1	First-ever long jump on August 5, 1901 by Peter O'Connor
2	Skateboarder Danny Way develops the MegaRamp (2002)
3	Basketballer Julius Erving wins the first-ever official Slam Dunk Contest (1976)
4	Edwards and Kravets both set triple jump world records at the '95 World Championships
5	In July of 2005, Danny Way jumped over the Great Wall Of China on his skateboard
6	David Belle invents Parkour and its popularity soars in the 1990s
7	Tom Sims invents the snowboard in 1963
8	Daredevil Robert Craig "Evel" Knievel's first stunt jump at Moses Lake, Washington (1965)
9	Shaun White's jaw-dropping performance on the half-pipe at the 2010 Winter Olympics
10	Ralph Samuelson invents waterskiing and performs leaps and stunts in 1922

LEAP OF FAITH

TOP 10 GREATEST NBA SLAM DUNK CONTEST PARTICIPANTS

The world's biggest basketball players compete for the best slam dunk in this annual NBA competition. Check out the guys that are leaping their way to the top of their game...

	PLAYER	NBA SLAM DUNK CONTEST TEAM/YEAR/PLACE	CAREER POINTS
1	Michael Jordan	Bulls/1985, 1987, 1988/2nd, 1st, 1st	32,292
3	Kobe Bryant	Lakers/1997/1st	30,252
2	Julius Erving	76ers/1984, 1985/2nd, 4th	30,026
4	Dominique Wilkins	Hawks/1984, 1985, 1986, 1988, 1990/3rd, 1st, 2nd, 2nd, 1st	26,668
5	Ray Allen	Bucks/1997/4th	23,203
6	Clyde Drexler	Trailblazers/1984, 1985, 1987, 1988, 1989/8th, 8th, 4th, 3rd, 2nd	22,195
7	Vince Carter	Raptors/2000/1st	21,427
8	Tom Chambers	SuperSonics/1987/6th	20,049
9	Scottie Pippen	Bulls/1990/5th	18,940
10	Tracy McGrady	Raptors/2000/3rd	18,381

YOU RATE! 1 to 100

FACT FLASH! CAREER POINTS 30,252

MICHAEL JORDAN

XTREME FACT

Perhaps the most famous basketball player of all time, Michael Jordan was nicknamed "Air Jordan" for the big jumps he would take during each Slam Dunk Contest. And despite not playing a professional game since 2003, Jordan is currently worth around $500 million, from his movie/TV career, and we can't forget his own awesome line of shoes!

CHECK IT OUT!

Kobe Bryant's fame skyrocketed with his impressive leaps in Slam Dunk contests, and he is now the highest scoring player to ever play for his team, the LA Lakers. His ball skills must run in the family as his father, Joe "Jellybean" Bryant, was a professional player for the Philadelphia 76ers and started showing Kobe how to play at the tender age of three years old!

STAT ATTACK

KOBE BRYANT

Date of birth .... August 23, 1978
Height .... 6.5 ft (2 m)
Weight .... 205 lb (93 kg)
Team .... Los Angeles Lakers
Olympic medals .... Two

GIVE IT A TRY... JOLLY JUMPERS

How far do you think you can jump from: a standing position upwards, a long jump, doing a triple jump? When the weather's great outside, get together with your friends and family and put on a competition! Let the games begin...

CHECK OUT THE INSANE LEAPS ON PAGE 108

...BUT, DO NOT TRY THESE AT HOME!

OUR TOP 10 UNOFFICIAL

SPORTS WITH THE MOST DANGEROUS JUMPS

Check out these sports, all involving death-defying leaps into the unknown...

1	**Sky surfing**
2	Base jumping
3	Wingsuit flying
4	Bungee jumping
5	Skydiving
6	Snowboarding
7	Stunt biking
8	Skiing
9	BMX biking
10	Skateboarding

SKY SURFING

XTREME FACT

Imagine snowboarding without any snow or ground! Sky surfing is when a skydiver jumps out of a plane with a board attached to his feet and performs surfing-style moves while falling, giving the illusion that he is surfing on air. However, it might look cool but it's a dangerous balancing act that can take years to learn.

FACT FLASH!
SKYDIVING FATALITIES DUE TO COLLISIONS
15 PERCENT

ANOTHER THING

BMX stunt biking started in concrete reservoirs in California, where brave bikers used the curves and ramps to perform crazy moves.

CHECK IT OUT!

With tight turns, big jumps and crowded tracks, BMX bikers need perfect balance and speed to avoid pile-ups, such as this one at the 2012 Olympic Games. New Zealand's Mars Willers (left of pic) used skill to escape the carnage.

IN FULL SWING

There are loads of sports that require a huge surge of energy from the player's arm, and the training required to get that swing perfect takes years. Here's how those awesome arms get put to great use...

TOP 10

SPORTS WITH THE FASTEST SWINGS

How fast can you get your arm to whip in a motion that sends a ball flying? These guys are the absolute speed demons of their chosen sport...

BADMINTON

XTREME FACT

Tan Boon Heong of Malaysia is doing a spectacular leap here to smash a shot in the mixed team at the 2011 World Badminton Championships. Putting a big jump behind his swing allows him to propel the shuttlecock with enough force to completely crush it!

FACT FLASH! SPEED 261.6 MPH

YOU RATE!
1 to 100

	SPORT	ATHLETE	NATIONALITY	YEAR	HEAD SPEED (KPH)	(MPH)
1	**Badminton**	**Tan Boon Heong**	**Malaysia**	**2010**	**421**	**261.6**
2	Racquetball	Egan Inoue	USA	1990s	307.39	191
3	Squash	Cameron Pilley	Australia	2011	281.64	175
4	Tennis	Samuel Groth	Australia	2012	263	163.4
5	Golf	Joe Miller	UK	2010	241.4	150
6	Lacrosse	Paul Rabil	USA	2010	178.64	111
7	Baseball	Justin Upton	USA	2012	171.4	106.5
8	Cricket (bowler)	Shoaib Akhtar	Pakistan	2003	161.3	100.2
9	Table Tennis	Lark Brandt	New Zealand	2003	112.5	70
10	Softball	Zara Mee	Australia	2005	111	69

CHECK IT OUT!

Here, Paul Rabil of the Boston Cannons lacrosse team takes a well-earned break during a game at Harvard Stadium in 2012. Lacrosse is very physical as players have to use a stick and a scoop action to launch a ball towards the goal at speed.

CHECK IT OUT!

Tiger Woods is celebrating here on the 18th green after winning the 1997 Masters tournament in Georgia, USA. Woods' club swinging has lead him to become the youngest and one of the most successful players in PGA history, with more career wins than any other golfer.

GIVE IT A TRY...
PERFECT PUTTER

Whacking a golf ball as hard as you can might look easy but it takes serious concentration and perfect aim. Head down to your local putting green or golf course with your friends or family and see if you can hit a hole-in-one!

ROGER FEDERER

XTREME FACT

Swiss tennis legend Roger Federer is victorious in this shot. This was match point against Andy Murray at the Wimbledon Lawn Tennis Championships in 2012. Wimbledon is the oldest tennis tournament in the world, dating back to 1877.

OUR TOP 10 UNOFFICIAL

MOST IMPORTANT SWINGS IN SPORT

FACT FLASH!
GRAND SLAM WINS
17

	THE SWING	THE RESULT
1	Tiger Woods' putt on the 18th hole at the 1997 Masters	Became the golf tournament's youngest-ever winner
2	Andy Murray's hooked forehand miss at Wimbledon 2012	Gave Roger Federer a record-breaking 17th Grand Slam tennis win
3	Joe Carter's 1993 World Series winning swing for the Jays	One of the most dramatic home runs in baseball history
4	Pat LaFontaine's 1987 NHL playoff goal in overtime	Ended the longest seventh and deciding game in NHL playoff history
5	Kyung-eun and Ha-na's deliberate bad shots at the Olympics 2012	Disqualified as the badminton pair played badly to influence the draw
6	Seve Ballesteros' 1976 birdie putt at the British Open	Then aged 19, he won the major and revitalized European golf
7	Pavel Bure's fifth goal against Finland in the 1998 Olympics	Ice hockey's "Russian Rocket" scored five in this incredible 7-4 win
8	Roger Maris' 61st home run for the Yankees in 1961	A baseball record that he took from Babe Ruth, and it stood for 37 years
9	Chen Jin's missed shot in the 2009 Championships	Gave Lin Dan an unmatched three consecutive badminton Championships
10	Goran Ivanišević's service winner at Wimbledon 2001	Won the tennis Grand Slam and he became the first-ever wild-card winner

IN FULL SWING

TOP 10 FASTEST TENNIS SERVES

You don't need to be a Wimbledon Champion to have a mighty strong serve. The Number One here is ranked 196th in the world, but he aces these competitors!

	NAME	COUNTRY	YEAR	SPEED (KPH)	(MPH)
1	**Samuel Groth**	**Australia**	**2012**	**263**	**163.4**
2	Ivo Karlović	Croatia	2011	251	155.96
3	Milos Raonic	Canada	2012	250	155.34
4	Andy Roddick	USA	2004	249	154.72
5	Joachim Johansson	Sweden	2004	245	152.24
6	Feliciano López	Spain	2008	242	150.37
7	John Isner	USA	2011	241	149.75
=	Taylor Dent	USA	2006	241	149.75
9	Ernests Gulbis	Latvia	2007	240	149.13
=	Greg Rusedski	UK	1998	240	149.13

YOU RATE!

1 to 100

ANDY RODDICK

XTREME FACT

Did you know that the Ancient Greeks used to play a version of tennis with their hands? Imagine trying to serve as fast as someone like Andy Roddick (right) with just your bare hands!

FACT FLASH! SPEED 163 MPH

COMPARE-O-METER

See how they match up to these speed demons!

SNOWBOARDER

SNOWBOARDING

202 kph
125.5 mph

FASTEST ANIMAL

PEREGRINE FALCON

325 kph
202 mph

CHECK IT OUT!

Here's the man behind the fastest tennis serve on Earth, Australia's Samuel Groth. The 25-year-old has been a professional tennis player since 2006. He is ranked 196th in the world at the moment, which goes to show that it's not just the Top 10 of the tennis world that have powerful serves... They had better all keep their eye on the underdogs, too!

World long drive record holder Mike Dobbyn takes a swing and watches his ball fly in Las Vegas, 2009

FARTHEST GOLF DRIVES (IN LONG DRIVE)

YOU RATE! 1 to 100

TOP 10

On a PGA (Professional Golfers' Association) Tour, the average distance of a golf ball drive is 287 yards. So, we thought we'd take a look at the LDA (Long Drivers Of America) legends, as they have whacked the ball REALLY far...

	NAME	NATIONALITY	DATE	DISTANCE (YARDS)	(M)
1	Mike Dobbyn	USA	2007	551	503.83
2	Sean Fister	USA	1974	515	470.92
3	Jason Zuback	Canada	2008	468	423.37
4	Carl Wolter	USA	2011	459	419.71
=	David Mobley	USA	2011	459	419.71
6	Vince Ciurluini	USA	2011	456	416.97
7	Joe Miller	UK	2011	452	413.31
8	Pat Dempsey	USA	2011	448	409.65
9	Jamie Sadlowski	Canada	2010	445	406.91
10	Craig Hagen	USA	2011	441	403.25

OUR TOP 10 UNOFFICIAL

ODDEST SWINGING SPORTS

	NAME	TECHNIQUE
1	Pelota mixteca	Punch a solid ball with special highly decorated gloves
2	Xare	This racket sport is similar to slingshot tennis
3	Jai Alai	Like squash but with scoops and incredibly fast
4	Speed-ball	Invented to train tennis players, involves a pole with a ball on a string
5	Frontenis	Like tennis, but the ball must hit the wall first then court
6	Speedminton	Super-fast badminton-esque battle with floor square
7	Racketlon	Multi-sport like Triathalon (table tennis, badminton, squash and tennis)
8	Matkot	Beach ball: wooden paddles, rubber ball, don't let it hit the sand
9	Paddle tennis	Solid wooden paddles, no strung racquets
10	Rapid ball	A new spin on squash with a "bouncier" ball, so less running

PELOTA MIXTECA

XTREME FACT

Created hundreds of years ago, here is pelota mixteca in action. It's a mash-up of tennis and volleyball, minus a net. Players wear special gloves to hit the ball. This photo shows Gustavo Gomez playing on one of the eight teams at an X Tournament of the game.

IN FULL SWING

TOP 10

LARGEST ATTENDANCE TO SPORTS WITH A SWING

Do you have a passion for a sport with a swing-skill? See if your best one has come out on top in our countdown...

CHECK IT OUT!

This is New York Yankees baseball player Alex Rodriguez, better known to his fans as A-Rod. He previously played for the Seattle Mariners and Texas Rangers, but a tempting $275 million contract lured him to the NY Yankees in 2007.

ICE HOCKEY

XTREME FACT

Bizarrely, fighting is accepted as a part of ice hockey. As long as players drop their sticks and gloves, they're allowed to get stuck in until the referee stops them!

YOU RATE!
1 to 100

	SPORT	EVENT	YEAR	ATTENDANCE RECORD
1	Golf	The Waste Management Phoenix Open	2012	173,210
2	Ice hockey	Michigan Wolverines vs Michigan State Spartans	2010	104,173
3	Cricket	Test between Australia and the West Indies	1961	90,800
4	Baseball	Telling's Strollers vs Hanna's Cleaners	1914	84,000
5	Women's golf	Valley's LPGA Tour*	2008	44,600
6	Tennis	Kim Clijsters vs Serena Williams	2010	35,681
7	Badminton	2012 World Championships	2012	32,000+
8	Lacrosse	Toronto Rock vs Arizona Sting	2005	19,432
9	Table Tennis	2012 World Championships	2012	16,000+
10	Softball	The Crimson Tide vs Auburn Tigers	2011	6,259

WEIRDEST SWINGIN' SPORTS

1	**Chess boxing: rounds alternate between boxing and a chess game set up in the ring**
2	Phasketboot: invented in 2011, it fuses basketball, football and ultimate frisbee
3	Muggle Quidditch: yes, Harry Potter fans, it's become an actual sport (but without the flying)
4	Unicycle polo: exactly as it sounds, playing polo with a unicycle instead of a horse
5	Cycle ball: swing the bicycle's wheel at a ball to score a goal
6	Clog Cobbing: who can throw the clog the furthest?
7	Conker smashing: that playground classic. Soak yours in vinegar to toughen it up
8	Crazy golf: an array of obstacles to try and stop you getting your ball in the hole
9	Pillow fight: yes, it's an all-female sport and there's a Pillow Fight League
10	Sheaf toss: swing that straw bundle over a bar using a pitchfork

SHUFFLE UP

Do you have a different idea about which are the best and weirdest swinging sports? Detail your own selection right here!

1 ....
2 ....
3 ....
4 ....
5 ....
6 ....
7 ....
8 ....
9 ....
10 ....

Know of any other crazy swing sports? Add them in... It's YOUR list!

CHESS BOXING

XTREME FACT

No, it's not a joke! Exactly as the title suggests, each bout involves a move of chess then a round of punching! Nils Becker (right) prepares for a battle of mind and muscle at the 2012 Championships in Germany. The first world championship was held in 2003.

CHECK IT OUT!

With the sheaf toss, this photo from August 8, 1955, shows that chucking a hefty sack over a bar never really goes out of fashion. Northleach Fete held in Gloucestershire, UK, still hosts the contest today.

THROW DOWN

So many sporting disciplines require a huge amount of skill in throwing something. Let's celebrate the many ways that we competitively launch objects into the air...

TOP 10 SPORTS WITH THE FARTHEST THROWS

When you compare all of the sports that involve throwing something, the Top 10 distance champs are a really surprising and eclectic mix...

	SPORT	INDIVIDUAL	COUNTRY	DATE	DISTANCE (M)	(FT)
1	Boomerang	David Schummy	Australia	Mar 15, 2005	427.8	1,403.5
2	Frisbee (Aerobie)	Erin Hemmings	USA	Jul 14, 2003	406.3	1,333
3	Disc golf	Dave Wiggins, Jr.	USA	Apr 13, 2012	255	836.61
4	Baseball	Glen Gorbous	Canada	Aug 1, 1957	135.89	445.83
5	Javelin	Uwe Hohn	Germany	Jul 20, 1984	104.8	343.83
6	American football	Various players	USA	N/A	90.53	297
7	Hammer throw	Yuriy Sedykh	Russia	Aug 30, 1986	86.74	284.6
8	Discus	Jürgen Schult	Germany	Jun 6, 1986	74.08	243.04
9	Soccer (thrown-in)	Danny Brooks	UK	Jan 18, 2010	49.78	163.32
10	Club throw	Mourad Idoudi	Tunisia	Sep 15, 2008	35.77	117.36

YOU RATE! 1 to 100

CHECK IT OUT!

Quarterback JaMarcus Russell of the Oakland Raiders certainly knows that it pays to throw well. When he signed up with the team in 2007, the six-year deal guaranteed him $31.5 million. Guess what other sport JaMarcus played in college? The javelin! Distance and accuracy are clearly in his blood...

JAVELIN

XTREME FACT

German javelin legend Uwe Hohn is the only person on the planet to ever throw more than 100 m! He was only 22 years old when he achieved the still unbeaten record distance of 343.83 ft (104.8 m). Imagine how tired his dog must be after playing fetch...

FACT FLASH! THROW 343.83 FT

OFF THE CHART

BASKETBALL

Elan Buller from Woodland Hills, California, USA, knows a thing or two about throwing. He holds the world record for the longest basketball shot successfully made at 104.7 ft (31.9 m)!

CHECK IT OUT!

This epic 1965 Boxing World Heavyweight Title fight saw Muhammad Ali face the wrath of the larger Sonny Liston at St. Dominic's Arena, but Ali knocked him out in the first round! The lightning blow became known as "the phantom punch", because most people at ringside didn't even see it. Here, champion Ali stands over the "lights out" Liston, shouting, "Get up sucker and fight!"

OUR TOP 10 UNOFFICIAL

MOST IMPORTANT THROWS IN SPORT

	THE THROW	THE RESULT
1	Muhammad Ali's 1965 "phantom punch"	Sonny Liston was counted out and Ali won boxing's World Heavyweight Championship
2	Jan Železný 2000 Olympic javelin throw	Gave him his third gold medal at consecutive Olympic Games
3	Terry Bradshaw's 1972 downfield pass	Won the Steelers the game with 30 seconds left, in one of the craziest plays in NFL history
4	Johnny Vander Meer's back-to-back no-hitters	In 1938, the baseball Hall Of Famer threw no-hitters in back-to-back starts
5	Michael Jordan's 20-foot jump shot	A 1998 championship-winning 20-foot jumper over a fallen Bryon Russell
6	Buster Douglas' 1990 uppercut	Mike Tyson ended up on the canvas making Douglas the heavyweight champion
7	Joe Montana's pass at Super Bowl XXIII	Better known for "the catch", this pass sealed the NFC Championship for the 49ers
8	Vinnie Johnson's 14-foot shot	Sealed a 2nd consecutive basketball championship for the Pistons with 0.7 secs remaining
9	Shot-putter Randy Barnes' 23.12 m throw	Gave the American the World Record in 1990 at UCLA
10	Rory Delap's 2008 45 m soccer throw-in	Landed in the penalty area and became an assist to Stoke's goal in a 2-1 victory over Arsenal

TOP 10

FASTEST BASEBALL PITCHERS

How fast do you think you can pitch a ball? These baseball players have the speed-skills that would be very intimidating to face from the plate...

AROLDIS CHAPMAN

YOU RATE!

1 to 100

	NAME	YEAR	PITCH SPEED (KPH)	(MPH)
1	**Nolan Ryan**	1974	173.97	108.1
2	Bob Feller	1946	173.17	107.6
3	Aroldis Chapman	2010	169.14	105.1
4	Joel Zumaya	2006	168.66	104.8
5	Mark Wohlers	1995	165.76	103
6	Jonathan Broxton	2009	165.12	102.6
7	Steve Dalkowski	1958	164.96	102.5
8	Brian Wilson	2009	164.47	102.2
9	Bobby Jenks	2005	164.15	102
=	Randy Johnson	2004	164.15	102

XTREME FACT

Here's 25-year-old Cincinnati Reds pitcher Aroldis Chapman doing his lightning ball thing against the St. Louis Cardinals on October 2, 2012. It was during his September 24, 2010, game against the San Diego Padres that he clocked his fastest-ever recorded pitch of over 105 mph (169 kph).

COMPARE-O-METER

See how those power-throws fair against these other T-10 chart toppers...

CHEETAH

FASTEST LAND ANIMAL

113 kph
70.2 mph

007's CAR

ASTON MARTIN DB5

315 kph
196 mph

CHECK IT OUT!

This is Nolan Ryan, who is pictured here during his time with the Houston Astros. He earned himself the nickname of "The Ryan Express" because of his hurricane pitch that regularly topped 99.4 mph (160 kph)!

Chris Ford, of the Boston Celtics, made the first three-point shot in NBA history at Boston Garden on October 12, 1979!

OUR **TOP 10** UNOFFICIAL

MOST SPECTACULAR BASKETBALL SHOTS

	NAME	TEAM	YEAR	THE SHOT
1	**Jerry West**	**Lakers**	**1970**	**Half-court shot puts the finals into overtime**
2	Sean Elliott	Spurs	1999	Last-second shot against the Trail Blazers in the playoffs
3	Alonzo Mourning	Hornets	1993	On-the-buzzer shot against the Celtics won the series
4	Reggie Miller	Pacers	1995	Constant three-pointers against the Knicks in the playoffs
5	Jeff Malone	Wizards	1984	Scored from beyond the baseline, beating the Pistons
6	John Stockton	Jazz	1997	Hit a last-second three-pointer to win the finals
7	Ralph Sampson	Rockets	1986	Made a buzzer-beating tip-shot to send the Rockets to the finals
8	John Paxson	Bulls	1993	Shot down the Suns in the 1993 NBA Finals with time running down
9	Robert Horry	Lakers	2002	A magic three-pointer pushed the Lakers past the Kings in the playoffs
10	Derek Fisher	Lakers	2004	A buzzer-beating shot to beat the Spurs in the playoffs

CHECK IT OUT!

Check out Utah Jazz's John Stockton as he shows how to shoot a perfect under-pressure shot. He played for the Jazz for a very impressive 19 years before retiring in 2003, aged 41 years old.

SEAN ELLIOTT

XTREME FACT

Sean Elliott (far right) of the San Antonio Spurs made his NBA debut on November 4, 1989. Before this, he won a gold medal with the US national team at the 1986 FIBA World Championships.

MUSCLE MOVEMENT

When it comes to thrill-seeking, a lot of sporting activities provide surges of adrenaline... Especially when you make your body travel at an insane speed like this bunch!

TOP 10 SPORTS THAT PROPEL THE FASTEST

Want to experience the thrill of going super-fast without the aid of an engine? These sports see humans achieve terrific speeds by just using their body and some cool equipment...

	SPORT	TOP SPEED ATTAINED (KPH)	(MPH)
1	Speed skydiving	526.9	327.4
2	Motor-paced cycling*	268.8	166.9
3	Speed skiing	251.4	156.2
4	Downhill cycling	222	138
5	Mountain biking	210.4	130.7
6	Snowboarding	202	125.5
7	Bobsledding	201	124.8
8	Cycling**	133	83
9	Longboarding (skateboard variant)	130.1	80.8
10	Track cycling (Velodrome)	85	52.8

*Using a special bicycle with a windshield behind a dragster
**Flat surface

YOU RATE! 1 to 100

FACT FLASH! SPEED 52.8 MPH

CHECK IT OUT!
Snowboarding used to be a fun pastime for the snowy slopes, but it zoomed into mainstream popularity when it became an Olympic sport in the 1990s.

TRACK CYCLING

XTREME FACT
This is Australia's Shane Perkins competing at the London 2012 Olympic Games. The strange shaped helmets and crouched cycling position used by the teams make the cyclists as aerodynamic as possible. Shane won the Olympic bronze medal for the men's sprint cycling final.

TOP 10 FASTEST SPRINTERS

With running, it's just you, the ground and some springy shoes. These are the quickest human beings on the planet, right now...

USAIN BOLT

YOU RATE! 1 to 100

XTREME FACT

Dubbed the fastest man on the planet, it's easy to see why. Bolt is not only the fastest sprinter, he also holds the world record for fastest 200 m and 4 x 100 m relays. He picked up SIX gold medals at the 2012 Olympics!

FACT FLASH! 100 M **9.58** SECONDS

	NAME	COUNTRY	DATE OF RACE	TIME (SECONDS)
1	Usain Bolt	Jamaica	Aug 16, 2009	9.58
2	Yohan Blake	Jamaica	Aug 23, 2012	9.69
=	Tyson Gay	USA	Sep 20, 2009	9.69
4	Asafa Powell	Jamaica	Sep 2, 2008	9.72
5	Nesta Carter	Jamaica	Aug 29, 2010	9.78
6	Maurice Greene	USA	Jun 16, 1999	9.79
=	Justin Gatlin	USA	Aug 5, 2012	9.79
8	Steve Mullings	Jamaica	Jun 4, 2011	9.80
9	Donovan Bailey	Canada	Jul 27, 1996	9.84
=	Bruny Surin	Canada	Aug 22, 1999	9.84

GIVE IT A TRY... WALK ABOUT

Have you heard of a pedometer? It's a great little device, used to measure your speed and the distance you travel. There are even apps to download for smartphones that'll do this, too. You could set up a challenge between you, your friends and family to find out exactly how fast each of you can run!

OFF THE CHART

JONNIE PEACOCK

20-year-old 100 m sprinter Jonnie Peacock took home gold for Great Britain at the 2012 Summer Paralympics. Prior to those events, he set a new 100 m world record in amputee sprinting in June 2012, with an amazing time of 10.85 secs! Sporting triumphs aside, Jonnie was awarded an MBE (Member of the Order of the British Empire) at the end of 2012. Go, Jonnie, GO!

FASTEST ON WATER
(UNASSISTED BY MOTORS)

TOP 10

Without the aid of engine thrust, how fast do you think water sports experts can propel themselves? Turns out it's a lot faster than you'd think...

	SPORT	RECORD HOLDER	COUNTRY	SPEED (KPH)	(MPH)
1	**Kiteboarding**	Rob Douglas	USA	103.1	64.1
2	Windsurfing	Steve Thorp	UK	93.5	58.1
3	Surfing	Mick Fanning	Australia	39.1	24.3
4	White Water Rafting	Currently unknown	N/A	30.6*	19*
5	Kayaking	Currently unknown	N/A	27.2**	16.9**
6	Skimboarding	Currently unknown	N/A	25***	15.5***
7	Waveski Surfing	Currently unknown	N/A	22***	13.7***
8	Rowing	Mahé Drysdale	New Zealand	18.3	11.4
9	Stand Up Paddle Boarding	Currently unknown	N/A	13.6*	8.5*
10	Swimming	Michael Phelps	USA	7.56	4.7

YOU RATE!
1 to 100

*River flow speed, Klutina River, Alaska
**Achieved with a hydrofoil "flyak"
***Attainable speed

FACT FLASH!
SPEED 64.1 MPH

CHECK IT OUT!

When kiteboarding champions unite! Here is Brock Callen (at the front), and Rob Douglas (the current world record holder for kiteboarding speed) behind him, training at Cape Poge, USA. Brock lives on Martha's Vineyard, which ocean fans will know is where they filmed Steven Spielberg's shark movie *Jaws*!

GIVE IT A TRY...
SKIPPING STONES

How good are you and your friends at skipping stones? Have you ever tried it? Seek out the flattest, smoothest, most oval-shaped stones, and, with a flick of the wrist, see how many times you can make it skip the water's surface before it sinks!

SURFING

XTREME FACT

Check out 32-year-old Australian Mick Fanning owning the waves. This shot was taken on August 27, 2012 at Teahupoo, French Polynesia. He was victorious for this Billabong Pro Teahupoo tournament. Hugely popular, Mick has nearly 100,000 twitter followers at @Mick_Fanning!

SPORTING TRICKSTERS

These guys and girls are all about the jaw-dropping tricks and flips that we love...

	NAME	COUNTRY	SPORT
1	**Amber Wing**	**Australia**	**Wakeboarding**
2	Carey Hart	USA	Motocross
3	Caroline Lejeune	France	Freestyle slalom skating
4	Keala Kennelly	Hawaii	Surfing
5	Sébastien Foucan	France	Parkour
6	Gretchen Bleiler	USA	Snowboarding
7	Warwick Stevenson	Australia	BMX Racing
8	Josh Tenge	USA	Sandboarding
9	Shaun White	USA	Snowboarding, Skateboarding
10	Tony Hawk	USA	Skateboarding

CHECK IT OUT!

Motocross and motorcycle legend and now off-road truck racer Carey Hart has a very famous rockstar wife... Pink! They got married in 2006 and have a daughter called Willow.

FACT FLASH!
SPEED
80.8
MPH

YOU RATE!
1 to 100

LONGBOARDING

XTREME FACT

Be wary if you're thinking of attempting crazy speeds on a longboard, because there are no brakes! Expert riders guide their longboard into S-shaped curves, which is called "carving". This gives them greater control of their speed.

FASTEST ON LAND
(UNASSISTED BY MOTORS)

When it comes to achieving breakneck speeds across land, without the help of an engine boost, these are the record-breaking legends...

	SPORT	RECORD HOLDER	COUNTRY	SPEED (KPH)	(MPH)
1	Motor-paced cycling*	Fred Rompelber	Netherlands	268.8	166.9
2	Speed skiing	Simone Origone	Italy	251.4	156.2
3	Downhill cycling	Eric Barone	France	222	138
4	Mountain biking	Markus Stöckl	Austria	210.4	130.7
5	Snowboarding	Darren Powell	Australia	202	125.5
6	Bobsledding	Romuald Bonvin	Switzerland	201	124.8
7	Cycling**	Sam Whittingham	Canada	133	83
8	Longboarding	Mischo Erban	Canada	130.1	80.8
9	Track cycling (Velodrome)	N/A	N/A	85***	52.8
10	Speed skating	Jeremy Wotherspoon	Canada	52.9	32.9

*Using a special bicycle with a windshield behind a dragster **Flat surface
***This sport is measured by lap times, but this speed is regularly achieved

125

ENGINE THRUST

The technology mankind has developed for engine power can now propel us to breakneck speeds we only thought possible years ago in science fiction...

TOP 10 FASTEST MACHINES IN SPORT

Brave drivers and pilots take the helm of mechanical beasts that make engine-powered sports such a thrill for us spectators to watch...

	SPORT	SURFACE	TOP SPEED (KPH)	(MPH)
1	Top fuel dragster	Track	515	320
2	Speedboat	Water	511	317.5
3	Airshow stunt plane	Air	426	264.7
4	Formula One car	Circuit	370	230
5	Motor rally (NASCAR, etc)	Circuit	342.4	212.8
6	Snowmobile	Snow terrain	338	210
7	Motorbike	Circuit	312	194
8	Jetski	Water	289.7	180
9	Monster truck	Course	154.5	96
10	Go-kart	Circuit	128.7	80

YOU RATE! 1 to 100

FACT FLASH! SPEED 212.8 MPH

TOP FUEL DRAG RACING

XTREME FACT

These racers don't run on any kind of normal gasoline. The engines feed on mostly nitromethane (hence, where the term "nitro" comes from). Acceleration? More like a jump to light-speed! How does zero to 100 mph (160 kph) in 0.7 secs sound? Yes, it sounds INSANE!

OUR TOP 10 UNOFFICIAL
GREATEST RACING DRIVERS

	DRIVER	NOTABLE ACHIEVEMENTS
1	Ayrton Senna	Three times Formula One World Driving Champion
2	Lewis Hamilton	21 wins and the 2008 Formula One Championship by the age of 28
3	Mario Andretti	Wins in Formula One, IndyCar, World Sportscar Championship and NASCAR
4	A.J. Foyt	Wins include the 24 Hours Of Le Mans, Daytona 500, 24 Hours Of Daytona
5	Mark Donohue	Competed in Trans-Am, Formula One, NASCAR and won five Indy 500s
6	Richard Petty	Known as "The King" as he won 200 races and seven NASCAR championships
7	Sebastian Loeb	The most successful driver in World Rally Car history, with 54 wins
8	Alex Zanardi	Drove a specially modified IndyCar after losing both legs in a crash
9	Michael Schumacher	306 Formula One starts, 155 podiums, 91 wins, and 7 championships
10	Jackie Stewart	Largely responsible for modernization of safety in motor racing

LEWIS HAMILTON
XTREME FACT

Never considered to be a shy guy, when he was just 10 years old and tearing up the karting scene, the UK's F1 star Lewis Hamilton informed his future McLaren bosses that he would drive for them!

FACT FLASH!
21 WINS

TOP 10 HIGHEST SCORING MONSTER JAM FREESTYLE WINNERS

Monster-sized trucks causing mayhem and destruction? Yes, please! Here are the 10 most successful trucks and their prize-winning drivers...

	TRUCK NAME	DRIVER(S)	FREESTYLE POINTS (2000-2012)
1	**Grave Digger**	**Dennis Anderson**	**362**
2	Avenger	Jim Koehler	267
3	Blue Thunder	Lyle Hancock, Tony Farrell, Linsey Weenk	253
4	Bounty Hunter	Jim Creten	249
5	Madusa	Debra Miceli	223
6	Monster Mutt	Todd Frolik, Bobby Z, Charlie Pauken	222
7	El Toro Loco	Lupe Soza, Marc McDonald	206
8	Maximum Destruction	Tom Meents	179
9	Air Force Afterburner	Paul Cohen, Damon Bradshaw	164
10	Black Stallion	Michael Vaters	144

YOU RATE!
1 to 100

GRAVE DIGGER

MONSTER MUTT
XTREME FACT
It's been 10 years since Monster Mutt first smashed things up in 2003. Ten drivers so far have tamed the canine-painted Mutt, which was devised and built in Chicago, USA.

FACT FLASH!
SCORE
222
POINTS

EXTRA! The Monster Truck's world-famous Monster Jam shifts 3.5 million tickets every year to gearheads with a love for big wheels and destruction! Each of the crazy trucks is created especially for the event and fans cheer for their preferred Monster, just like they would for their top wrestlers, except these metallic muscle-heads are a hell of a lot tougher!

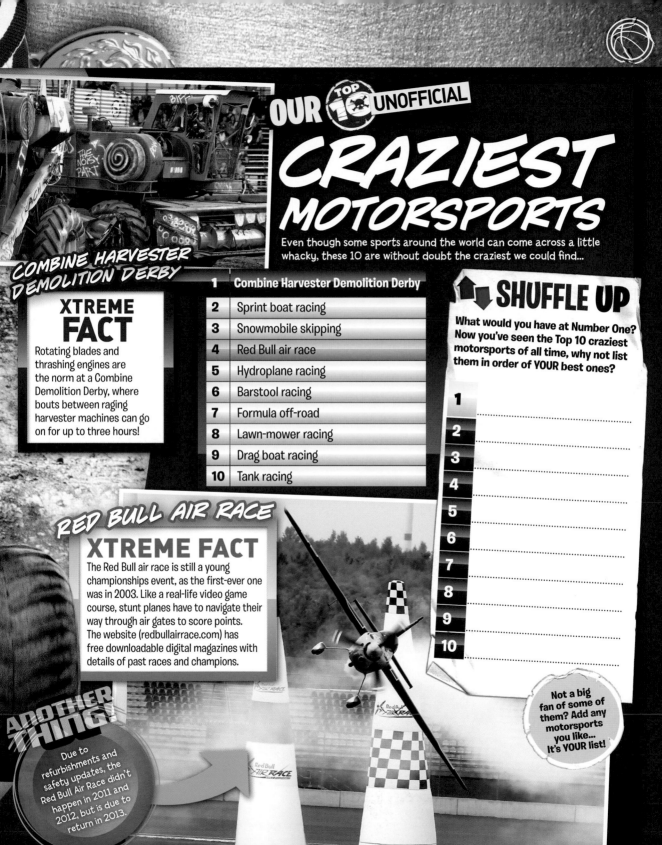

OUR **TOP 10** UNOFFICIAL

CRAZIEST MOTORSPORTS

Even though some sports around the world can come across a little whacky, these 10 are without doubt the craziest we could find...

COMBINE HARVESTER DEMOLITION DERBY

XTREME FACT

Rotating blades and thrashing engines are the norm at a Combine Demolition Derby, where bouts between raging harvester machines can go on for up to three hours!

1	**Combine Harvester Demolition Derby**
2	Sprint boat racing
3	Snowmobile skipping
4	Red Bull air race
5	Hydroplane racing
6	Barstool racing
7	Formula off-road
8	Lawn-mower racing
9	Drag boat racing
10	Tank racing

SHUFFLE UP

What would you have at Number One? Now you've seen the Top 10 craziest motorsports of all time, why not list them in order of YOUR best ones?

1 ....
2 ....
3 ....
4 ....
5 ....
6 ....
7 ....
8 ....
9 ....
10 ....

Not a big fan of some of them? Add any motorsports you like... It's YOUR list!

RED BULL AIR RACE

XTREME FACT

The Red Bull air race is still a young championships event, as the first-ever one was in 2003. Like a real-life video game course, stunt planes have to navigate their way through air gates to score points. The website (redbullairrace.com) has free downloadable digital magazines with details of past races and champions.

ANOTHER THING!

Due to refurbishments and safety updates, the Red Bull Air Race didn't happen in 2011 and 2012, but is due to return in 2013.

EXTREME DANGER

Extreme sports are unusual, adrenaline-filled activities. These are known as "extreme" because of how dangerous they are. However, some of the more "normal" sports are deadlier than you'd think...

TOP 10 MOST DECORATED X GAMES COMPETITORS

The X Games began in 1995, and covers all manner of action/extreme sports, including snowboarding and skateboarding. These are the 10 biggest medal winners of all time...

	NAME	COUNTRY	DISCIPLINE(S)	TOTAL MEDALS
1	**Dave Mirra**	USA	**BMX/Rally car**	24
2	Shaun White	USA	Snowboard, Skateboard	23
3	Andy McDonald	Canada	Skateboard	21
4	Pierre-Luc Gagnon	Canada	Skateboard	17
5	Travis Pastrana	USA	Motocross	15
=	Bucky Lasek	USA	Skateboard	15
7	Tony Hawk	USA	Skateboard	14
8	Barrett Christy	USA	Snowboard	10
=	Rune Glifberg	Denmark	Skateboard	10
10	Jamie Bestwick	UK	BMX	8

YOU RATE! 1 to 100

FACT FLASH! MEDALS 23

PIERRE-LUC GAGNON

XTREME FACT

Like many skateboarders, Canadian Pierre-Luc Gagnon started his career young, entering his first professional competition at age 12!

CHECK IT OUT!

Talk about being born to rule the snow... Shaun White is one of the greatest snowboarders of all time, with an insane 27 gold medals, including two for Olympic events and 14 from the X Games. But he doesn't just crush it on the snow, he also has eight medals (three of them gold) for skateboarding, as well!

SNOWBOARDING MASTERS & THEIR TRICKS

1	**Scotty Lago's 1620**
2	Shaun White's Double McTwist 1260
3	Joel Fuquay's Double Cork 1260
4	Pat Burgener's Switch Backside 1440 Triple Cork
5	Kimmy Fasani's Double Backflip
6	Travis Rice's Switch Backside Double Cork 1080
7	Eric Beauchemin's Double Back Rodeo
8	Torstein Horgmo Switch Backside 1260
9	Alek Oestreng's Hardway Backside 270
10	Travis Parker's Backflip 360

FACT FLASH!
MEDALS
24

DAVE MIRRA

XTREME FACT

BMX genius Dave Mirra knows how to cycle in style. At the 2006 X Games, he rode a gold-plated BMX, worth $7,500, in the competition! Sadly all that glitters isn't gold, as he didn't win any medals...

GIVE IT A TRY...
BE A TRICKSTER

Do you or any of your friends enjoy skateboarding, BMXing, or roller skating? Help each other develop cool, new tricks. Even if you don't take part, you could come up with some ace ideas!

CHECK IT OUT!

Scotty Lago has been snowboarding since he was just nine years old. However, of the six medals he's won, his only singular gold was for the sought-after "Best Method" at the X Games in 2011.

EXTRA! Want to see how spectacular these snowboarding tricks are? Search for them online to witness the gravity-defying madness for yourself...

TOP 10 MOST DECORATED X GAMES SKATEBOARDERS

From incredible jumps to becoming the kings of the half-pipe, here are the 10 most awarded 'boarders ever...

	NAME	COUNTRY	TOTAL MEDALS
1	**Andy MacDonald**	**Canada**	**22**
2	Pierre-Luc Gagnon	Canada	18
3	Bucky Lasek	USA	15
4	Tony Hawk	USA	14
5	Rune Glifberg	Denmark	10
6	Ryan Sheckler	USA	6
=	Paul Rodriguez	USA	6
=	Danny Way	USA	6
9	Shaun White	USA	5
=	Jake Brown	Australia	5

YOU RATE!

1 to 100

CHECK IT OUT!

Ryan Sheckler isn't just a world-class skateboarder... He's also a star of MTV's *Life Of Ryan*, which ran for three seasons between 2007-09 with a fly-on-wall reality-show style format. Sheckler didn't just have the camera crew focus on his skateboarding, they also captured the personal ups and downs of his family life. MTV produced 29 episodes in total.

TONY HAWK

XTREME FACT

Aside from being one of the most innovative skateboarders ever, Tony Hawk also has no less than 14 hit video games based on him and his style. Sales total more than 53 million units!

FACT FLASH!
MEDALS
14

HIGHEST AIR SPORTS

There are more sports you can do in the air than you'd think. The danger level is almost at maximum with these, so check out the astonishing heights this lot achieved...

	SPORT	NAME	HEIGHT (M)	(FT)
1	**Near-orbit skydive**	**Felix Baumgartner**	**39,045**	**128,100**
2	Free-fall parachute jump	Eugene Andreev	25,458	83,524
3	Hot-air ballooning	Vijaypat Singhania	21,027	68,986
4	Hang gliding	Judy Leden	11,826	38,800
5	Wingsuit flying	Jhonathan Florez	11,358	37,264
6	BASE jumping	Nic Feteris, Glenn Singleman	6,286	20,623
7	Powered paragliding	Ramón Morillas Salmeron	6,102	20,019
8	Cluster ballooning	Mike Howard, Steve Davis	5,600	18,373
9	Foot-launched powered hang gliding	Patrick Laverty	5,348	17,546
10	Paragliding	Robbie Whittall	4,526	14,849

YOU RATE!

1 to 100

NEAR-ORBIT SKYDIVE

XTREME FACT

Austrian skydiving legend Felix Baumgartner suffers from claustrophobia. This is the fear of small, confined spaces. Specialists were brought onto the project to help him get over the anxiety of being inside the pressurized suit, which was essential to his survival.

ANOTHER THING!

Felix can fly! He holds the record for being the first person to skydive across the English Channel wearing a wingsuit.

ZENITH
SWISS WATCH MANUFACTURE

FACT FLASH!
HEIGHT
128,100 FT

MISS EDGE

REDBULL

EXTREME DANGER

TOP 10 MOST DANGEROUS SPORTS

Even though extreme sports have a reputation for causing injuries, the most dangerous sports (by fatalities) surprised Team T-10, and will surprise you, too...

	SPORT	TOTAL FATALITIES	YOU RATE! 1 to 100
1	Motor racing	359	
2	Mountaineering	121	
3	Motorcycle racing	99	
4	Soccer	45	
5	Boxing	42	
6	Skiing	29	
7	Horse racing	24	
8	Scuba diving	23	
9	Cycling	20	
10	Parachuting	19	

BOXING XTREME FACT

The first boxing fatality happened way back in 1897. Jimmy Barry knocked out Walter Croot, who died of a brain injury from the blow.

TOP 10 GREATEST BOXERS WHO RETIRED UNDEFEATED

Every professional boxer wants to have a career full of wins with zero defeats, and these 10 legends achieved exactly that...

	NAME	COUNTRY	UNDEFEATED WINS	YOU RATE! 1 to 100
1	Rocky Marciano	USA	49	
2	Joe Calzaghe	Wales	46	
3	Somboon Phantasi	Thailand	43	
4	Sven Ottke	German	34	
5	Michael Loewe	Romania	28	
6	Edwin Valero	Venezuela	27	
7	Harry Simon	Georgia	25	
8	George Kandelaki	Thailand	24	
9	Pichit Sitbangprachan	Namibia	24	
10	Scott Daley	USA	24	

FACT FLASH! UNDEFEATED IN 43 FIGHTS

OFF THE CHART FLOYD MAYWEATHER JR.

Although Floyd Mayweather, Jr. has won all 43 of his fights to date (including eight world titles), until he retires, we can't feature him in this Top 10. As he doesn't get hit much, he's earned himself the nickname of "Pretty Boy".

TAKING IT FURTHER

We decided to come up with some ways that extreme sports legends could push themselves to the limit, and beyond...

1	**Bungee jump over a crocodile-infested river**
2	Parachute from a helicopter then snowboard upon landing
3	Hang-glide over a cliff and land on a moving boat
4	Waterski in shark-infested waters
5	Nighttime BMXing in the woods
6	Wingsuit skydive into a canyon gorge
7	Mountain climbing using just their hands
8	Bungee jump from the basket of a hot-air balloon
9	Canoeing down the Amazon River (full of river monsters)
10	Base jump in a built-up city

CHECK IT OUT!

American daredevil stuntman Evel Knievel was almost as famous for his epic crashes as he was for the stunts themselves. In this shot from 1975, above, he lost control of his motorbike after clearing 13 single-deck buses in London. He broke his pelvis in the fall.

✓ BASE JUMP IN A BUILT-UP CITY

XTREME FACT

Here's the famous Russian base jumper Anton Chervyakov literally taking it to the next level on September 27, 2012. He jumped off the Kuala Lumpur Tower, which stretches up 1,381 ft (421 m) over the capital city of Malaysia. Madness!

OUR **TOP 10** UNOFFICIAL

ULTIMATE SPORTING DAREDEVILS

Here are Team T-10's all-time fave adrenaline addicts and the amazing stunts they're famous for performing...

	NAME	STUNTS
1	**Evel Knievel**	Motorcycle jumps over buses, cars and canyons
2	Felix Baumgartner	Record-breaking skydive from the edge of space
3	Alain Robert	Climbs buildings without a safety rope
4	Eddie Kidd	Jumped the Great Wall Of China on a motorcycle
5	Ormer Locklear	Daredevil pilot walked on a plane's wings
6	Gary Connery	Skydive without a parachute
7	David Smith Jr.	He is, simply, "the human cannonball"
8	Philippe Petit	Tightrope walked between NY's Twin Towers
9	Danny Way	Countless terrifying skateboard records
10	Jackie Chan	Does all his own crazy movie stunts

THE A-TEAMS

There is no "I" in team, and these are the groups of sports stars who really know how to be successful by working together...

TOP 10

TEAMS WITH THE LARGEST STADIUM

Great teams need great places to hone their skills, and these 10 are lucky enough to train in some massive structures...

CHECK IT OUT!

Michigan Stadium had a major renovation in 2010, costing to the tune of $226 million! Seeing as it was originally constructed in 1927, it was really due for a makeover. The stadium is the sporting home to over 109,000 fans, so it's no wonder it's known as The Big House.

FACT FLASH!
CAPACITY
109,901

YOU RATE!
1 to 100

	TEAM	SPORT	LOCATION	STADIUM	CAPACITY
1	Korea DPR	Soccer	Pyongyang (North Korea)	Rungrado May Day	150,000
2	Mohun Bagan Athletic Club & Mohammedan Sporting Club	Soccer	Kolkata (India)	Salt Lake	120,000
3	Michigan Wolverines	American football	Ann Arbor (USA)	Michigan	109,901
4	Penn State Nittany Lions	American football	Pennslyvania (USA)	Beaver	106,572
5	Club América	Soccer	Mexico City (Mexico)	Estadio Azteca	105,000
6	Tennessee Volunteers	American football	Knoxville (USA)	Neyland	102,455
7	Ohio State Buckeyes	American football	Columbus (USA)	Ohio	102,329
8	Alabama Crimson Tide	American football	Tuscaloosa (USA)	Bryant-Denny	101,821
9	Texas Longhorns	American football	Austin (USA)	Darrell K Royal-Texas Memorial	100,119
10	Australian National Cricket Team	Cricket	Melbourne (Australia)	Melbourne Cricket Ground	100,018

OUR TOP 10 UNOFFICIAL

TEAMS WITH THE COOLEST NICKNAMES

	TEAM	NICKNAME
1	**Manchester United**	**The Red Devils**
2	Real Madrid	The Vikings
3	The New York Yankees	The Bronxs Bombers
4	Dallas Cowboys	America's Team
5	Texas Rangers	The Power Rangers
6	Philadelphia Flyers	The Broad Street Bullies
7	Spanish National Soccer Team	La Furia Roja (The Red Fury)
8	Los Angeles Dodgers	The Boys In Blue
9	Atlanta Falcons	Dirty Birds
10	New Orleans Saints	The Aints

NEW YORK YANKEES

XTREME FACT

Many sports teams have been around for a long time, but the New York Yankees are one of the oldest: it's been a New York-based team for 110 years, since 1903!

GIVE IT A TRY...
JOIN A LOCAL TEAM

Are you a member of a local sports team? Find out what facilities there are and see if you can become a team player!

MANCHESTER UNITED

XTREME FACT

Manchester United's numerous wins and awards include the famous "treble" of 1998-99, where they won the European Cup, FA Cup and were Premier League champions. The team has attracted some soccer-star greats, including Dutch international Robin van Persie, shown celebrating in this pic (left) with teammate Wayne Rooney.

FACT FLASH!
WORTH
2.23 BILLION DOLLARS

THE A-TEAMS

TOP 10 MOST SUCCESSFUL OLYMPIC NATIONS

The best way to work out the Top 10 Olympic nations of all time is by combining all the medals of all the Olympic games...

YOU RATE! 1 to 100

CHECK IT OUT!

USA's Allyson Felix had a phenomenal 2012 Olympics. Not only did she pick up three gold medals (for the 200 m, 4x400 m relay and 4x100 m relay), but her 4x100 m relay team clocked a new world record of 40.82 secs!

	COUNTRY	GOLD	SILVER	BRONZE	TOTAL MEDALS
1	USA	1062	854	738	2,654
2	Russia	473	376	355	1,204
3	Great Britain	245	275	282	802
4	France	229	250	286	765
5	Germany	244	254	265	763
6	Italy	235	198	222	655
7	Sweden	191	197	224	612
8	China	192	165	162	519
9	Hungary	167	146	169	482
10	Australia	143	154	179	476

TOP 10 NATIONS THAT HAVE NEVER WON AN OLYMPIC MEDAL

These are the nations with the lowest amount of athletes at London 2012, and they're all still awaiting an elusive Olympic medal. There's always Rio in 2016, guys!

YOU RATE! 1 to 100

	COUNTRY	ATHLETES AT 2012
1	Dominica	2
=	Gambia	2
=	Sierra Leone	2
4	Brunei Darussalam	3
=	Chad	3
=	Kiribati	3
7	Bangladesh	5
=	Burkina Faso	5
9	Cambodia	6
10	Guam	8

CAMBODIA

XTREME FACT

Just 20 years old, Sorn Davin, Cambodia's tae kwon do expert, proudly held the flag for her team in the 2012 Olympics opening ceremony.

MOST POPULAR TEAMS ON FACEBOOK

TOP 10

Of all the sports teams on the planet, which are the most (Facebook) liked? These 10 crush all the competition...

SHUFFLE UP

What would you have at Number One? Take a look at this Top 10 list and put them in the order of the ones YOU support the most!

YOU RATE!
1 to 100

1
2
3
4
5
6
7
8
9
10

	TEAM	SPORT	"LIKES"
1	FC Barcelona	Soccer	37,333,483
2	Real Madrid	Soccer	33,480,628
3	Manchester United	Soccer	29,091,530
4	LA Lakers	Basketball	15,233,966
5	Chelsea	Soccer	14,135,735
6	AC Milan	Soccer	12,565,187
7	Arsenal	Soccer	12,013,031
8	Liverpool	Soccer	10,682,337
9	Chicago Bulls	Basketball	7,362,499
10	Miami Heat	Basketball	6,999,476

Know of any other awesome teams? Add them in... It's YOUR list!

CHECK IT OUT!

Part of the reason for FC Barcelona's popularity may be due to the fact that they have the amazing Lionel Messi in their ranks. Unbelievably, he was awarded the much sought-after European Golden Shoe award for Leading Goalscorer in both seasons 2009-10 and 2011-12.

LA LAKERS

XTREME FACT

As one of the most successful and celebrated basketball teams of all time, the LA Lakers have certainly had its superstars, including Kobe Bryant, Earvin "Magic" Johnson and 7.1 ft (2.16 m) giant Shaquille O'Neal. The trio has set countless records, including Bryant's score of 12 for "most three-point field goals in a game"!

YOU'RE ON YOUR OWN

For some sports, you don't have the support of a team... It's just you, your skills and the rush of adrenaline to propel you towards medal glory!

TOP 10 MOST POPULAR SOLO SPORTS STARS

We've taken 10 of the biggest moneymakers in solo sports, put the dollars aside, and found out how they measure up against each other on Facebook...

	NAME	SPORT	FACEBOOK PAGE "LIKES"
1	Roger Federer	Tennis	12,600,000
2	Rafael Nadal	Tennis	11,500,000
3	Valentino Rossi	Motorcycle racing	5,300,000
4	Manny Pacquiáo	Boxing	3,500,000
5	Phil Mickelson	Golf	3,000,000
6	Tiger Woods	Golf	2,700,000
7	Floyd Mayweather Jr.	Boxing	1,900,000
8	Dale Earnhardt Jr.	NASCAR	1,500,000
9	Michael Schumacher	F1 racing	308,000
10	Fernando Alonso	F1 racing	304,000

YOU RATE! 1 to 100

VALENTINO ROSSI

XTREME FACT

Valentino Rossi (below) certainly takes his stardom seriously... Check out his website (valentinorossi.com) for flashy displays and full-on celebrity stylings! This pic shows him warming up for the 2012 MotoGP World Championship.

CHECK IT OUT!

Aside from Rafael Nadal's amazing 11 championship wins, he also won the gold for tennis at the 2008 Olympics. He started ruling the court at a very young age, with major junior events won at the age of eight, and turning professional at just 15!

FACT FLASH! 5.3 MILLION "LIKES"

TOP 10

MOST SUCCESSFUL OLYMPIANS

Competing at an Olympic level is surely the greatest honour for any sports star, as you're competing with the planet's best for your nation. These 10 go beyond the gold...

YOU RATE!
1 to 100

	NAME	DISCIPLINE	COUNTRY	TOTAL MEDALS WON
1	**Michael Phelps**	**Swimming**	**USA**	**22**
2	Larisa Latynina	Gymnastics	Russia	18
3	Nikolai Andrianov	Gymnastics	Russia	15
4	Boris Shakhlin	Gymnastics	Russia	13
=	Edoardo Mangiarotti	Fencing	Italy	13
=	Takashi Ono	Gymnastics	Japan	13
7	Paavo Nurmi	Athletics	Finland	12
=	Bjørn Dæhlie	Cross-country skiing	Norway	12
=	Birgit Fischer	Canoeing	Germany	12
=	Sawao Kato	Gymnastics	Japan	12

VALENTINA VEZZALI

OFF THE CHART

Fencer Valentina Vezzali (above, on the right, battling South Korea's Nam Hyun-Hee at the 2012 Olympics) has a total of nine medals, comprised of six gold, one silver and two bronze.

MICHAEL PHELPS

XTREME FACT

This medal-winning Olympic megastar set up the Michael Phelps Foundation, a non-profit organization, to help others stay healthy by swimming, especially children.

TOP 10

MOST SUCCESSFUL MMA FIGHTERS

The battle is over! Mixed Martial Arts (MMA) has many super-tough stars, but these have won the most fights in their weight divisions...

	FIGHTER	COUNTRY	DIVISION	WINS
1	**Anderson Silva**	**Brazil**	**Middleweight**	33
2	Tony Lopez	USA	Super Heavyweight	32
3	Georges St-Pierre	Canada	Welterweight	23
4	Jose Aldo	Brazil	Featherweight	22
5	Dominick Cruz	USA	Bantamweight	19
6	Ben Henderson	USA	Lightweight	18
7	Demetrious Johnson	USA	Flyweight	17
=	Jon Jones	USA	Light Heavyweight	17
9	Cain Velasquez	USA	Heavyweight	11
10	Ronda Rousey	USA	Womens	7

YOU RATE!
1 to 100

FACT FLASH!
WINS
17

JON JONES

XTREME FACT

Here's Jon Jones in action against former teammate Rashad Evans on April 21, 2012, in a battle for the Light Heavyweight belt in Atlanta, Georgia, USA. Jones kept his title and beat Evans, easily, on points.

VINNIE JONES

XTREME FACT

He's been a soccer star, a big-screen Hollywood hit and Vinnie Jones has even shone in a TV ad! The super-tough Jones starred in an infomercial to raise awarenesss of how to perform CPR to save heart attack victims.

ANOTHER THING!

Seen *X-Men: The Last Stand*? Vinnie Jones is in it, hidden under loads of fake muscles as Juggernaut!

OUR TOP 10 UNOFFICIAL

SPORTS STARS IN MOVIES

	NAME	SPORT	MOVIES INCLUDE...
1	Dwayne Johnson	Wrestling	Journey 2: The Mysterious Island
2	Dan Marino	American football	Ace Ventura: Pet Detective
3	Wayne Gretzky	Ice hockey	D2: The Mighty Ducks
4	Lennox Lewis	Boxing	Ocean's Eleven
5	Carl Weathers	American football	Rocky III
6	Vinnie Jones	Soccer	X-Men: The Last Stand
7	Estella Warren	Synchronized swimming	Planet Of The Apes
8	David Prowse	Weightlifting	Star Wars saga
9	Dennis Rodman	Basketball	The Comebacks
10	Michael Jordan	Basketball	Space Jam

CHECK IT OUT!

You may have heard of Dennis Rodman because of his glittering basketball career, but did you know he also had a lot of success as a wrestler? Between 1997 and 2004, Rodman had battles with wrestling legends, such as "Macho Man" Randy Savage!

SPORT ZONE

YOUR SHOUT!

Check out these questions. Can you answer them without looking back through the book?

The winning shots have been performed, the statistics have been gathered and now it's over to YOU for an interactive recap on Sport Zone!

YOU RATE!

TOP 10

T-10 SPORTS STUFF

Go back through the entire sports section and unite your team of "You Rate" scores here. Then you'll be able to see YOUR overall winner!

	NAME/SPORT	"YOU RATE" SCORE
1		
2		
3		
4		
5		
6		
7		
8		
9		
10		

JUST FOR KICKS

WHICH SPORT?

Can you remember which sport with kicks has had the largest-ever crowd attendance? See how many clues you need below before you can work out what it is...

1. This event took place over 60 years ago in Rio de Janeiro.
2. The legendary match was between Brazil and Uruguay.
3. A brain-frazzling 199,854 attended the game, an all-time sporting record.

SPORT:
....

LEAP OF FAITH

WHICH SPORTSMAN?

Date of birth .... August 23, 1978
Height .... 6.5 ft (1.98 m)
Weight .... 205 lb (93 kg)
Team .... Los Angeles Lakers
Olympic Medals .... Two

NAME:
....

IN FULL SWING

Can you list the three swingin' sports that have had the largest attendances?

1. ....
2. ....
3. ....

MUSCLE MOVEMENT

Whose medal-winning legs do these belong to? Put a tick next to the sprinter you think it is...

- [ ] **Usain Bolt**
- [ ] **Asafa Powell**
- [ ] **Jonnie Peacock**
- [ ] **Justin Gatlin**
- [ ] **Tyson Gay**

THE A-TEAMS

TRUE OR FALSE...

1. The Most Popular Teams On Facebook list only contains soccer and basketball teams. T ☐ F ☐

2. Russia has won more gold medals than the USA in the Successful Olympic Nations. T ☐ F ☐

THROW DOWN

Can you remember the boxer who knocked out Sonny Liston in this World Heavyweight Title fight from 1965?

NAME: ....

ENGINE THRUST

Got a remote-controlled car or truck? Try setting up an assault course for the vehicle to tackle. Get your friends to have a try and see who can complete it the quickest!

EXTREME DANGER

Ready for a bit of extreme number crunching? See if you can work out how many medals were won by all the Top 10 Most Decorated X Games Competitors...

TOTAL MEDALS: ....

YOU'RE ON YOUR OWN

WHO'S THAT STAR?

This Italian legend races motorcycles for a living. He rides the #46 bike in the Ducati Team and is number three on our Most Popular Solo Sports Stars. Worked out who it is yet?

NAME: ....

ANSWERS ON PAGE 312

FORCES OF NATURE!

Although the human race has managed to create some astounding things since we first started to walk the Earth, the one thing that's always been out of our control is the natural world. From earthquakes and volcanoes, to violent storms and tidal waves, Mother Nature can often take a dark, devastating turn...

LAND DEMOLITION

The ground beneath your feet might feel stable most of the time, but when Mother Nature decides to go into a rage unleashing earthquakes, volcanoes and avalanches, boy, can she be brutal...

TOP 10 BIGGEST EARTHQUAKES

An earthquake with a magnitude of 8.75 is equal to the volcanic island of Krakatoa in Indonesia erupting (in 1883)... A force so powerful it was felt around the planet!

FACT FLASH!
RICHTER SCALE
9.1-9.3

SUMATRA

YOU RATE! 1 to 100

	LOCATION	DATE	MAGNITUDE (RICHTER SCALE)
1	Valdivia (Chile)	May 22, 1960	9.5
2	Alaska (USA)	Mar 27, 1964	9.2
3	Sumatra (Indonesia)	Dec 26, 2004	9.1-9.3
4	Tōhoku region (Japan)	Mar 11, 2011	9.0
=	Kamchatka (Russia)	Nov 4, 1952	9.0
6	Sumatra (Indonesia)	Nov 25, 1833	8.8-9.2 (Est*)
7	Ecuador (Colombia)	Jan 31, 1906	8.8
=	Maule (Chile)	Feb 27, 2010	8.8
=	Arica (Chile)	Sep 16, 1615	8.8 (Est*)
10	Krakatoa (Indonesia)	Aug 26, 1883	8.75

* Estimated measurement

XTREME FACT

This photo (above) shows the vast devastation caused by earthquakes and the tsunamis they create. Meulaboh in Sumatra, Indonesia, was hit by the Indian Ocean tsunami on December 26, 2004. It was caused by an earthquake that shook for nearly 10 minutes and ended up claiming over 200,000 lives.

EXTRA!

The Richter magnitude scale was created to measure the energy of an earthquake. The scale goes from zero to 10 (which has never been scientifically recorded). This measurement system was developed in 1935 by two very smart physicists, Charles Richter and Beno Gutenberg.

CHECK IT OUT!

One of the saddest aftereffects of a natural disaster like an earthquake is the opportunistic crimes that can occur. In some cases, people have come together to see lost items returned. Looting is a rare occurence but in Chile's Maule, in 2010, soldiers were deployed to ward off those looking to take advantage of the situation.

ODDEST NATURAL DISASTERS

CHECK IT OUT!

Here, you can see the extreme damage wreaked by the mysterious Tunguska blast of 1908. There have been countless conspiracy theories, articles and books on the subject, blaming everything from a meteor to aliens!

	EVENT	LOCATION	YEAR	DETAILS
1	**The Tunguska blast**	**Tunguska (Russia)**	**1908**	An explosion 1,000 times more powerful than the Hiroshima bomb, with no evidence of the cause. Everything from a comet to a black hole, and even aliens, have been blamed...
2	The ten-year storm	USA	1930-40	A series of devastating dust bowl storms that struck over a 10-year period
3	Mass deaths	Lake Nyos (Cameroon)	1986	Thousands killed overnight by what scientists believe were volcanic gases erupting
4	Fire devil	Kantō (Japan)	1923	A colossal vortex of air and fire that killed nearly 40,000 people in 15 minutes
5	The great smog	London (UK)	1952	Heavy, dense fog and burning of coal led to 12,000 breathing-related deaths
6	Florida sinkholes	Florida (USA)	1994	The appearance of a 15-storey cavity in the Earth's surface, right under a toxic waste site
7	Elephant stampede	Chandka Forest (India)	1972	A crippling drought sparked a devastating stampede by elephants, killing 24 people
8	No summer	USA, Canada, Europe	1816	Blizzards throughout the summer months
9	Killer hailstorms	Gopalganj (Bangladesh)	1986	The biggest hailstorm recorded killed nearly 100 people with giant hailstones
10	Tri-state tornado	Indiana (USA)	1925	An F5 tornado (on the Fujita scale) wrecked three US states without stopping

More than 450 desperate rescuers worked at the site of the Siachen Glacier avalanche in Pakistan

TOP 10 MOST FATAL AVALANCHES

They may look exciting in the movies, but the harsh reality is that avalanches are deadly natural phenomena, which can cause a huge amount of death and destruction...

	LOCATION	EVENT	YEAR	FATALITIES
1	**Peru**	**Huascarán avalanche (caused by the Ancash earthquake)**	**1970**	**20,000**
2	Peru	Huascarán avalanche	1962	4,000
3	Austria, Switzerland	649 avalanches (the "winter of terror")	1951	265
4	Pakistan	Siachen Glacier avalanche	2012	201 (inc 145 presumed)
5	Afghanistan	Salang avalanches (minimum of 36 avalanches)	2010	172
6	Russia	Kolka-Karmadon rock ice slide	2002	125
7	Pakistan	Kohistan avalanche	2010	102
8	USA	Wellington, Washington avalanche	1910	96
9	Canada	Frank slide (buried part of Frank's mining town in the Northwest Territories)	1903	90
10	Afghanistan	Afghanistan avalanches (hit the north-eastern province of Badakhshan)	2012	50

BIGGEST VOLCANIC ERUPTIONS

ANOTHER THING!

Volcanic lava can reach temperatures of up to 2,192 °F (1,200 °C)! No wonder it causes such devastation!

There hasn't been a serious volcanic eruption for some time, but when these bad boys blow, the amount of material they discharge is incredible...

	NAME	LOCATION	YEAR	AMOUNT OF VOLCANIC DISCHARGE (CUBIC KM)	(CUBIC MI)
1	Unknown	The Tropics	1258	200-800	48-192
2	Mount Tambora	Lesser Sunda Islands (Indonesia)	1815	150	36
3	Unknown	New Hebrides (Vanuatu)	1452-53	36-96	8.6-23
4	Kolumbo	Santorini (Greece)	1650	60	14.4
5	Huaynaputina	Peru	1600	30	7.2
=	Long Island (Papua New Guinea)	New Guinea	1660	30	7.2
7	Krakatoa	Indonesia	1883	21	5
=	Quilotoa	Ecuador	1280	21	5
9	Santa Maria	Guatamala	1902	20	4.8
10	Pinatubo	Luzon (Philippines)	1991	6-16	1.4-3.8

YOU RATE!
1 to 100

CHECK IT OUT!

When some volcanoes erupt, they spit out ash and lava in staggering volumes. The Philippines' Mount Pinatubo's plume of ash reached an unbelievable 11 mi (19 km) high when she woke up in 1991, and the eruption was felt across the world!

KRAKATOA

XTREME FACT

The volcanic eruption of Krakatoa in 1883 was so powerful it destroyed two-thirds of the island of the same name, killing more than 36,000 people. To give you an example of its power, that's like the force of 13,000 atomic bombs!

GIVE IT A TRY...
BABY VOLCANO

Build yourself a model volcano (out of a plastic bottle filled with water and a cardboard cone around it). Create an eruption by adding baking powder to the water and letting it foam out over the top to simulate a volcano!

TOP 10

NATURAL DISASTER MOVIES

Sometimes in the movie world, nature plays a very powerful role! From planet-smashing asteroids to city-melting molten rock, the human race (almost) escapes all of these disasters...

	MOVIE	YEAR	WORLDWIDE GROSS ($ MILLION)
1	2012	2009	766,812,167
2	Armageddon	1998	554,600,000
3	The Day After Tomorrow	2004	527,939,919
4	Twister	1996	494,700,000
5	Deep Impact	1998	348,600,000
6	The Perfect Storm	2000	327,000,000
7	Dante's Peak	1997	178,127,760
8	Volcano	1997	122,823,468
9	Earthquake	1974	79,666,653
10	The Core	2003	73,498,611

YOU RATE! 1 to 100

Source: IMDB.com

SHUFFLE UP

Do you prefer volcanoes over earthquakes or meteors over tornadoes? Make your own list of your all-time fave film disasters!

1
2
3
4
5
6
7
8
9
10

Know of any other mega-disaster movies to add? It's YOUR list!

2012 XTREME FACT

On the release of this end-of-the-world disaster movie, many cinemas decided to have some fun with its title. For evening screenings, some venues would begin the film at exactly 20:12! That's the kind of nerdy movie stuff that Team T-10 applauds.

FACT FLASH! GROSSED **766.8 MILLION DOLLARS**

SAVAGE OCEANS

Water covers more than 70 per cent of the Earth. Although oceans can be full of wonder and majesty, they can also become unforgiving and deadly...

TOP 10 TALLEST TSUNAMI

Tsunami is Japanese for "harbour wave", and these devastating natural phenomena are the by-product of things like earthquakes and landslides. Here are the biggest of the past few hundred years...

	LOCATION	YEAR	HEIGHT OF TSUNAMI (M)	(FT)
1	Lituta Bay, Alaska (USA)	1958	524	1,719
2	Spirit Lake, Washington (USA)	1980	260	853
3	Vajont Dam (Italy)	1963	250	820
4	Mount Unzen, Kyushu (Japan)	1792	100	328
5	Ishigaki & Miyakojima Island (Japan)	1771	79.9	262
6	Lisbon (Portugal)	1755	20.1	66
7	Messina (Italy)	1908	12.2	40
8	Hōei (Japan)	1707	9.8	32
9	Meiji-Sanriku (Japan)	1896	9.1	30
10	Haiti	2010	3.1	10

YOU RATE!
1 to 100

FACT FLASH!
HEIGHT
1,719 FT

STAT ATTACK

LITUTA BAY

Location.............................Alaska, USA
Length ....9 mi (14.5 km)
Width...............................2 mi (3.2 km)
Megatsunami.........................Occurred July 9, 1958
Fatalities............ Amazingly, only five people died

HAITI

XTREME FACT

Here, you can see the effects of the downpours caused by Hurricane Tomas on the island of Haiti on November 5, 2010. Fortunately, the violent wind and rain didn't cause too much damage to the region although, if the winds had changed, it could have been much worse.

DEADLIEST FLOODS

Extreme weather causes rivers to break their banks, while earthquakes often lead to tsunamis. Floods kill a jaw-dropping number of people...

YOU RATE!
1 to 100

	LOCATION/EVENT	YEAR	FATALITIES
1	China	1931	2.5-3.7 million
2	Yellow River, Huang He (China)	1887	900,000-2 million
3	Yellow River, Huang He (China)	1938	500,000-700,000
4	Indian Ocean tsunami (several)	2004	230,000-310,000
5	Banqiao Dam failure/Typhoon Nina (China)	1975	231,000
6	Yangtze River floods (China)	1935	145,000
7	Messina earthquake and tsunami (Italy)	1908	123,000
8	St Felix's flood (Netherlands)	1530	100,000+
9	Hanoi/Red River Delta floods (N Vietnam)	1971	100,000
=	Lisbon earthquake and tsunami	1755	100,000

OFF THE CHART

TŌHOKU, JAPAN

One of the most catastrophic natural disasters of recent times was the Tōhoku earthquake and tsunami, which devastated Japan on March 11, 2011. Officials have determined the loss of life to be between 15,859 to 18,880 people.

FACT FLASH!
95 PERCENT
OF OUR OCEANS ARE UNMAPPED

OUR TOP 10 UNOFFICIAL

STRANGEST AQUATIC MYSTERIES

	MYSTERY	DETAILS
1	Bermuda Triangle	The expanse of water between the three coastal points of Florida, Puerto Rico, and Bermuda has been blamed for boats disappearing, weird weather patterns, and some theorize it's a location of alien activity
2	Lost City of Atlantis	Greek philosopher Plato first mentioned this in 360 BC. Is there really a massive island that sank to the bottom of the Atlantic ocean?
3	The Mary Celeste	Discovered abandoned in 1872 (with sails set and intact). Sea monsters have been blamed for the crew's disappearence
4	Underwater voices	In 1997 and 1999, strange sounds were detected coming from the ocean's depths, including one that sounded like "Julia". Creepy!
5	UFO on seabed	Oceanic researcher Peter Lindberg captured sonar recordings that could prove a UFO is on the seabed between Finland and Sweden
6	Alaskan sea monster	In 2009, fisherman Kelly Nash captured amazing footage in Nushagak Bay, Alaska, which appears to show a sea serpent swimming
7	Ghost ships	Spectral, crewless vessels have been sighted sailing with purpose (not just drifting). But is it just a trick of the light?
8	Mermaids	In 1998, diver Jeff Leach took photos of a mermaid off the coast of Hawaii. Experts say they had not been doctored
9	The Montauk monster	A bizarre dead animal was found on the coast of New York in 2008. Some say it was the result of an alleged time-travel experiment
10	The Philadelphia Experiment	Were the US military involved with new technologies to bend space-time to "cloak" warships back in 1943?

TOP 10 LARGEST SHIPS SUNK BY NATURE

From natural disasters to colossal collisions on the high seas, the ocean's bed is now the resting place of many giant, man-made vessels...

	SHIP	COUNTRY	YEAR SUNK	HOW IT SANK	GROSS REGISTERED TONNAGE	YOU RATE!
1	SS Atlantic Express	Greece	1979	Collision with a tanker in tropical storms	293,000	*1 to 100*
2	Costa Concordia	Italy	2012	Ran aground on sharp rocks	114,000	
3	MV Derbyshire	UK	1980	Sank in tropical storms	92,000	
4	RMS Titanic	UK	1912	Collision with an iceberg	46,000	
5	Andrea Doria Liner	Italy	1956	Collision with another ship in fog	30,000	
6	MV Princess of the Stars	Philippines	2008	Capsized during a typhoon	24,000	
7	SS Edmund Fitzgerald	USA	1975	Sank in storm and rough seas	16,000	
8	RMS Republic	UK	1909	Collision with another ship in fog	15,000	
=	RMS Empress of Ireland	Canada	1914	Collision with another ship in fog	14,000	
10	MS al-Salam Boccaccio	Egypt	2006	Capsized and sank in heavy storms	5,600	

RMS TITANIC

XTREME FACT

It's likely that you will know the fateful story of this ship from the 1997 James Cameron movie *Titanic*. Before the ship struck the iceberg that sunk her on April 15, 1912, she departed from Southampton on her first-ever voyage. This photo, right, from April 10, was taken just five days before her tragic end, when 1,514 people died.

FACT FLASH!
FATALITIES
1,514

ANOTHER THING!
Titanic's legacy was the creation of the International Convention for the Safety of Life at Sea (SOLAS) to stop similar disasters happening again.

BEEN & SEEN

Tick the natural phenomena you've seen with YOUR own eyes!

- ☐ TORNADO
- ☐ ICEBERG
- ☐ LIGHTNING
- ☐ COASTAL ROCKS
- ☐ BLIZZARD
- ☐ HIGH WINDS
- ☐ SNOWSTORM
- ☐ HAILSTORM
- ☐ GIANT WAVE
- ☐ CORAL REEF

CITIES MOST AT RISK OF FLOODING

People all over the world have no choice but to live in areas prone to natural disasters. For these cities, it's flooding that is the problem...

	AREA/REGION	COUNTRY	CURRENT EXPOSED POPULATION	FUTURE EXPOSED POPULATION
1	**Kolkata**	**India**	1,929,000	14,014,000
2	Mumbai	India	2,787,000	11,418,000
3	Dhaka	Bangladesh	844,000	11,135,000
4	Guangzhou	China	2,718,000	10,333,000
5	Ho Chi Minh City	Vietnam	1,931,000	9,216,000
6	Shanghai	China	2,353,000	5,451,000
7	Bangkok	Thailand	907,000	5,138,000
8	Rangoon	Myanmar/Burma	510,000	4,965,000
9	Miami	USA	2,003,000	4,795,000
10	Hai Phòng	Vietnam	794,000	4,711,000

Source: OECD

KOLKATA

XTREME FACT

Located in Western Bengal in India, Kolkata has suffered several cyclonic storms over the years and the monsoon rains are a seasonal occurrence. A typical year of rainfall sees 70.9 in (180 cm) drop onto Kolkata, which is nearly 6 ft of water!

CHECK IT OUT!

Filmmaker James Cameron has been fascinated by the story of Titanic for many years. As well as his 1997 film of the same name, he also made a 3D documentary in 2003 about its wreckage called *Ghosts Of The Abyss*.

HEAVEN-SENT

With changing worldwide temperatures, cases of weird and extreme weather are on the rise. These are some of the most powerful forces of nature our world can serve up...

TOP 10 DEADLIEST TORNADOES

Also called cyclones or twisters, these spinning funnels of air always leave a trail of destruction in their wake. These are the incidents that caused the most human deaths...

	LOCATION	COUNTRY	DATE	FATALITIES
1	Daultipur, Salturia	Bangladesh	Apr 26, 1989	1,300
2	East Pakistan	(now Bangladesh)	Apr 14, 1969	923
3	Missouri, Illinois, Indiana	USA	Mar 18, 1925	695
4	Manikganj, Singair, Nawabganj	Bangladesh	Apr 17, 1973	681
5	Valletta's Grand Harbour	Malta	Sep 23, 1551	600
6	Magura, Narail	Bangladesh	Apr 11, 1964	500
=	Sicily	Italy	Dec 1851	500
=	Madaripur, Shibchar	Bangladesh	Apr 9, 1984	500
9	Belyanitsky, Ivanovo, Balino	Russia	Jun 9, 1984	400
10	Natchez, Mississippi	USA	May 6, 1840	317

INDIANA, USA

XTREME FACT

They say a picture speaks a thousand words, and this image really conveys the damage the 1925 Tri-state tornado did to Princeton in Indiana, USA. It was one of the THREE states that were pummeled by this relentless and devastating storm.

TOP 10 FASTEST CYCLONIC STORMS, HURRICANES & TYPHOONS

YOU RATE! 1 to 100

When Mother Nature whips up a storm, the winds can reach truly terrifying speeds...

	NAME	YEARS	AFFECTED AREAS	HEIGHEST SPEED (KPH)	(MPH)
1	Cyclone Zoe	2002-03	Solomon Islands, Fiji, Vanuatu, Rotuma	350	217.5
2	Cyclone Inigo	2003	Indonesia, Australia	335	208.2
=	Typhoon Violet	1961	Pacific Ocean	335	208.2
4	Super Typhoon Ida	1958	Japan	325	202
5	Super Typhoon Opal	1964	Kosrae, Chuuk, Philippines	315	195.7
=	Super Typhoon Kit	1967	Japan	315	195.7
=	Typhoon Joan	1959	Taiwan, China	315	195.7
=	Super Typhoon Sally	1964	Philippines, China	315	195.7
9	Typhoon Tip	1979	Guam, Japan	305	189.5
10	Cyclone Glenda	2006	Australia	300	186.4

AMAZING LIGHTNING PICTURES

One of the scariest and most exciting sights of nature can be a powerful thunderstorm. Check out these incredible examples...

1 Location: **Pretoria (South Africa)**
Photographer: **Mitchell Krog**

2 Location: **New Mexico (USA)**
Photographer: **Nancy Newell**

3 Location: **Taipei (Taiwan)**
Photographer: **Sharleen Chao**

4 Location: **New York (USA)**
Photographer: **Unknown**

5 Location: **Namib desert (Namibia)**
Photographer: **Ed Collacott**

6 Location: **Johannesburg (South Africa)**
Photographer: **Mitchell Krog**

7 Location: **Dhaka (Bangladesh)**
Photographer: **Parvez Khaled**

8 Location: **London (UK)**
Photographer: **Craig Allen**

9 Location: **Colorado (USA)**
Photographer: **Pat Gaines**

10 Location: **Magaliesburg (South Africa)**
Photographer: **Mitchell Krog**

MOST DESTRUCTIVE HAILSTORMS

When hail hits hard enough, it can almost be like a massive machine gun spraying icy bullets from the sky. Here are the hailstorms on recent record that have caused the most damage...

	LOCATION	DATE	DAMAGE ($)
1	St. Louis, Missouri (USA)	Apr 10, 2001	2 billion+
2	Dallas-Fort Worth, Texas (USA)	Jun 13, 2012	2 billion
3	Dallas-Fort Worth, Texas (USA)	May 5, 1995	1.1 billion
4	Oklahoma City, Oklahoma (USA)	May 10 & 16, 2010	1 billion
5	Denver, Colorado (USA)	Jul 20, 2009	770 million
6	Denver, Colorado (USA)	Jul 11, 1990	625 million
7	Calgary, Alberta (Canada)	Sep 7, 1991	600 million
=	Wichita, Kansas (USA)	Jun 19, 1992	600 million
9	Chicago, Illinois (USA)	May 18, 2000	572 million
10	Calgary, Alberta (Canada)	Jul 12, 2010	400 million

YOU RATE! 1 to 100

FACT FLASH! DAMAGE **2 BILLION+ DOLLARS**

ST. LOUIS

XTREME FACT

St. Louis has been the target of some unbelievably large hailstorms over the years. Most recently, on April 28, 2012, it was hit by winds of up to 60 mph (96 kph), and the size of hailstones increased from the size of a golf ball (which is big enough!) to as large as a baseball!

OFF THE CHART

ANOTHER THING!

Hailstones form at around 10,000 ft (3,000 m) when ice pellets collide with water. The largest hailstone ever recorded was the size of a human head!

CALGARY & WINNIPEG, CANADA

On July 24, 1996, Calgary and Winnipeg in Canada suffered $300 million worth of damage from vicious hailstorms. The hailstones that fell were reportedly as big as oranges!

CHECK IT OUT!

These are some BIG hailstones! If you were to cut these open, they would look like the inside of an onion, with layers of ice alternating between clear and cloudy. This weird effect is caused by the way the hailstones formed as they were bounced around within the cloud by strong winds. Hailstones finally fall to Earth when they become too big and heavy for the wind to keep afloat, so stronger winds can mean bigger hailstones. Hail of this size usually comes with destructive storms and even tornaodes, so if you see any this size, take cover and watch out...

OUR TOP 10 UNOFFICIAL
WEIRDEST OBJECTS TO FALL FROM THE SKY

Could it be storms scooping up these objects or something stranger? You won't believe the bizarre things that have plummeted to Earth...

	OBJECT	LOCATION	DATE
1	Frogs	Naphlion (Greece)	May 1981
2	Spiders	Argentina	Apr 6, 2007
3	Cone shaped metallic object	Novosibirsk (Russia)	Mar 20, 2012
4	Fish	Great Yarmouth (UK)	Aug 6, 2000
5	Golf balls	Punta Gorda, Florida (USA)	Sep 1, 1969
6	Huge metal sphere	Brazil	Feb 23, 2012
7	Jelly rain	Pentlands (UK)	17 Oct, 2008
8	Frogspawn	Port-au-Prince (Haiti)	May 5, 1786
9	Whale-sized object	Litchfield, Connecticut (USA)	Apr 12, 2012
10	100 starlings	Somerset (UK)	Mar 7, 2010

FISH
XTREME FACT
Fish have fallen from the sky many times in the past, with occurrences in Australia, Singapore and the USA. Scientists believe the most likely reason is a cyclone or waterspout sucking them up then dropping them off.

HUGE METAL SPHERE
XTREME FACT
The people of Riacho dos Poços, a village in Brazil, got a shock when a 110 lb (50 kg) metal sphere crashed very close to a resident's home. The military collected the object, which has so far not been officially identified...

CHECK IT OUT!

Stories and historical records of frogs and toads falling from the sky date back to biblical times. Storms can have incredible power, especially cyclonic storms, so it isn't surprising that some animals get swept up and then "dropped off" somewhere else once the vortex has moved on or died down. There has even been a report of an alligator dropping from the stormy sky!

AROUND THE WORLD

From the highest rocky peaks to the deepest unexplored waters, let's take a look at the weird and wonderful natural phenomena that exist on this planet...

TOP 10 HIGHEST WATERFALLS

If you've ever seen a waterfall up close, you'll never forget how breathtaking it is. Check this bunch out... Some are over half a mile high!

YOU RATE!
1 to 100

	NAME	LOCATION	HEIGHT (M)	(FT)
1	Angel Falls	Bolívar State (Venezuela)	979	3,212
2	Tugela Falls	KwaZulu-Natal (South Africa)	948	3,110
3	Cataratas las Tres Hermanas	Ayacucho (Peru)	914	3,000
4	Olo'upena Falls	Molokai, Hawaii (USA)	900	2,953
5	Catarata Yumbilla	Amazonas (Peru)	896	2,940
6	Vinnufossen	Møre og Romsdal (Norway)	860	2,822
7	Balåifossen	Hordaland (Norway)	850	2,788
8	Pu'uka'oku Falls	Hawaii (USA)	840	2,756
=	James Bruce Falls	British Columbia (Canada)	840	2,756
10	Browne Falls	South Island (New Zealand)	836	2,743

TUGELA FALLS

XTREME FACT

Located in KwaZula-Natal in South Africa, Tugela Falls is the world's second highest waterfall. It has five drops in total, measuring 3,110 ft (948 m) in height overall. A very popular tourist attraction it may be, but the journey to see the falls up close can take up to eight hours on foot, with a rickety chain ladder as part of the experience.

STAT ATTACK

ANGEL FALLS

Place.................................Bolívar State, Venezuela

Location type ....Dense jungle within Canaima National Park

Named after.................Pilot Jimmie Angel who flew over it

Drops...47

Highest drop ....2,648 ft (807 m)

HIGHEST MOUNTAINS

Mountains have always fascinated mankind. Reaching up over 26,000 ft (8,000 m) towards the sky, these jagged giants awaken our primal instinct to explore and climb...

YOU RATE!
1 to 100

	NAME	RANGE	LOCATION	HEIGHT (M)	(FT)
1	**Mount Everest**	**Mahalangur Himalaya**	**China/Nepal border**	**8,848**	**29,029**
2	K2	Baltoro Karakoram	Pakistan/China border	8,611	28,251
3	Kangchenjunga	Kangchenjunga Himalaya	India/Nepal border	8,586	28,169
4	Lhotse	Mahalangur Himalaya	China/Nepal border	8,516	27,940
5	Makalu	Mahalangur Himalaya	China/Nepal border	8,485	27,838
6	Cho Oyu	Mahalangur Himalaya	China/Nepal border	8,188	26,864
7	Dhaulagiri	Dhaulagiri Himalaya	Nepal	8,167	26,795
8	Manaslu	Manaslu Himalaya	Nepal	8,163	26,781
9	Nanga Parbat	Nanga Parbat Himalaya	Pakistan	8,126	26,660
10	Annapurna	Annapurna Himalaya	Nepal	8,091	26,545

KANGCHENJUNGA

XTREME FACT

During a British expedition in 1925, the sighting of a strange creature was the start of a mystery called the Kangchenjunga Demon. This yeti-type being is said to roam the icy plains...

DEEPEST LAKES

They can look like tranquil places to relax by with a picnic, but did you know that some of the world's lakes are extraordinarily deep and filled with mysterious tales?

YOU RATE!
1 to 100

	NAME	LOCATION	DEPTH (M)	(FT)
1	**Baikal**	**Siberia (Russia)**	**1,637**	**5,371**
2	Tanganyika	Tanzania, Democratic Republic of the Congo, Burundi, Zambia	1,470	4,823
3	Caspian Sea	Iran, Russia, Turkmenistan, Kazakhstan, Azerbaijan	1,025	3,363
4	Vostok	Antarctica	1,000	3,281
5	O'Higgins-San Martin	Chile, Argentina	836	2,743
6	Pinatubo	Philippines	800	2,625
7	Malawi	Mozambique, Tanzania, Malawi	706	2,316
8	Issyk Kul	Kyrgyzstan	668	2,192
9	Great Slave	Canada	614	2,015
10	Crater	Oregon (USA)	594	1,949

OFF THE CHART

LOCH NESS

The world-famous Loch Ness in Scotland doesn't quite make the Top 10, but is still VERY deep at 436 ft (133 m)! If there is a Loch Ness Monster, there's certainly plenty of water for it to remain hidden in...

COLDEST PLACES

The next time you complain that "it's freezing", remember the following sub-zero temperatures...

	LOCATION	DATE	TEMPERATURE (°C)	(°F)	
1	**Vostok Station (Antarctica)**	Jul 21, 1983	-89.2	-128.6	YOU RATE! 1 to 100
2	Amundsen-Scott South Pole Station (South Pole)	Jun 23, 1982	-82.8	-117	
3	Dome A (East Antarctica)	Jul 2007	-82.5	-116.5	
4	Verkhoyansk & Oymyakonm Sakha Republic (Russia)	Feb 6, 1933	-68	-90	
5	North Ice (Greenland)	Jan 9, 1954	-66.1	-87	
6	Snag, Yukon (Canada)	Feb 3, 1947	-63	-81	
7	Prospect Creek, Alaska (USA)	Jan 23, 1971	-62	-80	
8	Ust-Shchuger (Russia)	Dec 31, 1978	-58.1	-72.6	
9	Malgovik, Västerbotten (Sweden)	Dec 13, 1941	-53	-63.4	
10	Mohe County (China)	Feb 13, 1969	-52.3	-62.1	

CHECK IT OUT!

Vostok Station is a Russian research outpost in deepest Antarctica. It was set up during the second Soviet exploration of the South Pole region on December 16, 1957. Although the area seems like it's a place very few would dare to go, let alone live and work, Vostok is one of 76 research stations in this freezing region.

HOTTEST PLACES

We're a funny bunch, aren't we? Whether it's too hot or too cold, we are never happy... But here are some really extreme temperatures!

FACT FLASH!
TEMPERATURE
134
DEGREES FAHRENHEIT

DEATH VALLEY

XTREME FACT

Death Valley is an appropriate name for the hottest place on Earth! Straddling Nevada and California, the native American Timbisha people still live here. "Death Valley" is not a translation from an indigenous description, it was named that by English settlers back in 1849, possibly as a warning of its extreme heat.

	LOCATION	DATE	TEMPERATURE (°C)	(°F)	
1	**Death Valley (USA)**	Jul 10, 1913	56.7	134	YOU RATE! 1 to 100
2	Kebili (Tunisia)	Jul 7, 1931	55	131	
3	Tirat Zvi (Israel)	Jun 21, 1942	54	129	
4	Kuwait International Airport (Kuwait)	Aug 3, 2011	53.5	128.3	
=	Mohenjo-daro, Sindh (Pakistan)	May 26, 2010	53.5	128.3	
6	Basra (Iraq)	Jun 14, 2010	52	125.7	
=	Jeddah (Saudia Arabia)	Jun 22, 2010	52	125.7	
8	Illizi Province (Algeria)	Aug 18, 2011	51	123.8	
9	Oodnadatta (Australia)	Feb 2, 1960	50.7	123.3	
10	Doha (Qatar)	Jul 14, 2010	50.4	122.7	

OFF THE CHART

KALMYKIA, RUSSIA

Russia is famous for its abundance of snow and extremely chilly conditions, but this isn't always the case... It's a huge place after all! In Kalmykia (south-west Russia), a record high temperature of 4113.7°F (45.4°C) was recorded on July 12, 2010. That was one hot summer!

ANOTHER THING!

Clouds come in many shapes and sizes and are often mistaken for UFOs. Lenticular clouds are shaped just like huge flying saucers.

GIVE IT A TRY...
RECREATE WEATHER

The natural recurring phenomena in the list below are truly extraordinary to look at. Using pens, paints or textiles, be experimental and try to recreate your best one as a piece of art! Look them up online and pick one you like the look of. Then it's time to get creative...

MAMMATUS CLOUDS
XTREME FACT

These incredible-looking clouds are created by different combinations of wind direction, temperature and moisture. Weirdly, there are currently no exact scientific explanations for these odd clouds and how they are formed...

OUR TOP 10 UNOFFICIAL
RECURRING PHENOMENA

	NAME	DETAILS
1	Mammatus clouds	Thousands of orb-like clouds that look like bubble wrap in the sky
2	Aurora Borealis	Charged particles high up in the atmosphere cause this magical light show
3	Penitentes	Snow forming at high altitude creates these blade-like icy spikes
4	Ice circles	Thin slices of circular ice form on the surface of slow-moving cold water
5	Supercells	Spectacular-looking thunderstorms that often look like a huge UFO-type cloud
6	Light pillars	Ice pillars reflecting light create these supernatural-looking light lines
7	Catatumbo river at Lake Maracaibo (Venezuela)	The lightning at this location is continuous
8	Fire rainbow, Idaho (USA)	Light refracting through ice crystals in the sky causes this unique rainbow
9	Black Sun (Denmark)	Migrating starlings en masse (up to a million) swirl in the sky, hence the name
10	Moonbow	Light reflects off the surface of the Moon to create this kind of rainbow

TOP 10 LONGEST RIVERS

You may have a river near where you live, but we bet it's nowhere near as long as these huge rivers, which cover vast expanses of the Earth...

RIVER/COUNTRY(S)	LENGTH (KM)	(MI)
1 Amazon-Ucayali-Apurímac	**6,800**	**4,425**
Brazil, Peru, Bolivia, Colombia, Ecuador, Venezuela, Guyana		
2 Nile-Kagera	6,695	4,160
Ethiopia, Eritrea, Sudan, Uganda, Tanzania, Kenya, Rwanda, Burundi, Egypt, Democratic Republic of the Congo, South Sudan		
3 Yangtze	6,300	3,915
China		
4 Mississippi-Missouri-Jefferson	6,275	3,899
USA (98.5%), Canada (1.5%)		
5 Yenisei-Angara-Selenga	5,539	3,442
Russia (97%), Mongolia (2.9%)		
6 Yellow River	5,464	3,395
China		
7 Ob-Irtysh	5,410	3,362
Russia, Kazakhstan, China, Mongolia		
8 Paraná-Río de la Plata	4,880	3,032
Brazil (46.7%), Argentina (27.7%), Paraguay (13.5%), Bolivia (8.3%), Uruguay (3.8%)		
9 Congo-Chambeshi	4,700	2,920
Democratic Republic of the Congo, Central African Republic, Angola, Republic of the Congo, Tanzania, Cameroon, Zambia, Burundi, Rwanda		
10 Amur-Argun	4,444	2,761
Russia, China, Mongolia		

CHECK IT OUT!
Here it is, the world-famous Mississippi that runs through TEN states in the USA! Appropriately, its name originates from another word that means "great river".

OUR TOP 10 UNOFFICIAL AMAZING ROCK FORMS

	NAME	LOCATION
1	**Uluru**	**Northern Territory (Australia)**
2	Ergaki Hanging Rock	Central Siberia (Russia)
3	Queen's Head	Yehliu Geopark (Taiwan)
4	Devil's Tower	Black Hills, Wyoming (USA)
5	Fairy Chimneys	Pasabag Valley (Turkey)
6	Wave Rock	Hyden (Western Australia)
7	Ko Tapu	Khao Phing Kan (Thailand)
8	Balancing Rock	Garden of the Gods, Colorado (USA)
9	Reed Flute Cave	Guilin, Guangxi (China)
10	Giant's Causeway	County Antrim (Northern Ireland)

CHECK IT OUT!

Wave Rock is an astounding 361 ft (110 m) long and 49 ft (15 m) high, but that isn't the most amazing thing about it. Samples have been dated as 2,700 MILLION years old!

LARGEST CRATERS

Some of the most spectacular rocky sights you can see are craters, colossal dents caused by comets or meteorites smashing into the Earth's surface...

	NAME	LOCATION	AGE (MILLIONS OF YEARS)	DIAMETER (KM)	(MI)
1	**Vredefort**	**Free State (South Africa)**	**2,023**	**300**	**186.4**
2	Sudbury	Ontario (Canada)	1,849	250	155
3	Chicxulub	Yucatán (Mexico)	65	170	105
4	Kara	Nenetsia (Russia)	70.3	120	75
5	Manicouagan	Québec (Canada)	215	100	62
=	Popigai	Siberia (Russia)	35.7	100	62
7	Acraman	South Australia	580	85-90	53-55
8	Chesapeake Bay	Virginia (USA)	35.5	85	53
9	Puchezh-Katunki	Nizhny Novgorod Oblast (Russia)	167	80	50
10	Morokweng	Kalahari Desert (South Africa)	145	70	43

YOU RATE! 1 to 100

MANICOUAGAN

XTREME FACT

Canada's Manicouagan crater has got to be one of the most spectacular natural sights on this planet. It was created after an impact, or possibly multiple impacts, of asteroids some 215 million years ago. This fantastic satellite image of the crater was taken on June 1, 2001.

FACT FLASH! WIDTH **186.4** MI

CHECK IT OUT!

Named after a nearby town, the Vredefort crater in South Africa is the biggest on Earth by a long shot. Scientists have calculated that it may be more than two BILLION years old. LANDSAT, NASA and the US Geological Survey's satellite took this photo of Vredefort in April 1991, which really shows its size...

COMPARE-O-METER

See how the super-craters match up to these...

LENGTH OF MANHATTAN ISLAND

MANHATTAN ISLAND
25 50 75 100 125 150

21.6 km
13.4 mi

WORLD'S LONGEST BRIDGE

DANYANG-KUNSHAN GRAND BRIDGE
25 50 75 100 125 150

164.8 km
102.4 mi

FORCES OF NATURE!

YOUR SHOUT!

Check out these questions. Can you answer them without looking back through the book?

It's time for another break. Are you sitting comfortably? Then we'll begin...
This is your interactive section full of things to test YOUR T-10 memory!

YOU RATE!

T-10 FORCES OF NATURE

Hope you didn't rip through this section like a whirlwind because now it's time to look back at YOUR ratings for the Forces of Nature zone, and list all of your top ones here!

	NAME	"YOU RATE" SCORE
1		
2		
3		
4		
5		
6		
7		
8		
9		
10		

LAND DEMOLITION

NAME THE YEAR?

Can you remember which year the elephant stampede in Chandka Forest, India, took place? The terrible event happened after a crippling drought sparked a devastating stampede by elephants, killing 24 people.

....

TRUE OR FALSE...

1. The biggest earthquake ever recorded measured over 10 on the Richter scale. ☐ T ☐ F

2. The top two most fatal avalanches both took place in Peru. ☐ T ☐ F

3. The highest grossing natural disaster movie of all time was called 2001. ☐ T ☐ F

SAVAGE OCEANS

See how many clues it takes before you can recall the name of this colossal ship that became victim to the ocean...

1. This luxurious Italian cruise ship got into trouble off Isola del Giglio, in Tuscany, Italy, in 2012.

2. The monster ocean liner ran aground on sharp rocks.

3. Her gross registered tonnage was 114,000, and it is the second largest ship to ever sink at sea.

SHIP:
....

HEAVEN-SENT

Can you name the cities where these amazing photographs of lightning were taken?

A

CITY:
....

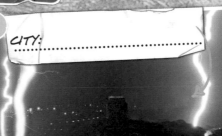

B

CITY:
....

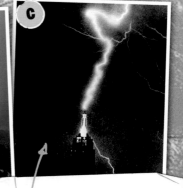

C

CITY:
....

AROUND THE WORLD

See if you can list the names of the top three highest waterfalls and highest mountains. No cheating!

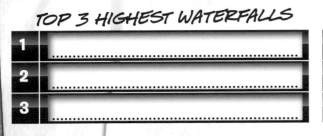

TOP 3 HIGHEST WATERFALLS

1	
2	
3	

TOP 3 HIGHEST MOUNTAINS

1	
2	
3	

ANSWERS ON PAGE 312

MUSIC MASH-UP

Music is, quite simply, amazing. It may just be a combination of sounds, but when we find a piece of music that we emotionally connect with, it can make us happy, sad, reflect on memories or get up and dance like crazy! Set your volume to 10, as we prepare to ROCK OUT...

CHART TOPPERS

From the biggest guitar riffs to the sweetest fizzy pop songs, in this zone we're going to be finding out the biggest successes from across ALL the music genres...

FACT FLASH!
DOWNLOADS
8.186 MILLION

TOP 10 MOST DOWNLOADED SONGS EVER

It's time to settle any arguments you've had with your friends about what are the most popular MP3s ever... It's THESE 10!

YOU RATE!
1 to 100

	SONG	ARTIST	UNITS SOLD
1	I Gotta Feeling	The Black Eyed Peas	8,186,000
2	Rolling In The Deep	Adele	7,640,000
3	Party Rock Anthem	LMFAO	7,463,000
4	Somebody That I Used To Know	Gotye ft. Kimbra	6,885,000
5	Poker Face	Lady Gaga	6,866,000
6	Just Dance	Lady Gaga ft. Colby O'Donis	6,720,000
7	Low	Flo Rida ft. T-Pain	6,565,000
8	Boom Boom Pow	The Black Eyed Peas	6,544,000
9	Call Me Maybe	Carly Rae Jepsen	6,474,000
10	I'm Yours	Jason Mraz	6,436,000

Source: Billboard

BLACK EYED PEAS

XTREME FACT

Fergie (full name Stacy Ann Ferguson) didn't join the band until 2002. She sung on The Black Eyed Peas' breakthrough hit *Where Is The Love?* (released June 16, 2003), but the band had been a trio since 1995.

STAT ATTACK

CARLY RAE JEPSEN

Born	November 21, 1985
Debut album	*Tug Of War* (2008)
Singles	8
"Call Me Maybe" Top 10 in...	29 countries

TOP 10 MOST POPULAR MUSIC GENRE

These results surprised us too, but Team T-10 love that rock is towering above all the other musical genres. We LOVE big guitars and drums!

	GENRE	TRACK SALES
1	**Rock**	**323,800,000**
2	Pop	303,800,000
3	R&B/Hip Hop	249,300,000
4	Country	162,100,000
5	Dance/Electronic	53,000,000
6	Christian/Gospel	34,400,000
7	Latin	21,100,000
8	Holiday/Seasonal	12,100,000
9	Jazz	8,800,000
10	World	8,700,000

Source: Billboard

YOU RATE! 1 to 100

CHECK IT OUT!

Although Kings Of Leon had massive success in 2008 with their fourth album *Only By The Night*, they began their career with a five-track EP called *Holy Roller Novocaine*, released on February 18, 2003.

R&B/HIP HOP

XTREME FACT

The roots of hip-hop are in 1970s New York City in The Bronx (USA), where pioneers of the style began mixing pre-existing records into new songs!

GIVE IT A TRY...

FORM A SUPERGROUP

Do you play an instrument, or do you prefer to sing? Get together with some like-minded music-mad friends and form a band! You could even mash together the different genres you all love.

EMINEM

XTREME FACT

Eminem's real name isn't that much of a mystery when you say it slowly... it sounds like "M" and "M"... because he's Marshall Mathers III. 2015 will mark Eminem's twentieth year making music!

FACT FLASH!
UNITS SOLD
53.6 MILLION

TOP 10

BIGGEST SELLING ARTISTS EVER

Whether you rock a guitar, or sing power ballads, of every musical artist, these 10 are the sales champions...

YOU RATE!
1 to 100

	ARTIST	UNITS SOLD
1	Garth Brooks	68,617,000
2	The Beatles	64,158,000
3	Mariah Carey	53,939,000
4	Metallica	53,642,000
5	Celine Dion	51,759,000
6	George Strait	43,932,000
7	Eminem	41,950,000
8	Tim McGraw	40,993,000
9	Alan Jackson	39,630,000
10	Pink Floyd	37,969,000

Source: Billboard

CHECK IT OUT!

Metallica bassist Roberto Trujillo joined the heavy metal outfit in 2003. During his long career he's also played for the likes of Black Label Society, and hellraiser rock'n'roll legend Ozzy Osbourne!

172

TOP 10 BIGGEST SELLING DIGITAL ALBUMS 2012

Each year the popularity for digital downloads has increased, and 2012 was a phenomenal year for the format, especially for these ten artists...

	ALBUM	ARTIST	UNITS SOLD
1	21	**Adele**	1,040,000
2	Red	Taylor Swift	863,000
3	Babel	Mumford & Sons	778,000
4	Up All Night	One Direction	562,000
5	Some Nights	Fun.	558,000
6	Lumineers	Lumineers	474,000
7	Overexposed	Maroon 5	451,000
8	My Head Is An Animal	Of Monsters And Men	424,000
9	Making Mirrors	Gotye	387,000
10	Sigh No More	Mumford & Sons	384,000

Source: Billboard

YOU RATE! 1 to 100

STAT ATTACK

ADELE

Full name ....Adele Laurie Blue Adkins
Born .... May 5, 1988
Studied/trained ...BRIT School, Croydon, UK
Debut single..................... Hometown Glory
(October 22, 2007)

FACT FLASH!
UNITS SOLD
558 THOUSAND

FUN.
XTREME FACT

Fun. (and that full stop isn't a mistake... it's how the band spell their name!) are trio Nate Ruess, Jack Antonoff and Andrew Dost, who hail from New York City, USA. Aside from their albums, they've contributed the song *Sight Of The Sun* to the TV show *Girls*' soundtrack.

TOP 10

BIGGEST SELLING ARTISTS OF 2012

It's a really mixed bag of genres, but the most successful ones aren't too much of a surprise...

YOU RATE!

1 to 100

	ARTIST	UNITS SOLD
1	**Adele**	**5,167,000**
2	Taylor Swift	4,062,000
3	One Direction	2,978,000
4	Mumford & Sons	2,149,000
5	Justin Bieber	1,897,000
6	Jason Aldean	1,855,000
7	Whitney Houston	1,789,000
8	Maroon 5	1,540,000
9	Carrie Underwood	1,497,000
10	Luke Bryan	1,432,000

Source: Billboard

FACT FLASH!
UNITS SOLD
4 MILLION

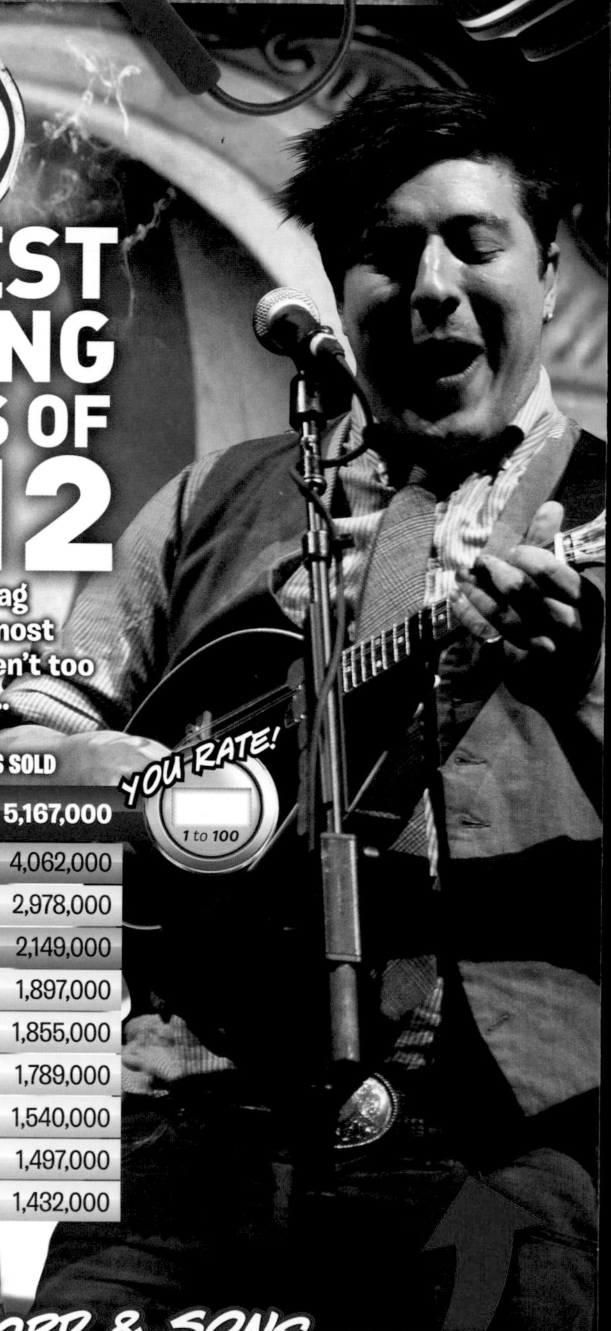

CHECK IT OUT!

Never before has singing chirpily about never getting back together with an ex led to such huge success! Here's Taylor Swift rocking the 2012 MTV EMAs (European Music Awards), where she picked up Best Live Act, Best Female, and Best Look!

MUMFORD & SONS
XTREME FACT

Before the success of their debut 2009 album *Sigh No More*, Mumford & Sons took the approach that many bands do: release EPs (which means "Extended Play") first: *Mumford & Sons* EP (July 7, 2008) and *Love Your Ground* EP (November 8, 2008) on limited edition 10" vinyls.

TOP 10 BIGGEST SELLING DIGITAL SONGS 2012

Buying digital downloads has never been easier, with more and more companies offering the format. Here are the biggest from 2012...

YOU RATE!
1 to 100

	SONG	ARTIST	UNITS SOLD
1	Somebody That I Used To Know	Gotye ft. Kimbra	6,801,000
2	Call Me Maybe	Carly Rae Jepsen	6,472,000
3	We Are Young	Fun. ft. Janelle Monae	5,948,000
4	Payphone	Maroon 5 ft. Wiz Khalifa	4,757,000
5	Starships	Nicki Minaj	3,979,000
6	What Makes You Beautiful	One Direction	3,881,000
7	Some Nights	Fun.	3,839,000
8	Stronger	Kelly Clarkson	3,823,000
9	Gangnam Style	PSY	3,592,000
10	One More Night	Maroon 5	3,461,000

Source: Billboard

FACT FLASH!
UNITS SOLD
6.8 MILLION

CHECK IT OUT!

Celebrating what was arguably Canadian Carly Rae Jepsen's year (in 2012, her song *Call Me Maybe* was number one in 19 countries), she performed on New Year's Eve 2012 in Times Square, New York, USA.

SOMEBODY THAT I USED TO KNOW...

XTREME FACT

This global smash hit by Belgian born Australian Gotye also features New Zealand popstar Kimbra on vocals. It seems singers love going by one name/word these days! Gotye's real name is Wouter De Backer, and Kimbra's full name is Kimbra Lee Johnson.

COMPARE-O-METER

Here are some more massive music stats!

KATY PERRY AIRPLAY

SELENA GOMEZ FOLLOWERS

KATY PERRY RADIO AIRPLAY

SELENA GOMEZ TWITTER FOLLOWERS

1,395,000
Detections

13,108,025
Followers

TOP 10

MOST STREAMED ARTISTS 2012

Here at T-10 Towers, we aim to bring you the best lists. Here, we've combined audio AND video streams for the ultimate chart...

	ARTIST	STREAMS
1	Taylor Swift	216,000,000
2	Nicki Minaj	210,000,000
3	Rihanna	204,000,000
4	Katy Perry	177,000,000
5	Eminem	174,000,000
6	One Direction	168,000,000
7	Adele	163,000,000
8	Beyoncé	141,000,000
9	Chris Brown	139,000,000
10	Carly Rae Jepsen	135,000,000

Source: Billboard

YOU RATE!
1 to 100

CHECK IT OUT!

Incredibly, at just 25 years old (born February 20, 1988), Rihanna has already released SEVEN albums! And she's not short of awards either, having won an astounding 18 Billboard Music Awards. She's unstoppable!

FACT FLASH!
STREAMS
204 MILLION

KATY PERRY

XTREME FACT

Although her debut as Katy Perry was 2008's *One Of The Boys*, she did release the album *Katy Hudson* (also her real name) in 2001!

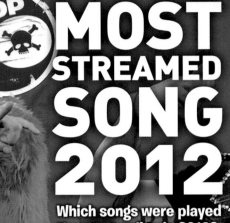

TOP 10 MOST STREAMED SONG 2012

Which songs were played the most online in 2012? These 10, and check out the amazing play counts for the megahits...

YOU RATE!
1 to 100

	SONG	BAND/GROUP	STREAMS
1	**Call Me Maybe**	**Carly Rae Jepsen**	**119,764,000**
2	Payphone	Maroon 5 ft. Wiz Khalifa	62,004,000
3	We Are Never Ever Getting Back Together	Taylor Swift	61,098,000
4	Mirror	Lil Wayne ft. Bruno Mars	53,536,000
5	As Long As You Love Me	Justin Bieber ft. Big Sean	51,850,000
6	Boyfriend	Justin Bieber	51,196,000
7	Wide Awake	Katy Perry	49,773,000
8	Party Rock Anthem	LMFAO	48,414,000
9	Lights	Ellie Goulding	47,988,000
10	Starships	Nicki Minaj	47,187,000

Source: Billboard

PARTY ROCK ANTHEM

XTREME FACT

In Italy, the 2012 MTV TRL (Total Request Live) Awards show presented LMFAO Best Video for *Party Rock Anthem*, which has been in countless TV shows too, including *Glee* and *Gossip Girl*!

CHECK IT OUT!

Sometimes the truth behind a song's lyrics is simpler than you think... Ellie Goulding wrote the song *Lights* about her fear of the dark! She's said that if she falls asleep in the dark, she'll often get up to turn a light on for comfort. Aw, bless you Ellie!

FAN FORUM

Team T-10 are massive fans of loads of musicians and singers, but how many of YOUR top pop and rock stars are in these fan-led countdowns?

TOP 10

MOST "LIKES"
ON THEIR OFFICIAL FACEBOOK PAGE

Music stars are not just defined by album sales and radio play, it's also very important how many fans "Like" their official Facebook pages...

	ARTIST/BAND	"LIKES"
1	**Rihanna**	**62,545,301**
2	Eminem	62,517,481
3	Shakira	56,257,196
4	Lady Gaga	53,637,695
5	Michael Jackson	52,734,693
6	Katy Perry	48,514,397
7	Justin Bieber	47,738,449
8	Linkin Park	46,287,472
9	Lil Wayne	40,941,008
10	Bob Marley	40,688,266

YOU RATE!
1 to 100

FACT FLASH!
"LIKES"
53.6 MILLION

SHUFFLE UP

Who would you have at Number One? Now you've seen the Top 10 most "Liked" music stars on Facebook, why not list them in order of YOUR top popsters?

1 ....
2 ....
3 ....
4 ....
5 ....
6 ....
7 ....
8 ....
9 ....
10 ....

Not a big fan of some of them? Add any stars you like... It's YOUR list!

CHECK IT OUT!

The legendary pop star passed away on June 25, 2009, but his popularity lives on. The official Facebook page dedicated to *This Is It*, the documentary about the rehearsals for his ill-fated tour, has nearly three million "Likes". The HIStory World Tour (Sep 7, 1996-Oct 15, 1997), his last, saw him perform to 4.5 million fans in 35 countries.

LADY GAGA

XTREME FACT

Lady Gaga calls her fans Little Monsters, and those "monsters" remain hungry for her music! She's shifted more than 42 million digital downloads, and won 207 awards from 295 nominations. The singer has even got her own perfume, Fame, which has over 15,000 "Likes" on its own Facebook page.

STAT ATTACK

LIL WAYNE

Born .... September 27, 1982
First album .... Tha Block Is Hot (1999)
Latest album .... I Am Not A Human Being II (2013)
Awards 80
Myspace plays .... Over 570 million

LIL WAYNE

XTREME FACT

Behind every stage name is the name the music star was born with... Lil Wayne's real name is Dwayne!

OUR TOP 10 UNOFFICIAL

SOCIAL NETWORKING-RELATED MUSIC SITES

There are so many ways to interact with fellow music fans. Check these out...

1	Spotify
2	Facebook
3	Last.FM
4	Myspace Music
5	Jango
6	Google Play
7	Live365
8	Pandora
9	MOG
10	Yahoo Music

GIVE IT A TRY... PARTY PLAYLISTS!

Which bands and singers do you and your friends love? Do you have wildly different tastes? Ever checked out a recommended band and then become a fan? Get together with your friends and each make up your own playlists. Then listen to each others' playlist, but without looking at it, and judge on what you hear... Like *The Voice*!

FACT FLASH!
"LIKES"
40.9 MILLION

TOP 10 ARTISTS WITH THE MOST WEB SEARCHES 2012

When it comes to looking for information online, there are 10 artists who are searched for more often and by more people than any others...

	ARTIST/BAND	SEARCHES
1	Lady Gaga	578,000,000
2	Justin Bieber	496,000,000
3	Rihanna	384,000,000
4	Cher	340,000,000
5	Nicki Minaj	296,000,000
6	Britney Spears	277,000,000
7	Katy Perry	263,000,000
8	Shakira	239,000,000
9	Madonna	230,000,000
10	Jennifer Lopez	214,000,000

YOU RATE! 1 to 100

CHECK IT OUT!

Nicki Minaj (who has the awesome real name of Onika Tanya Maraj) has seen her popularity explode over the past few years, since her 2010 debut album *Pink Friday*. 2012's *Pink Friday: Roman Reloaded* may be a deluxe, few-more-songs version of her debut, but it still sold more than a quarter of a million copies during its first week. Her Myspace page, launched in 2006, has notched up more than 54 million plays... Quite an achievement!

FACT FLASH!
SEARCHES
296
MILLION

CHER OR CHER?

XTREME FACT

The search result of 340 million for Cher in the list (above) is for the female solo singer who has been a star for more than 50 years (right), not 19-year-old Cher Lloyd! Although, Ms. Lloyd is not doing too badly, with over 80 million search results... We bet she'd like to shift 195 million albums like Cher, though!

MUSE

XTREME FACT

Muse has always embraced the internet. On the official website (muse.mu) members can add themselves to a "world map". For the 2012 album *The 2nd Law*, a promotional video for *The 2nd Law: Unsustainable* mashed up news reports, data streams and robots!

CHECK IT OUT!

Linkin Park's fan club LPU (Linkin Park Underground) has been running for over 12 years and provides online video chats with the band, meet and greet events, and exclusive albums...

BEEN & SEEN

Tick the boxes by these music artists' names if you've visited their official website!

- [ ] NICKI MINAJ
- [ ] MUSE
- [ ] LADY GAGA
- [ ] RIHANNA
- [ ] FUN.
- [ ] BEYONCÉ
- [ ] MAROON 5
- [ ] COLDPLAY
- [ ] JESSIE J
- [ ] KATY PERRY

OUR TOP 10 UNOFFICIAL

COOLEST OFFICIAL ARTIST/GROUP WEBSITES

	ARTIST/GROUP	WEBSITE
1	Beyoncé	beyonce.com
2	Muse	muse.mu
3	The Civil Wars	thecivilwars.com
4	Linkin Park	linkinpark.com
5	Fun.	ournameisfun.com
6	Anneke van Giersbergen	annekevangiersbergen.com
7	Incubus	incubushq.com
8	Robyn	robyn.com
9	Soundgarden	soundgardenworld.com
10	Skrillex	skrillex.com

TOP 10 OFFICIAL MUSIC VIDEOS WITH THE MOST YOUTUBE "LIKES"

YouTube is an amazing way to share video content, but it can also lead to some very angry comments! Let's stay positive and look at the most liked videos...

YOU RATE! 1 to 100

	ARTIST/GROUP	SONG	RELEASE DATE	"LIKES"
1	Adele	Rolling In The Deep	Nov 29, 2010	1,307,505
2	One Direction	What Makes You Beautiful	Sep 11, 2011	1,117,228
3	Adele	Someone Like You	Jan 24, 2011	947,099
4	One Direction	Live While We're Young	Sep 28, 2012	861,290
5	Coldplay	Paradise	Sep 12, 2011	794,336
6	One Direction	One Thing	Jan 6, 2012	755,160
7	Jessie J ft. BoB	Price Tag	Jan 28, 2011	652,939
8	One Direction	Little Things	Nov 11, 2012	507,760
9	One Direction	Gotta Be You	Nov 11, 2011	434,427
10	Jessie J	Domino	Aug 29, 2011	382,467

ANOTHER THING!

If you Google "Jessie J Price Tag Cover" you will see over 20 million search results showing fans doing their own video versions!

CHECK IT OUT!

British popstar Jessie J has had huge likeability with *Price Tag* on YouTube... The videos for her other five singles (*Do It Like A Dude*, *Nobody's Perfect*, *Who's Laughing Now*, *Domino*, and *Laser Light*) have a total of over 1.3 million YouTube "Likes"! Convert that into a price tag and Ms. J is doing really rather well...

ONE DIRECTION XTREME FACT

Team T-10 is as amazed as the rest of the world at One Direction's global domination. And it's not just online where they rule, as their 2013 world tour sees them doing 116 live shows. On the first day that tickets were made available, 300,000 were snapped up!

FACT FLASH! VIEWS 1 BILLION+

JUSTIN BIEBER

XTREME FACT

He may be way up there on the YouTube chart, but statistics can sometimes be deceiving... It's worth noting that there are more than double the "Dislikes" for *Baby* than "Likes", which means his non-fans are pretty active online, too!

TOP 10

OFFICIAL MUSIC VIDEOS WITH THE MOST YOUTUBE VIEWS

YouTube views can make a big difference to a song's success, as these 10 prove with plays sky-rocketing to over a BILLION...

YOU RATE! 1 to 100

	ARTIST/GROUP	SONG	RELEASE DATE	VIEWS
1	PSY	Gangnam Style	Jul 15, 2012	Over 1 billion
2	Justin Bieber ft. Ludacris	Baby	Jan 18, 2010	818,244,327
3	Jennifer Lopez ft. Pitbull	On The Floor	Feb 8, 2011	620,984,923
4	Eminem ft. Rihanna	Love The Way You Lie	Aug 9, 2010	514,554,219
5	LMFAO ft. Lauren Bennett & GoonRock	Party Rock Anthem	Jan 25, 2011	511,230,148
6	Shakira ft. Freshlyground	Waka Waka (This Time For Africa)	May 7, 2010	499,721,397
7	Lady Gaga	Bad Romance	Oct 26, 2009	495,732,247
8	Michel Teló	Ai Se Eu Te Pego	Oct 10, 2011	472,617,587
9	Don Omar ft. Lucenzo	Danza Kuduro	Aug 15, 2010	403,711,054
10	Eminem	Not Afraid	Apr 29, 2010	373,560,942

TOP 10 SOLO ARTISTS WITH THE MOST FOLLOWERS ON TWITTER

From chatting to fans to retweeting links, the power of the micro-blogging system Twitter is undeniable. Here are the most followed solo artists...

	ARTIST	TWITTER HANDLE	FOLLOWING	FOLLOWERS
1	Lady Gaga	@ladygaga	137,046	31,246,211
2	Justin Bieber	@justinbieber	122,521	30,243,719
3	Katy Perry	@katyperry	117	28,994,471
4	Rihanna	@rihanna	890	26,691,688
5	Britney Spears	@britneyspears	412,343	21,867,468
6	Taylor Swift	@taylorswift13	82	20,767,033
7	Shakira	@shakira	72	18,692,911
8	Nicki Minaj	@NICKIMINAJ	1,991	14,947,800
9	Justin Timberlake	@jtimberlake	29	14,578,221
10	Selena Gomez	@selenagomez	746	13,108,025

YOU RATE!
1 to 100

PINK

OFF THE CHART

Just nudged off the chart is feisty pop-rocker Pink, with a still impressive 11,858,900 followers. But who does someone like Pink follow on Twitter? Her 196 include *New York Times* Food & Drink and rocker Alanis Morissette.

KATY PERRY

ANOTHER THING!
If you take into account the "followers to following" ratio, the clear champion is Katy Perry!

XTREME FACT

With more than 75 million digital downloads sold since her album *One Of The Boys* dropped in 2008, 28-year-old popstar Katy Perry is unstoppable. She has tweeted more than 4,000 times and enjoys tweeting playlists to her fans to spread the love of other bands and singers she enjoys. That's another reason why you rock, Katy!

TOP 10 GROUPS/BANDS WITH THE MOST FOLLOWERS ON TWITTER

It's not just the solo music stars who have made an impact on Twitter. These bands and vocal groups also command a very strong tweeting presence...

CHECK IT OUT!

Poor 30 Seconds To Mars... The rock band has a huge following on its Twitter account, but the lead singer/guitarist has even MORE followers on his own personal one! @JaredLeto has nearly 100,000 more than his band, with 941,513 followers hanging on to his every tweet...

STAT ATTACK

MAROON 5

Studio albums	4
Live albums	3
Singles	17
Tweets	1,826

FACT FLASH!
FOLLOWERS
2.118 MILLION

	GROUP/BAND	TWITTER HANDLE	FOLLOWING	FOLLOWERS
1	**Coldplay**	**@coldplay**	**2,254**	**8,772,336**
2	One Direction	@onedirection	2,078	7,815,054
3	Jimmy Eat World	@jimmyeatworld	119,559	2,500,974
4	Maroon 5	@maroon5	323	2,118,400
5	Pearl Jam	@pearljam	198	1,717,002
6	Counting Crows	@countingcrows	73	1,392,925
7	Zoé	@zoetheband	102	1,231,704
8	Weezer	@weezer	165	1,014,123
9	The Flaming Lips	@theflaminglips	3,403	795,227
10	30 Seconds To Mars	@30secondstomars	16	842,371

PRICE TAG

It's not all about the money, but we're sure that these mega-earners are not going to complain about their gargantuan paychecks...

TOP 10

HIGHEST EARNING SOLO ARTISTS IN 2012

When you're a solo artist not only is there hardly any equipment to lug around, but you don't need to split the profits with band members!

	ARTIST	EARNINGS ($)
1	Madonna	34,577,308
2	Bruce Springsteen	33,443,606
3	Roger Waters	21,160,131
4	Kenny Chesney	19,148,525
5	Tim McGraw	18,329,167
6	Jason Aldean	17,578,651
7	Justin Bieber	15,944,293
8	Adele	13,906,635
9	Celine Dion	12,927,494
10	Brad Paisley	12,848,724

Source: Billboard

YOU RATE! 1 to 100

FACT FLASH! EARNED IN 2012 **15.9 MILLION DOLLARS**

JAY-Z

OFF THE CHART

You might be surprised not to see Jay-Z in the Top 10, but he's not far behind with a more than adequate $7,011,905!

CHECK IT OUT!

How much would you like to be earning by the time you're 19? How does $15.9 million sound?! The power of the hairdo, eh? Bieber is only on his third album (well, second if you don't count his 2011 Christmas album *Under The Mistletoe*). And with his musical skills on the drums, guitar and piano, who knows what this multitalented guy will serve up in years to come...

TOP 10 HIGHEST EARNING BANDS/GROUPS IN 2012

Groups of musicians and singers have to earn enough to support the whole gang. Looking at these figures, these guys are doing just fine...

YOU RATE! 1 to 100

	BAND/GROUP	EARNINGS ($)
1	Van Halen	20,184,709
2	Dave Matthews Band	18,903,334
3	Coldplay	17,300,144
4	Lady Antebellum	12,968,992
5	Nickelback	11,121,419
6	Rascal Flatts	10,777,282
7	Trans-Siberian Orchestra	9,959,362
8	Red Hot Chili Peppers	9,477,807
9	The Rolling Stones	9,276,084
10	Rush	8,719,834

Source: Billboard

RED HOT CHILI PEPPERS

XTREME FACT

Anthony Kiedis, aged 50, (pictured, left) has been the frontman of psychedelic funk rockers Red Hot Chili Peppers for over 30 years! Their 10th album, *I'm With You* was released August 29, 2011.

FACT FLASH!
EARNED IN 2012
9.4 MILLION DOLLARS

LADY ANTEBELLUM

XTREME FACT

Nashville, Tennessee's country music superstars Lady Antebellum have notched up seven Grammy wins since they formed in 2006. Their triumphs include scooping the 2012 Grammy for Best Country Album for *Own The Night*.

COMPARE-O-METER

See how these do against the above's earnings...

THE BLACK KEYS
10 20 30 40 50 60
THE BLACK KEYS 2012 EARNINGS
$7,358,679

CARRIE UNDERWOOD
10 20 30 40 50 60
CARRIE UNDERWOOD 2012 EARNINGS
$11,942,956

PRICE TAG

TOP 10 MOST EXPENSIVE MUSIC VIDEOS

You don't necessarily have to spend a mountain of cash to make an effective music video, but you try telling that to these artists...

	ARTIST/GROUP	SONG/VIDEO	DATE OF SINGLE'S RELEASE	PRODUCTION COSTS ($)
1	Michael & Janet Jackson	Scream	May 31, 1995	7,000,000
2	Madonna	Die Another Day	Oct 22, 2002	6,000,000
3	Madonna	Express Yourself	May 9, 1989	5,000,000
4	Michael Jackson	Black Or White	Nov 11, 1991	4,000,000
=	Guns N' Roses	Estranged	Jan 14, 1994	4,000,000
6	Puff Daddy	Victory	Mar 17, 1998	2,700,000
7	MC Hammer	Too Legit To Quit	Oct 29, 1991	2,500,000
=	Mariah Carey	Heartbreaker	Sep 21, 1999	2,500,000
9	Busta Rhymes	What's It Gonna Be?	Mar 9, 1999	2,400,000
10	Celine Dion	It's All Coming Back To Me Now	Jul 29, 1996	2,300,000

YOU RATE!

1 to 100

VICTORY

XTREME FACT

No one has ever accused P. Diddy (aka Puff Daddy, aka Sean Combs) of not spending enough on his music videos. Part of *Victory*'s $2.7 million costs included hiring models Tamara Beckwith and Tara Palmer-Tomkinson (far left) to star in it.

FACT FLASH! COST

2.7 MILLION DOLLARS

CHECK IT OUT!

He may be a Hollywood A-lister, but actor Jared Leto didn't use this to his advantage when 30 Seconds To Mars became a band. In fact, the complete opposite. Their 2002 self-titled album contained no imagery of the band, no photos of Leto and no visible signs that he was in the band, except for a line-up reference in the sleeve notes. It wasn't until the 2006 single *The Kill* was released from their second album (*A Beautiful Lie*) that the band caught mainstream attention.

BEEN & SEEN

Tick the boxes by these official music videos if you've seen them!

- [ ] KATY PERRY **CALIFORNIA GURLS**
- [ ] PSY **GANGNAM STYLE**
- [ ] 30 SECONDS TO MARS **FROM YESTERDAY**
- [ ] RIHANNA **DIAMONDS**
- [ ] ALICIA KEYS **GIRL ON FIRE**
- [ ] FUN. **SOME NIGHTS**
- [ ] NICKI MINAJ **VA VA VOOM**
- [ ] THE HIVES **WAIT A MINUTE**
- [ ] BRUNO MARS **LOCKED OUT OF HEAVEN**
- [ ] GREEN DAY **THE FORGOTTEN**

ANOTHER THING

Have you noticed a resemblance between 30 Seconds To Mars' singer and drummer? You should, as the man behind the kit is Shannon Leto, Jared's brother!

GIVE IT A TRY...
MAKE A MUSIC VIDEO

With the technology available on smartphones these days, it's never been easier to shoot your very own music video! You could film a performance of a band you know, or just record you and your friends lip-synching to a song you know all the words to. So, get ROCKIN'!

OUR TOP 10 UNOFFICIAL
MOST EPIC MUSIC VIDEOS

	ARTIST/GROUP	SONG/VIDEO	RELEASE DATE	EPIC QUALITIES
1	Soundgarden	Black Hole Sun	Nov 30, 1993	Apocalypse, weird family, madness
2	Coheed and Cambria	The Suffering	Sep 20, 2005	Mermaids, centaurs, sea monsters
3	30 Seconds To Mars	From Yesterday	Nov 6, 2006	Samurai battles
4	Michael Jackson	Smooth Criminal	Oct 5, 1988	Gangsters, dance-offs
5	Muse	The 2nd Law: Unsustainable	Aug 10, 2012	Robotics, post-apocalyptic news broadcasts
6	Katy Perry	Hot N Cold	Sep 9, 2008	A romantic comedy wedding adventure
7	Talking Heads	Once In A Lifetime	Feb 2, 1981	Singer David Byrne's bizarre computer-aided moves
8	A-ha	Take On Me	Sep 16, 1985	Adventure through animation
9	Crash Test Dummies	Afternoons & Coffeespoons	Jun 6, 1994	Hospital/operation spoof
10	Meat Loaf	I Would Do Anything For Love	Oct 18, 1993	Beauty And The Beast love story

PRICE TAG

ARTIST/GROUP
WITH THE HIGHEST
GROSSING TOURS

Concert tickets may seem expensive sometimes, but putting on a huge tour costs a phenomenal amount. These elaborate tours did extremely well...

YOU RATE! 1 to 100

	ARTIST/GROUP	TOUR*	DATES	GROSS ($ MILLION)
1	U2	360°	2009-11	736,421,586
2	The Rolling Stones	A Bigger Bang	2005-07	558,255,524
3	AC/DC	Black Ice	2008-10	441,121,000
4	Madonna	Sticky & Sweet	2008-09	407,713,266
5	Roger Waters**	The Wall	2010-12	377,368,148
6	The Police	Reunion	2007-08	358,825,665
7	Celine Dion	Taking Chances	2008-09	279,200,000
8	Eagles	Long Road Out Of Eden	2008-11	251,112,882
9	Pink Floyd	The Division Bell	1994	250,000,000
10	Bruce Springsteen	Magic	2007-08	235,000,000

*If a band/artist had multiple tours, their highest grossing is featured
**Although Roger Waters was in Pink Floyd, this tour of The Wall album was a different band/live line-up

ANOTHER THING!

In 1994, this was the final time Pink Floyd would tour together under this band name.

FACT FLASH!
GROSSED
250
MILLION
DOLLARS

PINK FLOYD

XTREME FACT

The *Division Bell* tour was a feast for the eyes and ears: rotating stages, a replica of the Hollywood Bowl, inflatable airships... And it wasn't just a few shows. Pink Floyd took the show all over the world, with 110 performances!

MADONNA

XTREME FACT

Madonna's eighth tour featured the popstar powering through a 24-song set list, full of wild themes, including "Gypsy" where the stage was packed with folk musicians and dancers. The tour concluded in Israel on September 2, 2009.

FACT FLASH!
GROSSED
407.7
MILLION
DOLLARS

STAT ATTACK

RYAN GOSLING

Born .... November 12, 1980

T-10's best Gosling movie .... Crazy, Stupid, Love. (2011)

Active musician since 2007

Band name .... Dead Man's Bones

Albums released .. Dead Man's Bones (2009)

CHECK IT OUT!

Team T-10 thinks Zooey Deschanel rocks! Not only is she a brilliant actress (and hilarious in *New Girl*), but that VOICE! Zooey is in a duo called She & Him with a musician known as M Ward, and the pair have released three albums to date: *Volume One* (2008), *Volume Two* (2010) and *A Very She & Him Christmas* (2011). Zooey can also play the ukulele and piano, and has sung in many movies she's starred in, too.

RYAN GOSLING

XTREME FACT

He's been in the fame game longer than you'd think... Ryan Gosling started out performing on Disney's TV show *The Mickey Mouse Club* (alongside Christina Aguilera) when he was just 13 years old!

OUR TOP 10 UNOFFICIAL

ACTORS WHO ARE ALSO SINGERS/MUSICIANS

	ACTOR	SOLO/BAND
1	Kylie Minogue	Solo artist
2	Zooey Deschanel	She & Him
3	Jared Leto	30 Seconds To Mars
4	Hugh Laurie	Solo artist
5	Juliette Lewis	Juliette And The Licks
6	Taylor Momson	The Pretty Reckless
7	Jason Schwartzman	Phantom Planet/Coconut Records
8	Ryan Gosling	Dead Man's Bones
9	Scarlett Johansson	Solo artist
10	Tim Robbins	Tim Robbins And The Rogues Gallery Band

ON STAGE

Enjoying music at home on your media system or even on the move on your phone is one thing, but nothing really beats seeing a live performance...

TOP 10 BIGGEST TOUR ATTENDANCE

It must be amazing to look out from a stage at an ocean of fans, all there purely to see you. For these megastars, the attendance at their shows went through the roof...

YOU RATE! 1 to 100

	BAND/ARTIST	TOUR*	DATES	TOTAL ATTENDANCE
1	U2	360°	2009-11	7,272,046
2	The Rolling Stones	Voodoo Lounge	1994-95	6,336,776
3	Pink Floyd	The Division Bell	1994	5,500,000
4	AC/DC	Black Ice	2008-10	4,846,965
5	Michael Jackson	HIStory	1996-97	4,500,000
6	Madonna	Sticky & Sweet	2008-09	3,545,899
7	Cher	Living Proof	2002-05	3,500,000
8	The Police	Reunion	2007-08	3,300,912
9	Bruce Springsteen	The Rising	2002-03	3,232,384
10	Roger Waters**	The Wall	2010-12	3,056,048

*If a band/artist had multiple tours high in the list, their most attended is featured
**Although Roger Waters was in Pink Floyd, this tour of The Wall album was a different band/live line-up

MADONNA

XTREME FACT

Here she is... Madonna on stage in Bucharest as part of her *Sticky & Sweet* tour of 2009. For a 51-year-old popstar, she's got an incredible amount of energy!

FACT FLASH!
ATTENDEES
6.3 MILLION

CHECK IT OUT!

After a staggering 51 years, The Rolling Stones are still rockin'! Band member Keith Richards (above) was one of the inspirations for Johnny Depp's performance as Captain Jack Sparrow... The guitarist went on to play Sparrow's dad in the *Pirates Of The Caribbean* movies *At World's End* and *On Stranger Tides*!

OUR TOP 10 UNOFFICIAL

MOST AMAZING SET/STAGE PRODUCTION

	ARTIST/GROUP	SHOW/VENUE	SET/STAGE PRODUCTION
1	**Devin Townsend**	**Retinal Circus**	**Aliens, cat people, businessmen apes, dreamscapes, choirs**
2	Pink Floyd	The Wall	Huge stage props, including a massive wall, 30ft-high teacher
3	Iron Maiden	The Final Frontier	Crazy stage design, featuring inflatable monsters
4	Muse	Wembley Stadium	Trapeze artists, hot-air balloons
5	Take That	The Circus	Elephants, trapeze artists, a full circus
6	Rob Zombie	Hellbilly Deluxe	Graveyard, including guitarists rising from the graves
7	Aerosmith	Toxic Twin Towers Ball	Light shows, pyrotechnics, giant inflatables
=	Katy Perry	California Gurls	Candy cane and huge sweets as far as the eye could see
9	Michael Jackson	HIStory	Huge theatrics, including a tank on stage
10	Kiss	Rock The Nation	High-wire performances, spinning/elevating drum riser, pyrotechnics

TAKE THAT, THE CIRCUS

XTREME FACT

Over a million Take That fans saw the group's most lavish UK tour over 20 shows in 2009. Aside from the group dressing up and performing as clowns for one section, there were colossal pyrotechnics, high-wire stunts, singing in the rain, and a huge mechanical elephant!

OUR TOP 10 UNOFFICIAL

GROUPS WITH MORE THAN FIVE MEMBERS

	GROUP	MEMBERS
1	**I'm From Barcelona**	**28**
2	The Polyphonic Spree	21
3	Haggard	17
4	Bang Camaro	16
5	Earth, Wind & Fire	14
6	Arcade Fire	11
7	Edward Sharpe And The Magnetic Zeros	10
8	Godspeed You! Black Emperor	9
=	Slipknot	9
10	Madness	7

ON STAGE

TOP 10 LONGEST CONCERTS (RUNNING TIME)

Rock gods and goddesses can play really long live sets but, as shown here, the longest performances aren't the ones you'd expect...

	ARTIST/GROUP	DATE	LOCATION	SHOW LENGTH
1	John Cage	Sep 5, 2001*	Halberstadt (Germany)	12 years (to date, will last 639 years!)
2	Kuzhalmannam Ramakrishnan	Jul 5, 2009*	Kerala (India)	501 hr
3	Prasanth Manohar Gaikwad	Apr 19, 2009*	India	324 hr
4	Bodhi Foundation & Maharashtra Youth Development Organisation	Apr 14, 2009*	India	64 hr 5 min
5	Phish	Dec 31, 1999	Florida (USA)	7 hr 45 min
6	Manowar	Jul 5, 2008	Sofia (Bulgaria)	5 hr 1 min
7	Led Zeppelin	Jan 26, 1969	Boston (USA)	4 hr 30 min
8	Bruce Springsteen	Jul 31, 2012	Helsinki (Finland)	4 hr 6 min
9	Guns N' Roses	Dec 19, 2009	Tokyo (Japan)	3 hr 37 min
10	Foo Fighters	Sep 5, 2012	North Carolina (USA)	3 hr 30 min

*Date concert began

JOHN CAGE

XTREME FACT

John Cage (Sep 5, 1912-Aug 12, 1992) was one of the most influential and experimental composers. His piece ORGAN2/ASLSP (As SLow aS Possible) will take 639 years to perform! Check out: www.aslsp.org

FACT FLASH!
SHOW LENGTH
12+ YEARS

GIVE IT A TRY...
PUT ON A SUMMER FESTIVAL

Are you in a band? Know of any friends who are in a band? Get together and see if you can find a local community hall or park where you could plan your own mini-festival!

CHECK IT OUT!

Although they're one of the biggest rock bands in the world, Foo Fighters' debut self-titled album of 1995 doesn't feature a band at all... Dave Grohl (left) actually recorded all of the vocals, guitars, drums and bass sections himself... In one week!

TOP 10 ☠ LONGEST TOURS
(AMOUNT OF SHOWS)

Think the bands and singers that you love rock? But just how MUCH can they rock? How many shows in one tour can they do? Check out these superstars...

YOU RATE!
1 to 100

	BAND/ARTIST	TOUR	TOUR LENGTH	TOTAL SHOWS
1	Cher	Living Proof	Jun 14, 2002-Apr 30, 2005	326
2	Lady Gaga	The Monster Ball	Nov 27, 2009-May 6, 2011	201
3	Pink Floyd	A Momentary Lapse Of Reason	Sep 9, 1987-Jul 18, 1989	199
4	Roger Waters*	The Wall	Sep 15, 2010-Sep 18, 2012	192
5	Metallica	World Magnetic	Sep 12, 2008-Nov 21, 2010	187
6	AC/DC	Black Ice	Oct 28, 2008-Jun 28, 2010	167
7	Pink	Funhouse	Feb 24, 2009-Jul 25, 2010	163
8	U2	Zoo TV	Feb 29, 1992-Dec 10, 1993	157
9	The Police	Reunion	May 28, 2007-Aug 7, 2008	156
10	Eagles	Long Road Out Of Eden	Mar 20, 2008-Nov 19, 2011	155

*Although Roger Waters was in Pink Floyd, this tour of The Wall album was a different band/live line-up

OUR TOP 10 UNOFFICIAL
STRANGEST PLACES BANDS HAVE PLAYED LIVE

	BAND/ARTIST	LOCATION	DATE
1	The Presidents Of The United States Of America	Mount Rushmore	Feb 19, 1996
2	Ben Trevor	140 ft tree in Surrey (UK)	Jun 2, 2012
3	Arcade Fire	Inside an elevator, Paris (France)	Mar 26, 2007
4	Dan Le Sac vs Scroobius Pip	The British Library	Dec 14, 2008
5	Madness	Buckingham Palace rooftop	Jun 4, 2012
6	Johnny Cash	Folsom Prison (USA)	Jan 13, 1968
7	Darren Hayman	Belly of a ship	Jan 28, 2012
8	Jean Michel Jarre	Great Pyramids of Egypt	Dec 31, 1999
9	Alicia Keys	Great Wall Of China	Sep 25, 2004
10	Bon Iver	Hollywood Forever Cemetery	Sep 27, 2009

MADNESS

XTREME FACT
On June 4, 2012, British pop-rockers Madness performed on top of Buckingham Palace for the Queen's Diamond Jubilee celebrations, with over 12,000 people watching from the streets below.

LARGEST FESTIVALS

There are hundreds of music festivals held across the planet every year, but only 10 of them draw attendance figures as impressive as these...

	NAME	LOCATION	ATTENDANCE
1	Glastonbury	UK	175,000
2	Roskilde	Denmark	110,000
=	Werchter	Belgium	110,000
4	Rock al Parque	Columbia	88,600
5	T In The Park	Scotland	85,000
6	Exit	Serbia	75,000
=	Coachella	USA	75,000
=	Reading/Leeds	UK	75,000
9	Sziget	Hungary	65,000
10	Pukkelpop	Belgium	62,500

YOU RATE!
1 to 100

ANOTHER THING!

Coachella isn't just about the music... There's also a huge array of art, including sculptures and installations on show, for you to interact with.

GLASTONBURY

XTREME FACT

It was 43 years ago that the first-ever incarnation of the Glastonbury Festival was staged (September 19, 1970). It was called the Pilton Pop, Blues & Folk Festival, and 1,500 people attended. These days, the crowd numbers 175,000!

CHECK IT OUT!

The Arctic Monkeys performed at both Coachella and Lollapalooza festivals in 2012. Here is singer Alex Turner rocking it with a quiff from his band's festival set (above). The talented Alex doesn't just craft music with this group, he also wrote all of the songs for the hilarious 2010 movie *Submarine*.

OUR TOP 10 UNOFFICIAL

STANDOUT FESTIVAL SETS

Of all the live festival performances over the years, here are some that have rocked the music world, bigtime!

	BAND/ARTIST	FESTIVAL	COUNTRY	YEAR
1	**Foo Fighters**	**Reading/Leeds**	UK	2012
2	Paul McCartney	Coachella	USA	2009
3	Alanis Morissette	Pink Pop	Netherlands	2008
4	Beyoncé	Glastonbury	UK	2011
5	Nirvana	Big Day Out	Australia	1992
6	Jimi Hendrix	Woodstock	UK	1969
7	Gnarls Barkley	Lollapalooza	USA	2008
8	Katie Moore	Pop Montreal	Canada	2008
9	System Of A Down	Rock Am Ring	Germany	2011
10	Avengers In Sci-Fi	Rock In Japan	Japan	2012

STAT ATTACK

LOLLAPALOOZA

Year began 1991

Created by .... Perry Farrell (singer of Jane's Addiction)

Current status .... Touring festival

2012 acts included ..... Arctic Monkeys, Florence + The Machine, Jack White

2013 (new location) ...... Tel Aviv, Israel

BEYONCÉ

XTREME FACT

In 2011, Beyoncé Knowles made music history by being the first female artist to headline the main stage at Glastonbury in more than 20 years! She totally rocked her historic 90-minute set.

CHECK IT OUT!

Experimental rock band System Of A Down broke their five-year hiatus when they returned to the live scene in 2011 with a series of huge shows. The rockers' June 5, 2011 show at Rock Am Ring in Germany saw them perform a blistering 26-song set.

MUSIC MASH-UP

YOUR SHOUT!

Check out these questions. Can you answer them without looking back through the book?

A very slight intermission in musical proceedings is now required, to hand the microphone over to you and pump YOUR T-10 memory of all things loud!

YOU RATE!

T-10 MUSIC STUFF

Now, you can take off your dancing shoes and turn down the volume as you look back at your ratings for the Music Mash-up zone. List all of your poptastic faves that YOU scored here!

NAME	"YOU RATE" SCORE
1	
2	
3	
4	
5	
6	
7	
8	
9	
10	

CHART TOPPERS

GUESS WHOSE FRIZZ?

Can you name the group that this crazy head of hair belongs to? Here are some clues.. This party lovin' group feature in two seperate Chart Topper lists and their 2012 "Anthem" was streamed over 48 million times in the same year.

TRUE OR FALSE...

1. Adele tops three of the charts, including "Biggest Selling Artists Ever". ☐T ☐F

2. "Pop" is the music genre with the most amount of digital trck sales. ☐T ☐F

3. Taylor Swift's massive 2012 album was called "Red". ☐T ☐F

198

FAN FORUM

Put a tick next to the star that doesn't appear in the Top 10 Most Googled Music Artists 2012...

- ..... **Miley Cyrus**
- ..... **Justin Bieber**
- ..... **Lady Gaga**
- ..... **Nicki Minaj**
- ..... **Jennifer Lopez**
- ..... **Shakira**

WHICH ARTIST?

Born .... September 27, 1982
First album .... Tha Block Is Hot (1999)
Latest album .... I Am Not A Human Being II (2013)
Awards 80
Myspace plays .... Over 570 million

NAME:
....

PRICE TAG

Do you think you can name the ridiculously wealthy popstars hidden behind these, even more ridiculous, outfits?

HINT! SHE'S EVERY BOY'S TEENAGE DREAM

A

NAME:
....

HINT! THIS LADY LOVES THE PAPARAZZI

B

NAME:
....

ON STAGE

See if you can list the top three bands/artists of both the Tour Attendances and the Longest Tours...

TOP THREE BIGGEST TOUR ATTENDANCES

1 ....
2 ....
3 ....

TOP THREE LONGEST TOURS

1 ....
2 ....
3 ....

ANSWERS ON PAGE 312

EPIC STRUCTURES

Vertigo-inducing towers, gargantuan bridges, insane roller coasters... The world is full of brilliant buildings that take our breath away. It's not just the modern ones, though, that "WOW" us, as creations by the ancient architects often defy all explanation as to how they were even made! So, hard hats on, let's step inside a world of truly stunning structures...

SKYSCRAPING

It's the battle of the biggest things built on Earth, ever!
From the tallest towers through to the most radical roller
coasters and wildest water slides, we've got the most
massive structures MORE than covered for you...

TOP 10 TALLEST BUILDINGS

Every year there are announcements of new buildings being
built, and some projects threaten to make their way into this
Top 10. As of now, these are the titans of all towers...

FACT FLASH!
FLOORS
163

	BUILDING	COUNTRY	YEAR	FLOORS	HEIGHT (M)	(FT)
1	Burj Khalifa	United Arab Emirates	2010	163	828	2,717
2	Taipei 101	Taiwan	2004	101	508	1,667
3	Shanghai World Financial Center	China	2008	101	492	1,614
4	International Commerce Centre	China	2010	108	484	1,588
5	Petronas Twin Towers	Malaysia	1998	88	452	1,483
6	Zifeng Tower	China	2010	66	450	1,476
7	Willis Tower (was Sears Tower)	USA	1974	110	442	1,450
=	KK100 Development	China	2011	100	442	1,450
9	Guangzhou International Finance Center	China	2010	103	439	1,440
10	Trump International Hotel & Tower	USA	2009	98	423	1,388

Source: Council On Tall Buildings And Urban Habitat

YOU RATE!
1 to 100

BURJ KHALIFA

XTREME FACT
The official opening ceremony may
have been in January 2010, but guess
when the digging of the foundations
began? Way, way back in January 2004!
But then again, if you're gonna create
the tallest building in the world, it's
best not to rush it, huh?

CHECK IT OUT!
Can you handle some more amazing facts about
Petronas Twin Towers? In each tower there are
29 double-decker high-speed passenger elevators,
10 escalators and 765 flights of stairs!

WILLIS TOWER

XTREME FACT

Would you scale 1,450 ft (442 m) of the Willis Tower (formerly the Sears Tower) in Chicago if you were scared of heights? Well, that's what actor Christian Bale did for his Batman role in *The Dark Knight*. He even stood on a ledge to fire his pump-action sticky-bomb rifle. What a LEGEND!

BEEN & SEEN

Tick the box next to any of these sky-high features you've seen with your own eyes...

- ☐ **SPIRE**
- ☐ **20 FLOORS OR MORE**
- ☐ **EXTERNAL ELEVATOR**
- ☐ **HELIPAD**
- ☐ **TOP-FLOOR VIEWING GALLERY**
- ☐ **FLAGPOLE**
- ☐ **ROOF GARDEN**
- ☐ **GIANT BILLBOARD**
- ☐ **50 FLOORS OR MORE**
- ☐ **ROOF SWIMMING POOL**

OFF THE CHART

THE SHARD
LONDON, UK

It might be further down on the World's Tallest Building list, but London's Shard is one of the tallest buildings in Western Europe! At 1,017 ft (310 m) tall, the combination of offices, restaurants, a five-star hotel and residential apartments is incredible. Plus, it houses the highest viewing gallery in London, with 360° views of the city! Don't eat too much before visiting if you're not so hot with heights...

COMPARE-O-METER

Do the heights of these buildings blow your mind?
Check out THESE mad measurements...

HEIGHT OF MOUNT EVEREST
8,848 m
29,029 ft

GOLDEN GATE BRIDGE (LENGTH)
2,737 m
8,980 ft

CHANNEL TUNNEL (LENGTH)
50,450 m
165,516 ft

203

SKYSCRAPING

 ## TALLEST ROLLER COASTERS

You may think you've ridden some exhilarating (and terrifying) rides, but THESE 10 will test anyone's nerves for sheer height alone...

	RIDE	LOCATION	HEIGHT (M)	(FT)
1	Kingda Ka	Six Flags Great Adventure (USA)	139	456
2	Top Thrill Dragster	Cedar Point (USA)	128	420
3	Superman: Escape From Krypton	Six Flags Magic Mountain (USA)	126.5	415
4	Tower Of Terror II	Dreamworld (AUS)	115	377
5	Steel Dragon 2000	Nagashima Spa Land (JAP)	97	318
6	Millennium Force	Cedar Point (USA)	94.5	310
7	Leviathan	Canada's Wonderland (CAN)	93.3	306
8	Intimidator 305	Kings Dominion (USA)	93	305
9	Thunder Dolphin	Tokyo Dome City (JAP)	80.2	263
10	Fujiyama	Fuji-Q Highland (JAP)	79	259

YOU RATE! 1 to 100

INTIMIDATOR 305

XTREME FACT

Named after the late NASCAR driver Dale "The Intimidator" Earnhardt, this popular roller coaster in the US has a hair-raising top speed of 90 mph (145 kph), and can carry 1,350 passengers every hour!

TALLEST FERRIS WHEELS

The long-distant sights across the city and the heights that you soar to... Ferris wheels are lovely and relaxing rides, unless of course you get vertigo. If you do, avoid ALL of these...

	NAME	LOCATION	HEIGHT (M)	(FT)
1	Singapore Flyer	Singapore	165	541
2	The Star Of Nanchang	China	160	525
3	The London Eye	London, UK	135	443
4	Suzhou Ferris Wheel	China	120	394
=	Southern Star	Melbourne, Australia	120	394
=	The Tianjin Eye	China	120	394
=	Changsha Ferris Wheel	China	120	394
=	Zhengzhou Ferris Wheel	China	120	394
=	Sky Dream Fukuoka	Japan	120	394
10	Diamond And Flower Wheel	Tokyo, Japan	117	384

YOU RATE! 1 to 100

STAT ATTACK

LONDON EYE

Diameter.............................394 ft/120 m
Records held...................Most Visited UK Attraction, Tallest Ferris Wheel In Europe
Passengers....................3.5 million a year
Opened to public ....9 March 2000

Watching over London's River Thames, it's the London Eye

OUR TOP 10 UNOFFICIAL
GIANT ATTRACTIONS

Of all the mad and crazy big objects built around the world, we LOVE these...

	OBJECT	LOCATION	HEIGHT (M)	(FT)
1	**Thermometer**	**California (USA)**	**40.8**	**134**
2	The Angel Of The North	Tyne & Wear (UK)	20	65
3	Larry The Lobster	Kingston (Australia)	17	56
4	World's Largest Six-Pack of Beer	Wisconsin (USA)	16.5	54
5	Huge Axe	New Brunswick (Canada)	15	49
=	The Big Merino Ram (Rambo)	New South Wales (Australia)	15	49
7	Route 66 Rocking Chair	Missouri (USA)	14	46
8	Neon Gibson Guitar	Las Vegas (USA)	13.7	45
9	Giant Soft Drink Bottle	Waikato (New Zealand)	12.2	40
10	Huge Pitchfork	Iowa (USA)	12.5	41

FACT FLASH!
HEIGHT
305
FT

TOP 10 HIGHEST WATER SLIDE DROPS

Who doesn't LOVE a water slide?! But would you be brave enough to fling yourself down these massive monster shoots?

FACT FLASH!
DROP
108
FT

YOU RATE!
1 to 100

	RIDE	LOCATION	HEIGHT (M)	(FT)
1	Kilimanjaro	Águas Quentes (Brazil)	50	164
2	Insano	Beach Park (Brazil)	41	135
3	Summit Plummet	Blizzard Beach (USA)	37	121.4
4	Jumeirah Sceirah	Wild Wadi Water Park (Dubai)	33	108.3
5	Scorpion's Tail	Noah's Ark Water Park (USA)	30	98.4
6	World Waterpark	West Edmonton Mall (Canada)	25	82
7	Cliffhanger	Schlitterbahn, Texas (USA)	24	78.7
8	Leap Of Faith	Atlantis Paradise Island (Bahamas)	18	59.1
=	The Wedgie	Coomera (Australia)	18	59.1
10	AquaLoop	Moravske Toplice (Slovenia)	17	55.8

SKYSCRAPING

TOP 10 TALLEST DAMS

Dams are massive structures that retain water and often generate electricity via hydropower, as well. These concrete colossi are the 10 biggest in the world...

VAJONT DAM

XTREME FACT

This amazing structure completed in 1959 sits eerily in the valley of the Vajont River beneath Italy's Monte Toc as it is a disused dam following a disaster in October 1963. The locals call Monte Toc "The Walking Mountain" because of how often it's prone to landslides and floods, which is exactly what happened. Water was forced over the dam, which destroyed local villages, killing 1,909 of the residents.

COMPARE-O-METER

Here's how this tall wall measures up:

APOLLO SATURN V
100 200 300 400 500 600

APOLLO SATURN V

111 m
364.2 ft

LITUYA BAY TSUNAMI
100 200 300 400 500 600

BIGGEST TSUNAMI

576 m
1,720 ft

FACT FLASH!
HEIGHT
858
FT

YOU RATE!
1 to 100

	DAM	LOCATION	HEIGHT (M)	(FT)
1	**Nurek**	**Tajikistan**	**300**	**984**
2	Xiaowan	China	292	958
3	Grande Dixence	Switzerland	285	935
4	Inguri	Georgia	271.5	890
5	Vajont	Italy	261.6	858
6	Chicoasén	Mexico	261	856
=	Tehri	India	261	856
8	Álvaro Obregón	Mexico	260	853
9	Mauvoisin	Switzerland	250	820
=	Laxiwa	China	250	820

Source: Dr. Andy Hughes, Professor in Dam Engineering

TALLEST BRIDGES

YOU RATE! 1 to 100

Have you been across any big bridges before? Check how those measure up to these babies...

	BRIDGE	LOCATION	HEIGHT (M)	(FT)
1	**Millau Viaduct**	**Millau, France**	**343**	**1,125**
2	Bridge to Russky Island	Eastern Bosphorus strait	321	1,053
3	Akashi-Kaikyo	Japan	298.3	978.7
4	Stonecutters	Hong Kong	298	977.7
5	Great Belt East	Denmark	254	833.3
6	Golden Gate	San Francisco, USA	227.4	746
7	Foresthill	California, USA	223	731.6
8	Tatara	Honshu and Shikoku, Japan	220	721.8
9	Pont de Normandie	Normandy, France	215	705.4
=	Runyang	Jiangsu Province, China	215	705.4

AKASHI-KAIKYO

XTREME FACT

This titan of a suspension bridge spans the Japanese islands of Awaji and Kobe, with a total length of 2 mi (4 km). If it looks like it would take a long time to build, you'd be right. Construction began in 1988 but took 10 years to complete!

GIVE IT A TRY...
LOCAL BRIDGES

Why don't you look into the statistics of the bridges in your area? Arrange a trip to photograph any large bridges near you, then research the heights and histories.

TALLEST LIGHTHOUSES

What would a coastline be without a lighthouse? Well, it would be a lot less safe, as these are used to help sea vessels know their proximity to land!

FACT FLASH! HEIGHT **347.8** FT

	LIGHTHOUSE	LOCATION	HEIGHT (M)	(FT)
1	**Jeddah Light**	**Jeddah (Saudi Arabia)**	**113**	**370.7**
2	Perry Memorial Monument	Ohio (USA)	107	351
3	Yokohama Marine Tower	Yokohama (Japan)	106	347.8
4	Ile Vierge	Finistere's Shore (France)	82.5	271
5	Lighthouse of Genoa	Genoa (Italy)	77	253
6	Phare de Gatteville	Gatteville-le-Phare (France)	75	246
7	Lesnoy Mole Rear Range Light	St Petersburg City (Russia)	73	239
8	Mulan Tou	Hainan (China)	72	236
=	Baisha Men	Hainan (China)	72	236
10	Storozhensky Light	Lake Ladoga (Russia)	71	233

YOU RATE! 1 to 100

CHECK IT OUT!

Yokohama is a city on Tokyo Bay, on the main island of Honshu in Japan. The spectacular Yokohama Marine Tower was opened in 1961. It famously had alternating green and red lights sweeping the bay but these days a dazzling white light illuminates the way.

MASS APPEAL

It's not just the height of things we're interested in... We want to know all about the biggest structures there are on the planet in terms of mass and size! Here, we present to you the big boys from the world of builds...

OUR TOP 10 UNOFFICIAL

AWESOME NON-LAND STRUCTURES

1	International Space Station (as big as a soccer field)
2	MV Blue Marlin (transport ship that can carry 75,000 tonnes, that's 22 barges!)
3	Troll-A Offshore Gas Platform (world's heaviest platform is over 650,000 tonnes)
4	Hubble Space Telescope (as big as a bus, this records images in space)
5	Oil Platform P-51 (semi-submersible oil-drilling platform)
6	Envisat - Environmental Satellite (carries out environmental studies of Earth from space)
7	FPSO - Floating Production, Storage & Offloading Vessel (processes hydrocarbons & stores oil)
8	Hai Thach Central Processing Platform (60,000 tonnes)
9	ETLP - Extended Tension Leg Platform (offshore production of gas)
10	GBS - Gravity-based structure (suspended in water, held upright purely by gravity)

BEEN & SEEN

What huge buildings have you come across on your travels? Get together with your friends and have a brainstorm!

- [ ] CIRCUS BIG TOP
- [ ] SPORTS STADIUM
- [ ] INDOOR ARENA
- [ ] RAILWAY STATION
- [ ] INDOOR POOL
- [ ] AIRCRAFT HANGAR
- [ ] AIRPORT
- [ ] CATHEDRAL
- [ ] CASTLE
- [ ] MUSEUM

CHECK IT OUT!

Meet the Troll-A, Europe's biggest offshore gas platform in Norway. Its neck-craning 1,549 ft (472 m) height (and weight of over 620,000 tonnes) makes it the tallest structure to ever be moved from one place to another.

ANOTHER THING!

The amazing Hubble Space Telescope was launched in 1990, which means it's in its 23rd year of beaming space images to Earth!

COMPARE-O-METER

Want some more massive weights to compare these to?

TRUCK	JUMBO JET	STATUE OF LIBERTY
ARTICULATED TRUCK	JUMBO JET (INC. PASSENGERS)	STATUE OF LIBERTY
44 t	95 t	225 t

Heard of an area of land being described as an acre? It's just over 4,839 yd², NASA's Vehicle Assembly Building covers over EIGHT acres!

YOU RATE!

1 to 100

TOP 10 BIGGEST BUILDINGS

If you were to fill these buildings with comics, video games, whatever you wanted, these are the ones that would hold the most...

	BUILDING	LOCATION	VOLUME (CUBIC M)	(CUBIC FT)
1	Boeing Everett Factory	Washington (USA)	13,300,000	469,685,065
2	Target Import Warehouse	Washington (USA)	7,430,000	262,387,973
3	Jean-Luc Lagardère Plant	Blagnac (FRA)	5,600,000	197,762,133
4	Aerium	Brandenburg (GER)	5,200,000	183,636,266
5	Meyer Werft Dockhalle 2	Lower Saxony (GER)	4,720,000	166,685,226
6	NASA Vehicle Assembly Building	Florida (USA)	3,660,000	129,251,680
7	Palace Of The Parliament	Bucharest (ROM)	2,550,000	90,052,400
8	Palace Of Caserta	Caserta (ITA)	2,000,000	70,629,333
9	IHC Krimpen Shipyard	South Holland (NL)	1,300,000	45,909,067
10	Ericsson Globe	Stockholm (SWE)	600,000	21,188,800

NASA VEHICLE ASSEMBLY BUILDING

XTREME FACT

When you're building rockets, it's fair to say that you need quite a bit of room... Especially clearance space in the ceiling department! To make sure of that, this mountain of a building was made over 525 ft (160 m) tall! Constructed back in 1966, it's less busy now since the Space Shuttle retired in 2011 but, with space exploration continuing, who knows what elaborate machines could come out of its doors further down the line...

FACT FLASH!
VOLUME
129 MILLION FT³

BIGGEST CITIES

Some of us live in big cities, some of us in smaller villages. Do you live or know anyone who lives in one of the Top 10 most populated cities in the world?

	CITY	POPULATION
1	Greater Tokyo (Japan)	36.5 million
2	Jakarta (Indonesia)	26.1 million
3	New Delhi (India)	21.72 million
4	Shanghai (China)	20.8 million
5	Sáo Paulo (Brazil)	19.96 million
6	Mumbai (India)	19.70 million
7	New York City Met. Area (USA)	19.46 million
8	Mexico City (Mexico)	19.32 million
9	Õsaka/Kobe-Kyoto (Japan)	17 million
10	Seóul (South Korea)	9.78 million

YOU RATE!
1 to 100

CHECK IT OUT!

Tokyo is the capital of Japan, and it is one of the busiest and most vibrant cities in the world! Do you like video games? Then you would LOVE Tokyo, as many of the world's greatest game developers (including Game Freak, the team behind *Pokémon*, and Square Enix, who develop the *Final Fantasy* series) hail from here.

MUMBAI

XTREME FACT

Have you heard of Bombay? That was Mumbai's previous name. It is the most popular city in India, and the richest city, and Mumbai Harbour is home to six islands!

FACT FLASH!
PEOPLE
36.5
MILLION

OUR TOP 10 UNOFFICIAL

UNDERGROUND SPACES

	SPACE	USAGE	LOCATION
1	Cappadocia	Cave-like homes	Turkey
2	Coober Pedy	Cave-like homes	South Australia
3	SubTropolis	Office storage	USA
4	Double-decker City	Rail/shopping complex	Canada
5	PATH	Shopping complex	Canada
6	Seattle Underground	Abandoned housing	USA
7	Turda Salt Mine	Abandoned mine	Romania
8	G-Cans	Tokyo stormwater system	Japan
9	Object 825 GTS	Top secret soviet sub base	Russia
10	Cincinnati Transit	Abandoned subway	USA

CHECK IT OUT!

There are residents of Coober Pedy, Australia, who live in amazing underground homes! The first-ever subterranean realms were the result of opal mining (which the region is famous for). The funny thing was, the more digging that occurred, the more the homes grew. Nowadays, the modern changes found in the tunnel-homes include swimming pools and games rooms!

XTREME FACT

Those Egyptians really were the most amazing builders and sculptors! The Colossi of Memnon was created in 1350 BC, and represent pharaoh Amenhotep III, who reigned during Egypt's most prolific and astounding artistic period. At 59 ft (18 m) in height, the Colossi towers over all who gaze at its wonder.

BIGGEST STONE MONOLITHS

TOP 10

Monoliths are colossal stones that have been discovered during archaeological digs. Here are the biggest quarried and moved stones...

YOU RATE!

1 to 100

	MONOLITH	LOCATION	WEIGHT (T)
1	Thunder Stone	Saint Petersbur (Russia)	1,250
2	Stonehenge	Wiltshire (UK)	1,200+
3	Ramesseum	Thebes (Egypt)	1,000
4	Trilithon	Baalbek (Lebanon)	800
5	Colossi of Memnon	Thebes (Egypt)	700
6	Alexander Column	St Petersburg (Russia)	600
7	Western Stone, Jewish Holy Temple	Jerusalem (Israel)	560
8	Great Stele, King Ezana's Stele, Obelisk of Axum	Axum (Ethiopia)	520
9	Gomateshwara	Karnataka State (India)	400
=	Khafre's Pyramid	Giza (Egypt)	400

XTREME FACT

Is it an ancient calendar? A sacred burial ground? All we do know about Stonehenge is that mystery emanates from the stones that are believed to be up to 5,000 years old! The sizes of the stones are quite varied, with the biggest ones notching up a weight of about 50 tonnes!

GREAT LENGTHS!

Some of the longest structures mankind is responsible for building are truly awe-inspiring. We're not talking measurements in their thousands, we're talking about HUNDREDS of thousands...

TOP 10 LONGEST TUNNELS

Next time you're taking a stroll through or driving along one, imagine what it would be like moving through these monster-length tunnels...

FACT FLASH!
LENGTH
88,581 FT

YOU RATE!
1 to 100

	TUNNEL	LOCATION	LENGTH (M)	(FT)
1	**Thirlmere Aqueduct**	UK	154,497	506,874
2	Delaware Aqueduct	USA	137,000	449,470
3	National Water Carrier Of Israel	Israel	130,000	426,504
4	Päijänne Water Tunnel	Finland	120,000	393,696
5	Dahuofang Water Tunnel	China	85,320	279,918
6	Orange-fish River Tunnel	South Africa	82,800	271,650
7	Large Hadron Collider	Switzerland	27,000	88,581
8	Eucumbene-Snowy Tunnel	Australia	23,500	77,099
9	Eucumbene-Tumut Tunnel	Australia	22,200	72,834
10	Murrumbidgee-Eucumbene Tunnel	Australia	16,600	54,461

ANOTHER THING!

The Large Hadron Collider lies 574 ft (175 m) beneath the surface of the French-Swiss border, near Geneva, Switzerland.

COMPARE-O-METER

Here are some other HUGE dimensions!

WIDTH OF CASPIAN SEA
200k 400k 600k 800k 1m 1.2m

WIDTH OF THE CASPIAN SEA

435,000 *m*
1,427,148 *ft*

WIDTH OF TEXAS
200k 400k 600k 800k 1m 1.2m

WIDTH OF THE STATE OF TEXAS

1,062,167 *m*
3,484,757 *ft*

CHECK IT OUT!

The Large Hadron Collider is one of the biggest and most exciting tunnels ever built. Like something out of a science-fiction movie, particles can be accelerated to almost the speed of light, and then smashed together. So how important is it to collide them, and why are we doing this? Well, in this chamber, the biggest brains on the planet can test the theories of particles, the laws of nature, and pretty much increase our understanding of this thing we call life. So, overall, it's VERY important!

TOP 10 LONGEST BRIDGES

Bridges around the world reach some crazy lengths and these are another astounding example of engineering and construction...

YOU RATE! 1 to 100

	BRIDGE	LOCATION	TYPE	LENGTH (M)	(FT)
1	**Danyang-Kunshan Grand Bridge**	**China**	**Rail/Road**	**164,800**	**540,676**
2	Tianjin Grand Bridge	China	Rail	113,700	373,027
3	Weinan Weihe Grand Bridge	China	Rail	79,723	261,555
4	Bang Na Expressway	Thailand	Road	54,000	177,163
5	Beijing Grand Bridge	China	Rail	48,153	157,980
6	Lake Pontchartrain Causeway	USA	Road	38,442	126,121
7	Manchac Swamp Bridge	USA	Road	36,710	120,438
8	Yangcun Bridge	China	Rail	35,812	117,492
9	Hangzhou Bay Bridge	China	Road	35,673	117,036
10	Runyang Bridge	China	Road	35,660	116,993

LAKE PONTCHARTRAIN CAUSEWAY

XTREME FACT

When you construct a bridge of this magnitude, you've got to get serious about the supporting structures... Which is why there are (wait for it) 9,500 concrete pilings holding this up!

EXTRA! If you think this list is impressive, bear in mind that the exciting thing about bridge building is that it's a continuous industry. New technologies and new expanses require bridging all the time, and there are some huge ones being constructed even now as you read this. Need some examples? What about Mumbai's Trans-Harbour Link, set to be 72,178 ft (22,000 m) long when it opens in 2014. But keep your eye on this enterprise, because bridges keep getting bigger and better...

OUR TOP 10 UNOFFICIAL MOST TERRIFYING BRIDGES

	BRIDGE	LOCATION
1	**Hussaini Hanging Bridge**	**Pakistan**
2	Sidu River Bridge	China
3	Puente de Ojuela	Mexico
4	Iya Valley Vine Bridges	Japan
5	Trift Lake Bridge	Switzerland
6	Kakum National Park Canopy Walk	Ghana
7	Capilano Suspension Bridge	Canada
8	Living Root Bridge	India
9	Sarawak	Borneo
10	Braldu River Crossing	Pakistan

CHECK IT OUT!

Look like something out of an Indiana Jones movie? The Hussaini Hanging Bridge is real, and attracts daredevil tourists!

GREAT LENGTHS!

LONGEST ROLLER COASTERS

Here at Team T-10 we love all things theme-park based, but we had no idea that some of the greatest roller coasters are more than 6,500 ft long!

CHECK IT OUT!

The spectacular Fujiyama at the Fuji-Q High Land park in Yamanashi, Japan, takes its name from a combination of *Fuji* (King) and *Yama* (Mountain) and riding this one, you must really feel like the king of all the mountains! This $40 million ride lasts just over three-and-a-half minutes, and takes its brave riders to speeds of a cheek-flapping 80.8 mph (130 kph)!

FACT FLASH!
LENGTH
6,709
FT

STAT ATTACK

CALIFORNIA SCREAMIN'

Opened..................................... Feb 2001
Duration .... 2 mins 36 secs
Speed................. 55 mph (88.5 kph)
Made of ....Steel (over 5.5 million lbs of it!)

YOU RATE!
1 to 100

	ROLLER COASTER	LOCATION	LENGTH (M)	(FT)
1	Steel Dragon 2000	Nagashima Spa Land (Japan)	2,479	8,133
2	The Ultimate	Lightwater Valley (UK)	2,268.3	7,442
3	The Beast	Kings Island (USA)	2,243	7,359
4	Fujiyama	Fuji-Q High Land (Japan)	2,045	6,709
5	Millennium Force	Cedar Point (USA)	2,010.2	6,595
6	Formula Rossa	Ferrari World (UAE)	1,999.8	6,561
7	The Voyage	Holiday World (USA)	1,963.5	6,442
8	California Screamin'	Disney California Adventure (USA)	1,850.7	6,072
9	Desperado	Buffalo Bill's Resort (USA)	1,781	5,843
10	Gao	Mitsui Greenland (Japan)	1,735	5,692

COMPARE-O-METER

Here's a comparison to other big lengths!

GOLF TEE SHOT
471 m
1,545.3 ft

LONGEST ZIP LINE
2,130 m
6,988.2 ft

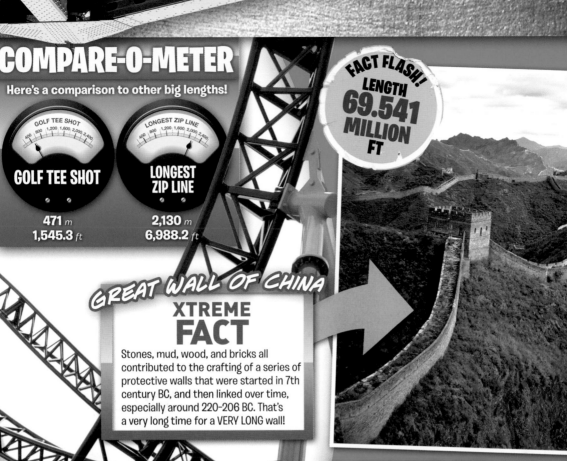

GREAT WALL OF CHINA

XTREME FACT

Stones, mud, wood, and bricks all contributed to the crafting of a series of protective walls that were started in 7th century BC, and then linked over time, especially around 220–206 BC. That's a very long time for a VERY LONG wall!

FACT FLASH!
LENGTH
69.541
MILLION
FT

TOP 10

LONGEST WALLS

When it comes to walls, we tend to think of those found in our house, etc. However, THESE take things into giant-sized territories...

YOU RATE!
1 to 100

	WALL	LOCATION	LENGTH (M)	(FT)
1	The Great Wall Of China	China	21,196,000	69,540,682
2	Berlin Wall	Germany	154,500	506,890
3	Hadrian's Wall	UK	117,482	385,440
4	Ancient Walls of Babylon	Mesopotamia	65,000	213,255
5	The Walls Of Ston	Croatia	5,500	18,044
6	Walls Of Troy	Turkey	1,200	3,937
7	Sacsayhuamán	Peru	600	1,969
8	Western Wall/Wailing Wall	Jerusalem	488	1601
9	The Great Zimbabwe	Zimbabwe	244	800
10	Vietnam Veterans' Memorial Wall	USA	150.4	493.5

TOP 10 LONGEST AIRPORT RUNWAYS

If you've ever taken off or landed in a plane, you'll know that runways are pretty long, but did you realize that some are more than 16,000 ft in length?!

ANOTHER THING!

How many airports do you think there are in the world? Ask your friends the same question, then hit them with the answer: 49,000. BOOM!

	AIRPORT	LOCATION	LENGTH (M)	(FT)
1	**Bamda/Bangda**	**China**	**5,500**	**18,045**
2	Ramenskoye	Russia	5,403	17,726
3	Ulyanovsk Vostochny	Russia	5,000	16,404
4	Embraer Unidade Gavião Peixoto	Brazil	4,967	16,296
5	Upington	South Africa	4,900	16,076
6	Denver International	USA	4,877	16,000
7	New Doha International	Qatar	4,850	15,912
8	Torrejón	Spain	4,818	15,807
9	Erbil International	Iraq	4,800	15,748
10	Harare International	Zimbabwe	4,725	15,502

YOU RATE!
1 to 100

DENVER INTERNATIONAL

XTREME FACT

This Colorado airport isn't just a hub for travel, there is an amazing array of art throughout the entire airport. The designers of Denver International Airport collaborated with many diverse artists to create an extensive series of installations, paintings and sculptures.

SPEED RACER

CRAZIEST MOVIE RACES

	MOVIE
1	Speed Racer
2	Talladega Nights: The Ballad Of Ricky Bobby
3	The Cannonball Run
4	Cars 2
5	Days Of Thunder
6	Herbie: Fully Loaded
7	Racing Stripes
8	Rat Race
9	A Day At The Races
10	The Fast And The Furious: Tokyo Drift

XTREME FACT

Did you know that the 2008 *Speed Racer* movie was based on a massively popular 1960s Japanese comic-turned-TV series called *Mach Go Go Go*? In the movie, the amazing cars were integrated into the most mind-bending race tracks, thanks to the skills of CGI (Computer Generated Imagery)! If you've never seen it and you love racing, check it out and then see if you can come up with a *Speed Racer* car design of your own.

TOP 10 LONGEST RACE CAR CIRCUITS

These tracks take a lot of planning and building, and they can go on for miles and miles, too...

	CIRCUIT	LOCATION	LENGTH (KM)	(MI)
1	Bahrain International/Endurance	Bahrain	6.3	3.9
2	Red Bull Ring/Österreichring	Austria	5.9	3.7
=	Silverstone Circuit/Grand Prix	UK	5.9	3.7
4	Suzuka/Grand Prix	Japan	5.8	3.6
=	Circuit Paul Ricard/Long Circuit	France	5.8	3.6
=	Autodromo Nazionale Monza	Italy	5.8	3.6
7	Yas Marina/Grand Prix	UAE	5.6	3.5
=	Korean International	Korea	5.6	3.5
9	Sepang International	Malaysia	5.5	3.4
=	Shanghai International	China	5.5	3.4

YOU RATE! 1 to 100

YAS MARINA

XTREME FACT

Car racing is an extremely exciting but also dangerous sport. Check out this photo of Italian driver Vitantonio Liuzzi colliding with German driver Michael Schumacher at the Yas Marina circuit in November 2010. Don't worry, though, they both escaped unhurt!

DESIGNED TO DELIVER

We celebrate some of the astounding structures that not only provide important services and are of historical awe, but these bunches of bricks tick the *fun* box, too!

CHECK IT OUT!

The Mehrangarh is a beautiful fort that towers over the land from its hilltop view in Rajasthan, India. The surrounding wall, all 6.2 mi (10 km) of it, protects the many treasures and palaces within, including a spectacular museum. And Batman fans, do you recognize this fort? What if we chanted, "Rise"? Yes, some of *The Dark Knight Rises* was filmed here in 2011!

FACT FLASH!
AREA
874,320
FT²

TOP 10 BIGGEST CASTLES

Team T-10 are huge fans of all things historical, and these ancient fortresses, still standing today, are the biggest on the planet...

YOU RATE!
1 to 100

	CASTLE	LOCATION	AREA (M²)	(FT²)
1	Malbork	Poland	143,591	1,545,600
2	Mehrangarh Fort	India	81,227	874,320
3	Prague	Czech Republic	66,761	718,609
4	Windsor	UK	54,835	590,239
5	Hohensalzburg	Austria	54,523	586,881
6	Spiš	Slovakia	49,485	532,652
7	Buda	Hungary	44,674	480,866
8	Himeji	Japan	41,468	446,357
9	Citadel of Aleppo	Syria	39,804	428,446
10	Edinburgh	Scotland	35,737	384,669

HOHENSALZBURG

XTREME FACT

Sitting on top of the Festungsberg mountain in the Austrian city of Salzburg, Hohensalzburg Castle dates back to the 11th century. At different times, the castle has been a fortress, a home for dignitaries, and it's been a prison!

BIGGEST AIRPORTS

Airports always look overwhelmingly huge when you're walking through one, but these ones are jaw-droppingly vast...

YOU RATE! 1 to 100

	NAME	LOCATION	AREA (KM²)	(MI²)
1	**King Fahd International**	**Saudi Arabia**	**1,256.1**	**485**
2	Montréal-Mirabel International	Canada	572.4	221
3	King Khaled International	Saudi Arabia	354.8	137
4	Denver International	USA	220.1	85
5	King Abdulaziz International	Saudi Arabia	168.3	65
6	Dubai World Central-Al Maktoum International	UAE	140	54
7	Dallas/Fort Worth International	USA	114	44
8	Charles de Gaulle	France	49.2	19
9	San Francisco International	USA	33.7	13
10	John F Kennedy International	USA	31.1	12

GIVE IT A TRY... TREE HOUSE

Get together with your friends (and some useful grown-ups) and discuss building your own tree house! Already have one? Think of some great ways to improve how it looks on the outside and add cool things inside, too.

OUR TOP 10 UNOFFICIAL

COOLEST TREE HOUSES

	TREE HOUSE	DESIGNER	HEADQUARTERS
1	**O2 Sustainability Tree House**	**Dustin Feider**	**USA**
2	4Treehouse	Lukasz Kos	Canada
3	Yellow Treehouse Restaurant	Pacific Environments NZ	New Zealand
4	Free Spirit Spheres	Tom Chudleigh	Canada
5	Reflective Tree Hotel	Tham & Videgård Arkitekter	Sweden
6	Äckerle Treehouse	Andreas Wenning/Baumraum	Germany
7	Takasugi-an Tea House	Terunobu Fujimori	Japan
8	Nescafé Treehouse	Takashi Kobayashi	Japan
9	Sam Stewart's Circular Tree House	TreeHouse Workshop	USA
10	Le Lit Perché	Alain Laurens/La Cabane Perchée	France

CHECK IT OUT!

You can go and stay inside a Free Spirit Sphere! There are a selection of them at a resort on Vancouver Island, Canada.

BIGGEST INDOOR ARENAS

Ever sat inside an indoor arena for a sporting event or music concert and wondered how many people the biggest ones can hold? Wonder no more...

YOU RATE!
1 to 100

	NAME	LOCATION	CAPACITY CROWD
1	Gwangmyeong Velodrome	South Korea	30,000
2	Mineirinho Arena	Brazil	25,000
=	Indira Gandhi Stadium	India	25,000
=	Belgrade Arena	Serbia	25,000
=	Coliseo Cubierto El Campín	Colombia	25,000
=	Petersberg Sports & Concert Complex	Russia	25,000
7	Greensboro Coliseum Complex	USA	23,500
8	Smart Araneta Coliseum	Philippines	23,000
=	Rupp Arena	USA	23,000
=	The O2 Arena	UK	23,000

CHECK IT OUT!

Not only is the Indira Gandhi Stadium the largest indoor sports arena in the whole of India, it's also the third-biggest in Asia! Its high-tech cycling velodrome (above) cost more than $33 million to build!

BIGGEST STADIUMS

Have you been to a stadium near where you live? They are monstrously massive, aren't they?! But chances are, you haven't experienced the majority of these beasts...

FACT FLASH!
CAPACITY CROWD
257,325

YOU RATE!
1 to 100

	NAME	LOCATION	CAPACITY CROWD
1	Indianapolis Motor Speedway	Indiana (USA)	257,325
2	Tokyo Racecourse	Tokyo (Japan)	223,000
3	Nürburgring	Nürburg (Germany)	220,000
4	Texas Motor Speedway	Texas (USA)	212,585
5	Shanghai International Circuit	Shanghai (China)	200,000
6	Estádio do Maracanã	Rio de Janeiro (Brazil)	199,854
7	Hampden Park	Glasgow (Scotland)	183,724
8	Talladega Superspeedway	Alabama (USA)	175,000
9	Daytona International Speedway	Florida (USA)	167,785
10	Charlotte Motor Speedway	North Carolina (USA)	167,000

TALLADEGA SUPERSPEEDWAY

XTREME FACT

The world-famous Talladega Superspeedway opened in 1969, but it started life as a very different and equally huge location. Long before cars competed there for trophies, the site was the World War II Anniston Air Force Base!

MOST VISITED THEME PARKS

The world is full of incredible theme parks and breathtaking rides, but how many people visit them every year? THIS many...

	NAME	LOCATION	ANNUAL ATTENDANCE
1	**Magic Kingdom, Walt Disney World Resort**	Lake Buena Vista, Florida (USA)	17,142,000
2	Disneyland, Disneyland Resort	Anaheim, California (USA)	16,140,000
3	Tokyo Disneyland, Tokyo Disney Resort	Chiba-Ken (Japan)	13,996,000
4	Tokyo DisneySea, Tokyo Disney Resort	Chiba (Japan)	11,930,000
5	Disneyland Park, Disneyland Paris	Marne-la-Vallée (France)	10,990,000
6	Epcot, Walt Disney World Resort	Lake Buena Vista, Florida (USA)	10,825,000
7	Disney's Animal Kingdom, Walt Disney World Resort	Lake Buena Vista, Florida (USA)	9,783,000
8	Disney's Hollywood Studios, Walt Disney World Resort	Lake Buena Vista, Florida (USA)	9,699,000
9	Universal Studios Japan	Osaka (Japan)	8,500,000
10	Islands of Adventure, Universal Orlando Resort	Orlando, Florida (USA)	7,674,000

YOU RATE!
1 to 100

WALT DISNEY WORLD RESORT

XTREME FACT

This Florida-based park, the most visited resort in the world, covers over 30,000 acres! Among the adventurous wonders are 31 hotels (for the indecisive out there), two water parks, four theme parks... the list goes on!

STAT ATTACK

BRIHADEESWARA TEMPLE

Located.................... Tamil Nadu, India
Purpose....................... Hindu temple
Dedicated to......... Shiva (Hindu god)
Date built.................... 11th century AD
Built by.............. King Raja Raja Chola I

CHECK IT OUT!

The ancient Brihadeeswara Temple is a true wonder made entirely of granite, which is uncommon for the area so it would've been transported in. Plus, at the entrance is a gigantic statue of a sacred bull called Nandi, said to be carved out of a SINGLE GRANITE ROCK!

OUR TOP 10 UNOFFICIAL SPIRITUAL STRUCTURES

	BUILD	LOCATION
1	**Great Pyramid of Giza**	**Egypt**
2	Sumerian Ziggurats	Mesopotamia
3	Göbekli Tepe	Turkey
4	Karnak	Egypt
5	The Pantheon	Italy
6	Brihadeeswara Temple	India
7	Hagia Sophia	Turkey
8	St. Peter's Basilica	Italy
9	Taj Mahal	India
10	Canterbury Cathedral	UK

BIZARRE BUILDS

From upside-down buildings to ancient spooky castles, there are plenty of weird and wonderful structures out there to explore...

GIVE IT A TRY... BUILDING DESIGN!

Why not design your own dream house? If these lists prove anything, it shows you can be as creative and imaginative as you like. Once you've designed it, try making a model of it with whatever materials you can get your hands on.

OUR TOP 10 UNOFFICIAL

STRANGEST BUILDINGS

	BUILDING	LOCATION
1	**Forest Spiral**	Germany

HOW STRANGE? These 105 apartments look like rock sedimentation crossed with a rainbow and an onion!

2	**Basket Building**	USA

LOOKS LIKE... A seven-floor high wicker basket! Think how many Blu-rays and video games you could get into that!

3	**Kansas City Public Library**	USA

BOUND TO BE ON THE LIST... because it's designed to look like 40 ft-wide leather-bound books on a shelf!

4	**Guggenheim Museum Bilbao**	Spain

ART ATTACK This sprawling art museum looks just like a futuristic battleship has docked into the city!

5	**Chapel of the Holy Cross**	USA

ROCKIN' Imagine a sleek, sophisticated, stone spacecraft emerging from Arizona's ancient desert rocks!

6	**Dancing House**	Prague

CEMENTING A FRIENDSHIP This looks just like two people dancing close together, cheek-to-cheek!

7	**Manchester Civil Justice Centre**	UK

FACT FILE: The entire building's 17 floors resembles a towering filing cabinet, complete with open drawers!

8	**National Library of Belarus**	Belarus

NEON UFO A diamond-shaped alien craft, covered in purple lights? No, it's actually Minsk's main library!

9	**WonderWorks**	USA

I'M WONDERING... Did a tornado do this? Nope, it was built to look upside-down, even inside does, too!

10	**House Attack at The Mumok**	Austria

MOVING HOME Easy to spot this in Vienna... A house has crashed into the roof of this contemporary museum!

GUGGENHEIM MUSEUM BILBAO

XTREME FACT

The Guggenheim art museum is a truly multicultural creation: it's in Spain's Basque Country, designed by Canadian Frank Gehry (now based in the US), and constructed by the multinational Ferrovial!

WONDERWORKS

XTREME FACT

If you're ever in Pigeon Forge, Tennese, USA, visit the upside-down world of the WonderWorks. It has over 100 interactive exhibits, including a challenge zone, complete with a rock climbing wall!

WONDERWORKS

TOP 10

TALLEST DEMOLISHED STRUCTURES

What goes up often must come down... Here are the most massive builds that have had to be brought down by controlled explosives experts!

CHECK IT OUT!

Imagine you lived near somewhere like the iconic Kingdome stadium, which was home to several Seattle sports stars, then picture the day of its planned demolition (March 26, 2000). Not only did thousands of residents gather to witness the building come down, they got something they didn't expect... The force of the blast caused a 2.3 earthquake reading on the Richter scale. BOOM!

YOU RATE!
1 to 100

	BUILDING	LOCATION	HEIGHT (M)	(FT)	WIPED OUT
1	**Omega Radio Tower**	**Trelew (Argentina)**	**366.1**	**1,201**	**1998**
2	Matla Power Station Smokestack	J'Burg (S Africa)	276.1	906	1982
3	Singer Building	New York (USA)	187.1	614	1968
4	Morrison Hotel	Illinois (USA)	160.3	526	1965
5	Trojan Nuclear Plant Cooling Tower	Oregon (USA)	152.1	499	2006
6	City Investing Building	New York (USA)	148.4	487	1968
7	J L Hudson Department Store	Michigan (USA)	133.8	439	1998
8	Sunshine Skyway Bridge (Old)	Florida (USA)	131.4	431	1991
9	Atlanta Air Traffic Control Tower	Georgia (USA)	121.3	398	2006
10	Kingdome	Washington (USA)	76.2	250	2000

TOP 10 TALLEST ABANDONED STRUCTURES

Like spectral giants, these buildings haunt skyline. Some stood empty for extended periods, and economic issues prevented others from being completed. Sadly, many remain unused...

	BUILD	LOCATION	HEIGHT (M)	(FT)
1	**Ostankino Tower**	**Moscow (Russia)**	**540.1**	**1,772**
2	Mystery Tower	Russia	300	1,000
3	Sathorn Unique Tower	Bangkok (Thailand)	149.35	490
4	Book Tower	Michigan (USA)	145	475.8
5	Henninger Turm	Frankfurt (Germany)	120	393.7
6	Gliwice Radio Tower	Upper Silesia (Poland)	118	387.1
7	Edifício São Vito	São Paulo (Brazil)	112	367.4
8	Sterick Building	Tennessee (USA)	111	364.2
9	Wacker Tower	Illinois (USA)	72.09	236.2
10	Michigan Central Station	Michigan (USA)	70	229.7

YOU RATE! 1 to 100

OSTANKINO TOWER

XTREME FACT

Designed by Russian designer/engineer Nikolai Nikitin, the Ostankino Tower is a radio/TV transmission tower, and has remained an iconic building in Moscow since its construction was completed in 1967. This tower was the first ever free-standing structure to be built taller than 1,640 ft (500 m).

CHECK IT OUT!

Ostankino Tower caught fire on August 27, 2000. In the tragedy, three people were killed and pretty much all of Moscow's TV broadcasts to the surrounding regions were knocked out. The fire safety systems failed to kick in so most of the tower's interior was completely destroyed in the flames. Then, on May 25, 2007, it caught fire again! There were no casualities and, thankfully, the blaze was taken care of by the city's firefighters.

FACT FLASH! HEIGHT 1,772 FT

CHECK IT OUT!

The enigmatic Edinburgh Castle sits atop the once-volanic Castle Rock, towering over the historic city of Edinburgh in Scotland. There are theories that before the castle was built, the land had residents on it as far back as 900 BC!

STAT ATTACK

EDINBURGH CASTLE

Occupied	From 12th century
Built upon	An extinct volcano
Annual visitors	More than 1.2 million
Reported ghostly sightings	

So many: dog wandering the grounds, headless drummer, phantom piper...

GIVE IT A TRY...
GHOST HUNTING

Ever been on a historic ghost walk? There are loads of them all over the world, and there's bound to be one near you. A well-informed guide takes you and your family/friends on a tour of a part of town and has plenty of spooky stories to tell along the way, perfect for Halloween!

CATACOMBS OF PARIS

XTREME FACT

Are you prepared for some creepy facts? The *Catacombes de Paris* contain the remains of six MILLION people. After 10 centuries of the dead being buried in the same location, which became diseased, this place then became the location to store the bones from all the cemeteries in Paris. With that many relocated remains, ghostly sightings are hardly surprising...

OUR TOP 10 UNOFFICIAL

MOST HAUNTED PLACES

	BUILDING	LOCATION
1	Edinburgh Castle	Edinburgh (Scotland)
2	Catacombs of Paris	Paris (France)
3	Monte Cristo Homestead	New South Wales (Australia)
4	Bhangarh Fort	Rajasthan (India)
5	Changi Beach	Changi (Singapore)
6	Diplomat Hotel/Dominican Hill	Baguio City (Philippines)
7	Berry Pomeroy Castle	Devon (UK)
8	Highgate Cemetery	London (UK)
9	Screaming Tunnel	Ontario (Canada)
10	The Stanley Hotel	Colorado (USA)

OSSEMENTS.DU CIMETIERE.DE INNOCENTS DEPOSES.EN AVRIL - 1786

EPIC STRUCTURES

YOUR SHOUT!

Check out these questions. Can you answer them without looking back through the book?

See? When we said this section was about EPIC structures, we weren't kidding around! Now it's time for a break, so here are some activities for you and your friends to complete together...

YOU RATE!

T-10 STRUCTURES

Go back through the Epic Structures section and find the 10 builds that you scored the highest in the "You Rate" buttons. Now list them in order below for YOUR ultimate T-10 structures!

	NAME OF STRUCTURE	"YOU RATE" SCORE
1		
2		
3		
4		
5		
6		
7		
8		
9		
10		

SKY SCRAPING

Can you link these cloud-busting builds with their correct heights?

1 Zifeng Tower

2 Taipei 101

3 Burj Khalifa

4 Shanghai World Financial Center

A 2,717 ft

B 1,667 ft

C 1,614 ft

D 1,476 ft

True or False: Kingda Ka, the world's tallest roller coaster, is taller than the fifth tallest building in the world.

T [ ] F [ ]

MASS APPEAL

CLOSE UP!

What is the name of the giant stone monolith (found in India) that is being worshipped here?

ANSWER: ....

GREAT LENGTHS

Can you place these monster constructions in descending order of their lengths?

- [.....] **Thirlmere Aqueduct** (Tunnel)
- [.....] **Danyang-Kunshan Grand Bridge** (Bridge)
- [.....] **Steel Dragon 2000** (Roller coaster)
- [.....] **The Great Wall Of China** (Wall)
- [.....] **Bamda/Bangda** (Runway)

BONUS POINT!
[............]
IS THE LENGTH OF STEEL DRAGON 2000

DESIGNED TO DELIVER

Take a look at the stadiums opposite and see if you can remember how many have a capacity exceeding 200,000...

STADIUMS	OVER 200,000 CAPACITY
TOKYO RACECOURSE.....................	[ ]
NÜRBURGRING.............................	[ ]
TALLADEGA SUPERSPEEDWAY ...	[ ]
TEXAS MOTOR SPEEDWAY..........	[ ]
ESTÁDIO DO MARACANÃ..............	[ ]

BIZARRE BUILDS

QUICK-FIRE QUESTIONS

1. What is odd about the WonderWorks building in the USA?

....

2. Which highly "haunted" place has walls made of human skulls?

....

3. Which is the tallest structure to have been most recently demolished?

....

4. Where does this "strange" building appear on our unofficial T-10 list?

[............]

ANSWERS ON PAGE 312

227

MOVIE SHOWTIME

Skyscraper-sized battling robots... Alien creatures that take over our cities... Time-travel quests to save the universe... In the movie world, we can experience all of these things and so much more! Team T-10 loves all things cinematic, so discovering the following Top 10s was nothing short of an absolute blast...

BLOCKBUSTERS

Summertime sees the biggest movie releases battling for the Number One slot. Here are the most successful action-packed thrill-rides ever made...

TOP 10 BIGGEST MOVIES OF ALL TIME

Here, we are mashing together all of the movie genres to discover the biggest hitters: from romance and comedy to action and thrillers, and everything in between...

	MOVIE	YEAR OF RELEASE	BOX OFFICE ($ BILLION WORLDWIDE)
1	Avatar	2009	2,782,275,172
2	Titanic	1997	2,185,372,302
3	The Avengers	2012	1,511,757,910
4	Harry Potter And The Deathly Hallows: Part 2	2011	1,328,111,219
5	Transformers: Dark Of The Moon	2011	1,123,746,996
6	The Lord Of The Rings: The Return Of The King	2003	1,119,929,521
7	The Dark Knight Rises	2012	1,081,041,287
8	Pirates Of The Caribbean: Dead Man's Chest	2006	1,066,179,725
9	Toy Story 3	2010	1,063,171,911
10	Pirates Of The Caribbean: On Stranger Tides	2011	1,043,871,802

Source: IMDB.com

YOU RATE! 1 to 100

FACT FLASH! BOX OFFICE **1.5 BILLION DOLLARS**

STAT ATTACK

THE AVENGERS

Director...................................Joss Whedon
Writer.......................................Joss Whedon
(Story by Joss Whedon and Zak Penn)
Music by.................................Alan Silvestri
Running time...............................143 min
US opening weekend takings:..$207,438,708

CHECK IT OUT!

Put May 1, 2015, in your calendars now for the return of the greatest superhero team ever in *The Avengers 2*. Writer-director Joss Whedon knocked it out of the park with the first *Avengers* movie, so we can't wait to see what he's got planned for the next one. Did you know Joss Whedon also created the beloved TV shows *Buffy The Vampire Slayer* (1997-2003), *Angel* (1999-2004) and *Firefly* (2002-03)?

SUPERHERO MOVIES

Team T-10 is a little bit obsessed with awesome superhero comic books, video games and, of course, movies! Here are the most successful costumed capers ever made...

YOU RATE!
1 to 100

	MOVIE	YEAR OF RELEASE	BOX OFFICE ($ WORLDWIDE)
1	**The Avengers**	2012	1,511,757,910
2	The Dark Knight Rises	2012	1,081,041,287
3	The Dark Knight	2008	1,004,558,444
4	Spider-Man 3	2007	890,871,626
5	Spider-Man	2002	821,708,551
6	Spider-Man 2	2004	783,766,341
7	The Amazing Spider-Man	2012	752,216,557
8	Iron Man 2	2010	623,933,331
9	Iron Man	2008	585,174,222
10	X-Men: The Last Stand	2006	459,359,555

Source: IMDB.com

SHUFFLE UP

What would you have at Number One? Now that you've seen the Top 10 superhero movies of all time, why not list them in order of YOUR faves?

1 ....
2 ....
3 ....
4 ....
5 ....
6 ....
7 ....
8 ....
9 ....
10 ....

Not a big fan of some of these? Add any superhero movies you like... It's YOUR list!

IRON MAN 2

XTREME FACT

In *Iron Man 2*, Scarlett Johansson plays Black Widow in her first appearance (before her larger role in *The Avengers*). Scarlett sensed other actresses were keen to get that role, too, including Natalie Portman (who ended up in *Thor*), Jessica Biel and Angelina Jolie. As Scarlett wanted the role so badly, she actually dyed her hair red before getting the part!

GIVE IT A TRY... CREATE A SUPERHERO!

Love superheroes as much as Team T-10? Why don't you invent a brand new one?! Get in touch with your friends, come up with some ideas and set a date as a challenge for when you all meet up and share your character designs. You never know, your imaginations could lead to the next batch of world-famous superheroes for comics and, of course, the movies inspired by them. Get creative!

231

TOP 10 ANIMATED MOVIES

From classic cel to stop-motion and, of course, 3D computer-generated adventures, here are the biggest animations, ever...

YOU RATE! 1 to 100

	MOVIE	YEAR OF RELEASE	BOX OFFICE ($ WORLDWIDE)
1	Toy Story 3	2010	1,063,171,911
2	The Lion King	1994	951,583,777
3	Finding Nemo	2003	921,738,870
4	Shrek 2	2004	919,838,758
5	Ice Age: Dawn Of The Dinosaurs	2009	886,686,817
6	Ice Age: Continental Drift	2012	875,268,222
7	Shrek The Third	2007	798,958,162
8	Shrek Forever After	2010	752,600,867
9	Madagascar 3: Europe's Most Wanted	2012	742,110,251
10	Up	2009	731,342,744

Source: IMDB.com

OUR TOP 10 UNOFFICIAL MOVIE VILLAINS

CHECK IT OUT!
Did you know that the creepy voice of Darth Vader did not belong to the actor who played him? British actor David Prowse played Lord Vader for episodes IV, V, and VI of the *Star Wars* saga, but American actor James Earl Jones provided the deep voice later.

	CHARACTER	MOVIE(S)
1	Loki	The Avengers/Thor
2	The Joker	The Dark Knight
3	Voldemort	The Harry Potter movies
4	Darth Vader	The Star Wars saga
5	Megatron	Transformers movies
6	Whiplash	Iron Man 2
7	Bane	The Dark Knight Rises
8	Venom	Spider-Man 3
9	Colonel Quaritch	Avatar
10	The T-800	Terminator Salvation

ICE AGE

XTREME FACT

The lovable but very accident-prone Scrat has starred in more than just the four hit *Ice Age* movies... He also starred in a series of DVD short tales, too! These include *Gone Nutty* (2002), *Surviving Sid* (2008) and the two-part *Scrat's Continental Crack Up* (2010 & 2011).

MOST MOVIES IN A FRANCHISE

TOP 10

It's pretty common for a popular character or franchise to enjoy multiple movie successes, but these 10 make all the others look like they're not even trying...

	FRANCHISE/CHARACTER	TOTAL MOVIES
1	Sherlock Holmes	37
2	James Bond	25
3	Star Trek	12
4	Batman	8
=	Harry Potter	8
6	The Avengers	7
=	Star Wars	7
8	X-Men	6
=	Superman	6
10	Ice Age	4

YOU RATE! 1 to 100

BATMAN

XTREME FACT

A total of five different actors have portrayed the Caped Crusader on the big screen, between 1966 and 2012, but Christian Bale has donned the Batsuit the most for Christopher Nolan's trilogy of *Batman Begins* (2005), *The Dark Knight* (2008) and *The Dark Knight Rises* (2012).

FACT FLASH! MOVIES 8

CHECK IT OUT!

Man Of Steel (released June 14, 2013) is the sixth time that Superman has flown into our cinemas, and he's still faster than a speeding bullet! The previous five movies collected a worldwide total of $889,412,997 at the box office, which is a lot, but when you consider *The Avengers'* worldwide box office is $1,511,757,910 for just one movie, it shows the hero in the red and blue outfit has still got a lot to prove.

BLOCKBUSTERS

TOP 10 BLU-RAY & DVD SALES

The Team T-10 home movie collection features most of these on Blu-ray and DVD... We bet yours does, too!

YOU RATE!
1 to 100

	MOVIE	YEAR OF RELEASE
1	Finding Nemo	2003
2	Pirates Of The Caribbean: The Curse Of The Black Pearl	2003
3	Shrek	2001
4	The Lord Of The Rings: The Fellowship Of The Ring	2001
5	The Lord Of The Rings: The Two Towers	2002
6	The Dark Knight	2008
7	Spider-Man	2002
8	Harry Potter And The Philosopher's Stone	2001
9	The Lord Of The Rings: The Return Of The King	2003
10	Shrek 2	2004

GIVE IT A TRY...
HAVE A MOVIE NIGHT!
The popcorn... The glow of the TV... There is nothing quite like a themed movie night, so set one up! See what cool themes you and your friends can come up with. Here, at Team T-10, we enjoy a "Murray and a curry", a selection of Bill Murray movies at home with an Indian meal!

THE LORD OF THE RINGS
XTREME FACT
The Lord Of The Rings saga took a total of $2,917,506,956 box office sales around the world, and that's not even counting *The Hobbit* prequel trilogy!

COMPARE-O-METER

See how the above have done against these...

BIGGEST SELLING ALBUM
THRILLER, MICHAEL JACKSON
110,000,000 *albums sold*

BIGGEST SELLING BOOK
A TALE OF TWO CITIES, CHARLES DICKENS
200,000,000 *books sold*

BEEN & SEEN

Tick the box next to the movies that you have in YOUR Blu-ray and DVD collection...

- [ ] IRON MAN 3
- [ ] SHREK
- [ ] THE AVENGERS
- [ ] TRANSFORMERS: DARK OF THE MOON
- [ ] THE AMAZING SPIDER-MAN
- [ ] ICE AGE: CONTINENTAL DRIFT
- [ ] THE DARK KNIGHT
- [ ] TOY STORY 3
- [ ] STAR WARS EPISODE I
- [ ] AVATAR

BEST
MOVIE-GOING SNACKS

1	**Sour Patch Kids sweets**
2	Peppermint Kandy Bar Kakes
3	Salted popcorn
4	Nachos with jalapeños & salsa
5	Hot dog, with all the trimmings
6	Coconut M&M's
7	Sweet popcorn
8	Banana milkshake
9	Coke float
10	Maltesers

SHUFFLE UP

What would you have as your Number One? Now you've seen Team T-10's all time best movie-going snacks, why not list them in order of YOUR tastiest treats?

1
2
3
4
5
6
7
8
9
10

Not a big fan of some of them? Add any snacks you like... It's YOUR list!

CHECK IT OUT!

Johnny Depp has played lovable rogue Captain Jack Sparrow four times now, with a fifth adventure believed to be in the works! And it's no surprise why, as the *Pirates Of The Caribbean* films have taken a staggering $3,727,735,967 in total sales at the box office. It's no wonder that interested actors agreed to be in number four without a script!

TOP 10 SCI-FI/ FANTASY MOVIES

Of all the amazing science fiction and fantasy tales that have exploded onto our cinema screens, these 10 are the box office champions...

	MOVIE	YEAR OF RELEASE	BOX OFFICE ($ WORLDWIDE)
1	Avatar	2009	2,782,275,172
2	The Avengers	2012	1,511,757,910
3	Harry Potter And The Deathly Hallows: Part 2	2011	1,328,111,219
4	Transformers: Dark Of The Moon	2011	1,123,746,996
5	The Lord Of The Rings: The Return Of The King	2003	1,119,929,521
6	Pirates Of The Caribbean: Dead Man's Chest	2006	1,066,179,725
7	Pirates Of The Caribbean: On Stranger Tides	2011	1,043,871,802
8	Stars Wars Episode I: The Phantom Menace	1999	1,027,044,677
9	Alice In Wonderland	2010	1,024,299,904
10	Harry Potter And The Philosopher's Stone	2001	974,755,371

Source: IMDB.com

YOU RATE!
1 to 100

ALICE IN WONDERLAND

XTREME FACT

Director Tim Burton and megastar Johnny Depp really do LOVE working together... *Alice In Wonderland* was their seventh movie together. And for such a complicated-looking movie, it only took 40 days to film it. But then, of course, the visual effects team spent a LOT longer than that crafting all the digital wizardry...

CHECK IT OUT!

When *Star Wars Episode I: The Phantom Menace* was released in 1999, it was the first *Star Wars* film for 16 years. Now that Disney has bought Lucasfilm (the company that created *Star Wars*), brand new movies for Episodes VII-IX will be released from July 15, 2015!

FACT FLASH!
BOX OFFICE
1 BILLION DOLLARS

TOP 10 COMEDY (LIVE-ACTION) MOVIES

Who doesn't love a good laugh? Exactly! These 10 comedies cover a huge range of movie genres and storytelling...

MIB3

XTREME FACT

Calling all *Transformers* movie fans! The movies' director, Michael Bay, made some early noises about directing *Men In Black 3*, but the job ultimately went to Barry Sonnenfeld, who directed the first two *MIB* movies.

YOU RATE!
1 to 100

	MOVIE	YEAR OF RELEASE	BOX OFFICE ($ MILLION WORLDWIDE)
1	Men In Black 3	2012	624,026,776
2	Mamma Mia!	2008	609,841,637
3	Men In Black	1997	589,390,539
4	Night At The Museum	2006	574,480,841
5	The Smurfs	2011	563,749,323
6	Meet The Fockers	2004	516,642,939
7	Bruce Almighty	2003	484,592,874
8	Home Alone	1990	476,684,675
9	Alvin And The Chipmunks: The Squeakquel	2009	443,140,005
10	Men In Black II	2002	441,818,803

Source: IMDB.com

OUR TOP 10 UNOFFICIAL

WEIRDEST MOVIE MERCHANDISE

	MOVIE	MERCHANDISE
1	Stars Wars Episode I: The Phantom Menace	French fast-food Dark Vador burger
2	The Hunger Games	Nail polishes relating to Panem's districts
3	Star Trek V: The Final Frontier	Marshmallow dispenser
4	The Twilight Saga: New Moon	Milk chocolate bar
5	The Avengers	Tony Stark's MK VII replica power band
6	Moonraker	Villain Jaws' metal teeth cast
7	Avatar	Na'Vi make-up kit
8	Thor	Dumbbell-shaped alarm clock
9	Transformers	Kids' Prime toy shaving kit
10	Robin Hood: Prince Of Thieves	Arrow-shaped breakfast cereal

CHECK IT OUT!

Yes, this really happened! In 2012, a Dark Vador burger had dyed black, burnt-looking buns to celebrate the release of the 3D version of *Star Wars Episode I: The Phantom Menace*.

BEFORE THE BIG SCREEN

Inspiration for movies can come from the most unexpected places... Often, it's a screenwriter's brilliant imagination, but sometimes toys, comics and novels are the spark!

FACT FLASH!
YEARS IN PRODUCTION
49

TOP 10

BIGGEST TOYS BEFORE THE MOVIE

Here are the most successful toy lines that ended up inspiring movie versions of their franchises...

GI JOE
XTREME FACT

GI Joe's popularity is still sky-high today, especially for character Snake Eyes. There's even a collectors' club for both vintage and current toy lines (gijoe.com).

HEAD TO HEAD

IN THE BLUE CORNER...		IN THE RED CORNER...
SNAKE EYES (GI JOE)		CAPTAIN AMERICA
✓ 10	CLASSIFIED STATUS	08 ✗
✓ 10	MARTIAL ARTS SKILLS	02 ✗
✗ 07	PHYSICAL STRENGTH	10 ✓
✗ 07	LEGENDARY STATUS	10 ✓
✗ 05	TEAMWORK	08 ✓

2

AND THE WINNER IS... CAPTAIN AMERICA! **3**

	TOY	PRODUCED BY	TOTAL MOVIES	YEARS TOYS IN PRODUCTION
1	Clue/Cluedo	Waddington/Parker Bros	1	64 (From 1949)
2	GI Joe	Hasbro	2	49 (From 1964)
3	Battleship	Hasbro	1	46 (From 1967)
4	He-Man & The Masters Of The Universe	Mattel	1	31 (From 1982)
5	Care Bears	Kenner	1	30 (From 1983)
=	My Little Pony	Hasbro	1	30 (From 1983)
7	Transformers	Hasbro	4	29 (From 1984)
8	She-Ra: Princess Of Power	Mattel	1	28 (From 1985)
9	American Girl	Mattel	1	27 (From 1986)
10	Bratz	MGA Entertainment	1	12 (From 2001)

YOU RATE!
1 to 100

GI JOE
ACTION SAILOR
by HASBRO

GI JOE
ACTION MARINE
by HASBRO

LONGEST-RUNNING COMIC BOOKS WITH MOVIES

Comic book-based movies have never been more popular, but how about the comics themselves that inspired them? Here are their legacies...

	COMIC CHARACTER(S)	CREATOR(S)	TOTAL MOVIE(S)	FIRST PUBLISHED/YEARS
1	**Batman**	Bob Kane	8	May 1939 (74 years)
2	Superman	Jerry Siegel, Joe Shuster	6	Jun 1939 (74 years)
3	Catwoman	Bob Kane, Bill Finger	3	Mar 1940 (73 years)
4	Captain America	Joe Simon, Jack Kirby	3	Mar 1941 (72 years)
5	Fantastic Four	Stan Lee, Jack Kirby	2	Nov 1961 (52 years)
6	Spider-Man	Stan Lee, Steve Ditko	4	Aug 1962 (51 years)
=	Thor*	Stan Lee, Jack Kirby	3	Aug 1962 (51 years)
8	The Hulk	Stan Lee, Jack Kirby	1	May 1962 (51 years)
9	Iron Man	Stan Lee	4	Mar 1963 (50 years)
10	X-Men	Stan Lee, Jack Kirby	6	Sep 1963 (50 years)

*Developed from Norse mythology

OFF THE CHART

THE AVENGERS

Sharing the 10th position, above, is *The Avengers*, also created by Stan Lee and artist Jack Kirby in September 1963!

THE ORIGIN OF CAPTAIN AMERICA!

FACT FLASH!

YEARS IN PRINT

72

CHECK IT OUT!

One of the longest-running comic characters of all time, comic books starring Steve "Captain America" Rogers have exceeded 210 million! For fans of Cap and Black Widow's scenes in *The Avengers*' movie, you'll be pleased to hear that you can get your hands on a comic collection (released in 2012) called *Captain America & Black Widow* (collecting issues #636 to #640)!

BEFORE THE BIG SCREEN

TOP 10 BIGGEST NOVELS WITH MOVIES

Countless novels have been made into hit movies, but these 10 are the most successful tales in book form before their adaptations occurred...

	NOVEL	AUTHOR	YEAR PUBLISHED	BOOK SALES	MOVIE ADAPTATIONS
1	A Tale Of Two Cities	Charles Dickens	1859	200,000,000	7
=	The Little Prince	Antoine de Saint-Exupéry	1943	200,000,000	5
3	The Lord Of The Rings (three volumes)	JRR Tolkien	1954-55	150,000,000	2
4	The Hobbit	JRR Tolkien	1937	100,000,000	2
=	And Then There Were None	Agatha Christie	1939	100,000,000	6
6	The Lion, The Witch And The Wardrobe	CS Lewis	1950	85,000,000	1
7	She	H Rider Haggard	1887	83,000,000	12
8	The Da Vinci Code	Dan Brown	2003	80,000,000	1
9	Anne Of Green Gables	Lucy Maud Montgomery	1908	50,000,000	2
=	Black Beauty	Anna Sewell	1877	50,000,000	5

YOU RATE! 1 to 100

THE LORD OF THE RINGS

XTREME FACT

The Lord Of The Rings is one novel divided into six books, two for each volume (*The Fellowship Of The Ring*, *The Two Towers* and *The Return Of The King*), much like the extended DVD sets have two discs per film!

TOP 10 BIGGEST ANIMATED TV SHOWS WITH MOVIES

Which are the most successful animated TV shows that have gone on to have hit movies based on them? Here they are!

	FIRST MOVIE VERSION	TOTAL MOVIES	BASED ON THE TV SHOW	YEARS ON-AIR (+ SPIN-OFFS)
1	Doraemon: Nobita's Dinosaur (1980)	33	Doraemon	35
2	The Transformers: The Movie (1986)	4	The Transformers	29
3	The Simpsons Movie (2007)	1	The Simpsons	24
4	Crayon Shin-chan (1993)	20	Crayon Shin-chan	21
5	Scooby-Doo (2002)	2	Scooby-Doo	20
6	The Rugrats Movie (1998)	3	The Rugrats	19
7	Garfield The Movie (2004)	2	Garfield	18
8	Tom And Jerry: The Movie (1992)	1	Tom And Jerry	18
9	Pokémon: The First Movie (1998)	2	Pokémon	16
10	The SpongeBob SquarePants Movie (2004)	1	SpongeBob SquarePants	14

YOU RATE! 1 to 100

DORAEMON

XTREME FACT

The time-travelling robo-cat's first movie was released in 1980, and the anime TV series has over 2,000 episodes to date.

CHECK IT OUT!

They say comedy perfection takes time, and *The Simpsons Movie* took over six years to complete! But will there be another movie? Maybe, considering the TV show *The Simpsons* is still going, clocking over 520 episodes!

TOP 10

BIGGEST LIVE-ACTION TV SHOWS WITH MOVIES

So many TV shows have been turned into movies, but these are the ones that clocked up the most airtime and inspired their own movies...

	FIRST MOVIE VERSION	TOTAL MOVIES	BASED ON THE TV SHOW	YEARS ON-AIR (+ SPIN-OFFS)
1	Dr. Who And The Daleks (1965)	2	Doctor Who	34
2	Star Trek: The Motion Picture (1979)	12	Star Trek	27
3	Mighty Morphin Power Rangers: The Movie (1995)	1	Mighty Morphin Power Rangers	20
4	Barney's Great Adventure (1998)	1	Barney & Friends	17
5	The Muppet Movie (1979)	9	The Muppet Show	14
6	Are You Being Served? (1977)	1	Are You Being Served?	13
7	Dragnet (1954)	2	Dragnet	13
8	The Mark Of Zorro (1920)	46	Zorro	9
9	Good Burger (1997)	1	All That	9
10	The Beverly Hillbillies (1993)	1	The Beverly Hillbillies	9

YOU RATE! 1 to 100

OFF THE CHART

THE A-TEAM

Have you seen the 2010 movie *The A-Team*? And, did you know it was based on a TV series that ran for four years, between 1983-87 (98 episodes), and regularly commanded over 20 million viewers? It revolved around a team of commandos who escaped from a maximum security stockade, as they were found guilty of a crime they didn't commit. Of all the characters in the series, BA Baracus (played by Mr. T, right), was a household fave.

FACT FLASH! YEARS ON TV 4

STAR TREK

XTREME FACT

Star Trek's legacy is astounding: no less than seven hit TV shows since 1966 (including an animated series) and 12 movies. Box office releases include 2013's *Star Trek Into Darkness*, featuring actor Benedict Cumberbatch, the star of smash hit TV show *Sherlock*.

BEFORE THE BIG SCREEN

MOVIES BASED ON HISTORIC EVENTS/ PEOPLE'S LIVES

However much we love them, the movie world isn't only about big robots and aliens. It's often inspired by real lives and incidents, too...

	MOVIE	YEAR OF RELEASE	BASED ON THE LIFE OF/EVENT	BOX OFFICE ($ WORLDWIDE)
1	Titanic	1997	Sinking of the RMS Titanic	2,185,372,302
2	Pearl Harbor	2001	1941 attack on Pearl Harbor	449,220,945
3	The King's Speech	2010	King George VI	414,211,549
4	Pocahontas	1995	Native princess Pocahontas	346,079,773
5	Catch Me If You Can	2002	Con man Frank Abagnale Jr	352,114,312
6	Apollo 13	1995	Apollo 13's real space mission	355,237,933
7	A Beautiful Mind	2001	Prodigy John Nash	313,542,341
8	The Blind Side	2009	NFL star Michael Oher	309,208,309
9	Marley & Me	2008	Marley the Labrador	242,717,113
10	Yes Man	2008	Writer Danny Wallace	223,241,637

Source: IMDB.com

YOU RATE!
1 to 100

GIVE IT A TRY...
YOUR STORY

Love movies? Why not write your own script?! Creative writing is a hugely rewarding process as you're in complete control of the characters, the story and everything. Go for it!

YES MAN

XTREME FACT

The central character may be called Carl, and he may be played by Jim Carrey, but did you know that *Yes Man* (2008) is based on the real-life experiences of British writer/ presenter/comedian Danny Wallace? He has a cameo in the movie, too. His book of the same name documented six months of him saying "yes" to any question!

FACT FLASH!
BOX OFFICE
2.18 BILLION DOLLARS

CHECK IT OUT!

Although the massively successful epic *Titanic* featured some characters that were written/created especially for the story (such as the central characters, played by Leonardo DiCaprio and Kate Winslet), many crew members were based on real passengers. Of course, the tragic incident really happened, causing 1,514 to lose their lives.

YOU RATE!
1 to 100

BIGGEST POP MUSIC DOCUMENTARIES

Over the past decade, documentaries on music stars have become more frequent than ever! Here are the 10 most successful pop-docs to date...

	MUSIC DOCUMENTARY	RELEASE DATE	BOX OFFICE ($ MILLION WORLDWIDE)
1	Michael Jackson's This Is It	Oct 28, 2009	261,183,588
2	Justin Bieber: Never Say Never	Feb 11, 2011	98,441,954
3	Hannah Montana & Miley Cyrus: Best Of Both Worlds Concert	Feb 1, 2008	70,642,036
4	Katy Perry: Part Of Me	Jul 5, 2012	32,439,363
5	Jonas Brothers: The 3D Concert Experience	Feb 27, 2009	23,186,960
6	Buena Vista Social Club	Jun 4, 1999	23,002,182
7	U2 3D	Jan 23, 2008	22,730,842
8	Glee: The 3D Concert Movie	Aug 12, 2011	18,663,238
9	Shine A Light	Apr 4, 2008	15,773,351
10	Mad Hot Ballroom	May 13, 2005	9,079,042

Source: IMDB.com

KATY PERRY

XTREME FACT

When Katy Perry's pop documentary came out in 3D in July 2012, the accompanying 3D glasses were Perry-fied, in red and white candy-cane colours!

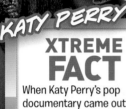

OUR **TOP 10** UNOFFICIAL

COOLEST LOCATIONS MOVIES HAVE BEEN FILMED

	MOVIE	LOCATION
1	Waterworld	Entirely on a floating set on the open ocean near Hawaii
2	Star Wars	Tunisian deserts were used for many of the alien planets
3	Apollo 13	Zero-G sequences were filmed in a plane going into a nosedive
4	Batman Begins	Gotham City is entirely a set, with CGI used for some external shots
5	The Avengers	NASA building doubled as SHIELD headquarters
6	The Lord Of The Rings	Middle-Earth exists... It's all on location in New Zealand
7	Jurassic Park	Hawaii's main island of Oahu was used to bring dinos back
8	Monsters	Mexico became the migration realm for the aliens
9	Harry Potter	London's King's Cross itself was used for the magical Platform 9¾
10	The Hunger Games	North Carolina, USA mountains doubled as the arena

CHECK IT OUT!

The Lord Of The Rings movies may have thousands of amazing special effects, but the location of New Zealand adds the most epic feel to the saga! Due to the popularity of the movies, avid fans can even experience tours that travel around several of the famous locations featured on screen.

THE MAKING OF

It's time to get under the skin of the movie-making process with lists and facts galore!

OUR TOP 10 UNOFFICIAL

MOST COMPLEX MAKE-UP

	CHARACTER	DESCRIPTION	PORTRAYED BY	MOVIE(S)
1	**Mystique**	**Blue make-up and prosthetics (full-body)**	**Rebecca Romijn**	**X-Men movies**
2	Abe Sapien	Fish-like head and limbs prosthetics	Doug Jones	Hellboy movies
3	Darkness	Full-body demon-like effects	Tim Curry	Legend
4	John Merrick	Disfigurement make-up/prosthetics	John Hurt	The Elephant Man
5	Mrs. Doubtfire	Head-to-toe old lady effects	Robin Williams	Mrs. Doubtfire
6	Dr. Evil	Bald cap, ageing and scars	Mike Myers	Austin Powers 2
7	The Monster	Undead effects/stitched body parts	Boris Karloff	Frankenstein movies
8	Lord Voldemort	Demon-like face/head reshaping	Ralph Fiennes	Harry Potter movies
9	Mad Hatter	Bleached skin and crazy hair	Johnny Depp	Alice In Wonderland
10	Sloth	Full-body deformed make-up	John Matuszak	The Goonies

THE MONSTER
XTREME FACT

Boris Karloff is the actor who made this character a famous monster in 1931. Don't forget, Frankenstein is the name of the scientist, NOT the monster he creates...

OUR TOP 10 UNOFFICIAL

ICONIC COSTUMES

	CHARACTER(S)	DESCRIPTION	MOVIE(S)
1	**Chewbacca**	**Hairy, furry giant**	**Star Wars saga**
2	Iron Man	Robotic-looking armour	Iron Man & Avengers movies
3	Marilyn Monroe's dresses	Iconic pink and white stylings	Gentlemen Prefer Blondes
4	Indiana Jones	The hat, whip and cream shirt	Indiana Jones saga
5	Dana Scully	Red hair and sharp suits	The X-Files movies
6	The Ghostbusters	Boiler suits and proton packs	Ghostbusters
7	Princess Leia	Swirly "bun" hairstyle and white gown	Star Wars
8	Edward Scissorhands	Hand-stitched clothing and scissors for hands	Edward Scissorhands
9	Aeon Flux	Asymmetric haircut and assassin clothing	Aeon Flux
10	Ringwraith (Nazgûl)	Hooded demonic horse riders	The Lord Of The Rings saga

CHECK IT OUT!
The cream jumpsuits, bold logos and proton packs (for the trio's all-important ghost-wrangling and entrapment) have become so iconic that fans of all ages still dress up as the Ghostbusters at conventions!

BIGGEST MOVIE BUDGETS

Those eye-popping adventures we all love so much cost a LOT of money to create... And these 10 are the biggest wallet-busters of them all!

YOU RATE!

1 to 100

	NAME	YEAR OF RELEASE	BUDGET ($ MILLION)
1	Pirates Of The Caribbean: At World's End	2007	300
2	Tangled	2010	260
3	Spider-Man 3	2007	258
4	John Carter	2012	250
5	Harry Potter And The Half-Blood Prince	2009	250
6	Avatar	2009	237
7	The Dark Knight Rises	2012	230
8	The Chronicles Of Narnia: Prince Caspian	2008	225
9	Pirates Of The Caribbean: Dead Man's Chest	2006	225
10	The Avengers	2012	220

FACT FLASH!
BUDGET
250 MILLION DOLLARS

CHECK IT OUT!

John Carter is a special-effects extravaganza with some mind-blowing technology behind its digital Martian monsters. However, the story isn't a modern creation at all... Creator Edgar Rice Burroughs had his first John Carter adventure published in a magazine over 100 years ago, in 1912!

THE DARK KNIGHT RISES

XTREME FACT

Actor Tom Hardy put on 30 lb (13.6 kg) in muscle to give Bane that uncompromising, brutal quality. This makes sense when you consider the movie's director Christopher Nolan said *The Dark Knight Rises*' theme was "pain"!

TOP 10

MOST EXPENSIVE MOVIES WITH SPECIAL EFFECTS

Of these, the most expensive effects-heavy movies made in the last seven years, three are from 2012! It goes to show how visual trickery is becoming bigger and better all the time...

YOU RATE!
1 to 100

	MOVIE	YEAR OF RELEASE	BUDGET ($ MILLION)
1	Pirates Of The Caribbean: At World's End	2007	300
2	Tangled	2010	260
3	Spider-Man 3	2007	258
4	John Carter	2012	250
=	Harry Potter And The Half-Blood Prince	2009	250
6	Avatar	2009	237
7	The Amazing Spider-Man	2012	230
=	The Dark Knight Rises	2012	230
9	The Chronicles Of Narnia: Prince Caspian	2008	225
10	Pirates Of The Caribbean: Dead Man's Chest	2006	225

CHECK IT OUT!

Although actor Bill Nighy performed the role of Davy Jones in two of the *Pirates Of The Caribbean* movies, his tentacular face ended up being replaced by an entirely digitally animated creation. Those special effects computer geniuses even wrote computer code to make each slimy tentacle move automatically!

THE AMAZING SPIDER-MAN

XTREME FACT

2012 was a significant year for Spidey... Not only did it see a brand new actor (Andrew Garfield) take on the role for a new series of the movies, it also marked the 50th anniversary of Spider-Man's creation.

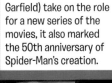

FACT FLASH!
BUDGET
225 MILLION DOLLARS

STAT ATTACK

PIRATES OF THE CARIBBEAN: AT WORLD'S END

Director.................................. Gore Verbinski
Writers .... Ted Elliot, Terry Rossio
Music by .... Hans Zimmer
Running time......................................169 min
US opening weekend..............$139,802,190

INSANE MOVIE EXPLOSIONS!

	MOVIE	YEAR OF RELEASE	EXPLOSION
1	**The Dark Knight**	2008	Gotham Hospital explosion
2	The Avengers	2012	Nuclear warhead into Chitauri
3	The Lord Of The Rings: The Two Towers	2002	Minas Tirith attack
4	Independence Day	1996	White House destruction
5	Godzilla	1998	Madison Square Garden blowing up
6	Iron Man 2	2010	Iron Man & War Machine's park attack
7	Star Wars Episode IV: A New Hope	1977	Destruction of the Death Star
8	Jaws	1975	Shark killed by air tank exploding
9	X-Men Origins: Wolverine	2009	Power plant destruction by Deadpool
10	Ghostbusters	1984	Closing the Zuul door explosion

TOP 10 BIGGEST MOVIE STUDIOS

Of all the movie studios out there, these are the most powerful 10 around right now...

YOU RATE! 1 to 100

	STUDIO	OWNED BY	OWNER'S REVENUE ($ BILLIONS)
1	**Universal Pictures**	**Comcast/General Electric**	203.142
2	Columbia Pictures	Sony Pictures	80.303
3	Walt Disney Pictures	The Walt Disney Company	40.893
4	20th Century Fox	News Corporation	33.706
5	Warner Bros. Pictures	Time Warner	28.974
6	Relativity	Relativity Media	17
7	DreamWorks Studios	Reliance Group	15.4
8	Paramount Pictures	Viacom	14.914
9	MGM	MGM Holdings	2.4-3
10	Lionsgate	Lionsgate Entertainment	1.584

LIONSGATE

XTREME FACT

Lionsgate are the production company behind one of the hottest properties right now, *The Hunger Games*. The sequel *The Hunger Games: Catching Fire* (out November 22, 2013) continues the saga, adapting the second book of the trilogy. How hot is this series? It has outsold the *Harry Potter* novels in four years since the 2008 release of the first novel...

STAR TALENT

You can't have movies without movie stars! It's time to take a look at the acting heavyweights who have a big influence on big screen success...

TOP 10 MOST BANKABLE MOVIE STARS

Based on all their lead roles in movies to date, these stars really do bring home the bacon... Gold-plated mountains of bacon!

	ACTOR	NO. MOVIES IN TOP 100	BOX OFFICE TOTAL U.S. ($)
1	Daniel Radcliffe	8	7,706,147,978
2	Johnny Depp	5	4,752,035,871
3	Robert Downey Jr.	5	3,788,742,560
4	Will Smith	5	3,240,553,962
5	Shia LaBeouf	4	3,456,396,502
6	Kristen Stewart	4	2,949,715,402
=	Robert Pattinson	4	2,949,715,402
8	Tobey Maguire	3	2,496,346,518
9	Daniel Craig	3	2,293,420,503
10	Harrison Ford	3	2,100,409,107

YOU RATE! 1 to 100

OFF THE CHART

TOM CRUISE

He's one of the most famous (and richest) movie stars in the world, and Tom Cruise is no slacker, with over 40 movies under his belt! Tom is also known for doing as much of his own daredevil stunt work as possible. What a trooper!

KRISTEN STEWART

FACT FLASH! BOX OFFICE TOTAL FOR LEADING ROLES **2.94** BILLION DOLLARS

XTREME FACT

In total, Ms. Stewart has been nominated for an eye-popping 53 awards... and went on to win 28 of them! Unfortunately for Kristen two of these wins have been infamous Golden Raspberry Awards, which included Worst Actress for *Snow White And The Huntsman* and *The Twilight Saga: Breaking Dawn: Part 2*.

COMPARE-O-METER

Here are some other mega-earners!

JUSTIN BIEBER'S
EARNINGS (2011-12)

$15,944,293

MADONNA'S
EARNINGS (2011-12)

$34,577,308

BEST ACTOR/ACTRESS ACADEMY AWARD WINNERS

It's very rare for an actor or actress to win more than one Academy Award, and grab a gold Oscar® statuette, but here are the lucky bunch who have...

YOU RATE!
1 to 100

	NAME	YEARS WON	TOTAL AWARDS
1	Katharine Hepburn	1934, 1968, 1969, 1982 (Best Actress)	4
2	Ingrid Bergman	1945, 1957 (Best Actress); 1975 (Best Supporting Actress)	3
=	Meryl Streep	1982, 2012 (Best Actress); 1979 (Best Supporting Actress)	3
=	Jack Nicholson	1975, 1997 (Best Actor); 1983 (Best Supporting Actor)	3
=	Walter Brennan	1936, 1938, 1940 (Best Supporting Actor)	3
6	Spencer Tracy	1937, 1938 (Best Actor)	2
=	Luise Rainer	1936, 1937 (Best Actress)	2
=	Tom Hanks	1993, 1994 (Best Actor)	2
=	Jane Fonda	1971, 1978 (Best Actress)	2
=	Daniel Day-Lewis	1989, 2007 (Best Actor)	2

OFF THE CHART

TWO OSCARS®

Other winners of two Academy Awards for Actor/Actress in a Leading Role are: Fredric March (1932, 1946); Bette Davis (1935, 1938); Vivien Leigh (1939, 1951); Gary Cooper (1941, 1952); Olivia de Havilland (1946, 1949); Marlon Brando (1954, 1972); Elizabeth Taylor (1961, 1967); Glenda Jackson (1969, 1973); Dustin Hoffman (1979, 1988); Sally Field (1979, 1984); Jodie Foster (1989, 1991); Hilary Swank (1999, 2004 for *Million Dollar Baby*, below); Sean Penn (2003, 2008).

ANOTHER THING!

Million Dollar Baby director Clint Eastwood is a big hitter, too... He has won four Academy Awards: two for Directing and two for Best Motion Picture!

JACK NICHOLSON

XTREME FACT

You'll know him best for playing The Joker in the earlier 1989 *Batman* movie, and here's the man behind that famous smile, Jack Nicholson, with the Academy Award he won in 1998 for Best Actor.

TOP 10

MOST RECURRING ROLES

When a movie character is successful, often the same actor is invited back to play that part many, many times...

ANOTHER THING! Total ticket sales for all eight *Harry Potter* movies? A magical total worldwide box office of $7,706,147,978 billion!

YOU RATE! 1 to 100

	ACTOR/ACTRESS	ROLE	NUMBER OF MOVIES FEATURING "ROLE"
1	Mickey Rooney	Andy Hardy	16
2	Basil Rathbone	Sherlock Holmes	14
3	Daniel Radcliffe	Harry Potter	8
=	Emma Watson	Hermione Granger	8
=	Rupert Grint	Ron Weasely	8
6	Leonard Nimoy	Dr Spock	7
=	Sean Connery	James Bond	7
=	Roger Moore	James Bond	7
9	Hugh Jackman	Logan/Wolverine	6
=	Ian McKellen	Gandalf	6

CHECK IT OUT!

After spending eight movies in each other's company for *Harry Potter*, it's time for Emma Watson, Daniel Radcliffe and Rupert Grint to embark on their individual movie careers. Rupert's set to play British skier Eddie "The Eagle" Edwards in a movie about his life and Emma's got many projects on the go, including an epic about Noah's Ark. Meanwhile, Daniel's got some very unusual movies coming up, including one about him sprouting horns!

HUGH JACKMAN

XTREME FACT

Going way beyond the action and stunts of his Wolverine performances, Hugh Jackman amazing singing abilities were centre stage in the musical *Les Misérables* (2012). Hugh's also had a hit Broadway show, too!

TOP TALLEST ACTORS OF ALL TIME

They may not all have appeared in a mainstream motion picture, but these 10 are the true towering titans of the movie world...

	NAME	COUNTRY	BEST KNOWN FOR...	HEIGHT (M)	(FT)
1	Al Tomaini	USA	Freaks Unlimited!	2.54	8.33
2	Alexander Sizonenko	Ukraine	Sedem Jednou Ranou	2.48	8.14
3	Mingming Sun	China	Rush Hour 3	2.36	7.74
4	Johann Petursson	Iceland	Being Different	2.34	7.68
5	Neil Fingleton	UK	X-Men: First Class	2.33	7.64
6	Jack Earle	USA	Jack And The Beanstalk	2.33	7.64
7	Lock Martin	USA	The Day The Earth Stood Still	2.32	7.61
8	Gheorghe Muresan	Romania	My Giant	2.32	7.61
9	Chris Greener	UK	The Rainbow Thief	2.30	7.55
10	Matthew McGrory	USA	Big Fish	2.29	7.51

PETER MAYHEW

OFF THE CHART

British actor Peter Mayhew, who plays Chewbacca in the *Star Wars* films, just misses out on a place in the Top 10, with a goliath height of 7.25 ft (2.21 m)!

OUR TOP 10 UNOFFICIAL

UNRECOGNIZABLE STARS

Sometimes the star of the big screen goes through such amazing make-up and wardrobe changes that we can barely tell who they really are!

	NAME	ROLE	MOVIE(S)	YEAR
1	Heath Ledger	The Joker	The Dark Knight	2008
2	Ron Perlman	Hellboy	Hellboy, Hellboy II: The Golden Army	2004 & '08
3	Lon Chaney	The Phantom	The Phantom Of The Opera	1925
4	Max Schrek	Count Graf Orlok	Nosferatu	1922
5	John Rhys-Davies	Gimli	The Lord Of The Rings saga	2001-03
6	Jason Flemyng	Dr. Jekyll & Mr. Hyde	The League Of Extraordinary Gentlemen	2003
7	Ralph Fiennes	Lord Voldemort	Harry Potter saga	2001-11
8	Bill Nighy	Davy Jones	Pirates Of The Caribbean movies	2006 & '10
9	Zoe Saldana	Neytiri	Avatar	2009
10	Johnny Depp	The Mad Hatter	Alice In Wonderland	2010

MOVIE SHOWTIME
YOUR SHOUT!

Check out these questions. Can you answer them without looking back through the book?

What a movie marathon! But the big screen fun isn't over yet... Now, it's over to you for an interactive cinematic section that YOU control!

YOU RATE! TOP 10

T-10 MOVIE STUFF

It's time to add up all of your top ones that you rated the highest, to compile your own list here. Compare with your friends' T-10 ratings, too!

	NAME	"YOU RATE" SCORE
1	....	....
2	....	....
3	....	....
4	....	....
5	....	....
6	....	....
7	....	....
8	....	....
9	....	....
10	....	....

BLOCKBUSTERS

TRUE OR FALSE...

1. *The Avengers* is not on the Top 10 Biggest Movies of All Time list   T   F

2. There have been over 40 Sherlock Holmes movies made   T   F

3. Two of the *Ice Age* movies are in the Top 10 Animated Movies list   T   F

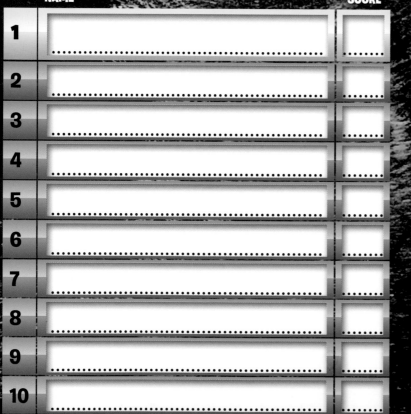

Can you name this character from the eighth biggest superhero movie of all time?

NAME:
....

BEFORE THE BIG SCREEN

Have a try at ranking these toys from 1 to 5 in order of their success before they were made into movies...

- [....] **GI JOE**
- [....] **SHE-RA**
- [....] **TRANSFORMERS**
- [....] **BATTLESHIP**
- [....] **HE-MAN**

Can you name the longest running comic book that inspired movies?

BONUS POINT!

MOVIES HAVE BEEN MADE OF THIS COMIC

....

Clue: This franchise has seen the hero battle The League of Shadows. What a joker!

THE MAKING OF...

See if you can work out who the actors are behind the mad make-up below and which movie they are starring in...

A

NAME:
....

MOVIE:
....

B

NAME:
....

MOVIE:
....

STAR TALENT

WHO'S THAT STAR?

The legendary actor, pictured on the right, has played one of the most famous recurring roles in the history of cinema. See how many clues you need before you work out who it is...

1. This British star is 83 years of age but first played his most famous role when he was 32

2. Daniel Craig now plays the role that he made famous

3. He played this role in seven movies, the same amount of times as Roger Moore

NAME:
....

ANSWERS ON PAGE 313

253

ONLY HUMAN

What separates us from the other animals of this planet? For one, opposable thumbs means we can operate devices pretty well. We're quite smart, too, but mainly it's our ideas. Through the development of unusual ideas and problem-solving, humans have gone on to achieve extraordinary things. Many of these are to be admired, but some, sadly, are frightening acts that we struggle to understand...

DARE TO GO...

The explorers who venture where others fear to go help us learn about the world around us. Here are some of the most significant events to date...

TOP 10 FASTEST AROUND THE WORLD BY SAILBOAT (EASTBOUND)

Any keen sailors out there? As Team T-10 are fascinated by the ocean, finding out who the fastest skippers are has made us want to head to the coast for, at the very least, an ice cream!

	NAME(S)	COUNTRY	YACHT	DATE	TIME
1	**Loïck Peyron**	**France**	**Banque Populaire V**	**Jan 2012**	**45d, 13h, 42m, 53s**
2	Franck Cammas	France	Groupama 3	Mar 2010	48d, 7h, 44m, 52s
3	Bruno Peyron	France	Orange II	Mar 2005	50d, 16h, 20m, 4s
4	Francis Joyon	France	IDEC	Jan 2008	57d, 13h, 34m, 6s
5	Steve Fossett	USA	Cheyenne	Apr 2004	58d, 9h, 32m, 45s
6	Bruno Peyron	France	Orange	May 2002	64d, 8h, 37m,24s
7	Olivier de Kersauson	France	Sport-Elec	Mar 1997	71d, 14h, 18m, 8s
8	Peter Blake, Robin Knox-Johnston	NZL, GB	Enza	Jan 1994	74d, 22h, 17m, 22s
9	Bruno Peyron	France	Commodore Explorer	Jan 1993	79d, 6h, 15m, 56s
10	Michel Desjoyeaux	France	Foncia	Jan 2009	84d, 3h, 9m

YOU RATE!
1 to 100

LOÏCK PEYRON

XTREME FACT

Successful sailing runs in the Peyron family: Loïck's younger brother Bruno is a yachtsman, too! Loïck was born on December 1, 1959, and has had a hugely triumphant career. Since 1979 he has won more than 60 awards, including the Jules Verne Trophy in 2012 for his around the world achievement.

OFF THE CHART

DEE CAFFARI

Eastbound is the easier of the two directions to travel around the world. Not many have ever attempted the Westbound route but, in May 2006, British sailor Dee Caffari did and became the first woman to travel around the world westerly, in 178 days... And she achieved it ALONE!

CHECK IT OUT!

Loïck Peyron's around the world success was achieved in the vessel called Banque Populaire V, which is a trimaran. This kind of boat has three hulls (hence the "tri" in the name). The biggest is the central one, with two smaller on either side. This style of boat actually dates back a long way, 4,000 years ago, to be precise! Native Pacific Islanders developed the technology way back then, and it has hardly changed since. However, at 130 ft (40 m) in length, Banque Populaire V is the world's biggest trimaran.

FACT FLASH!
AROUND THE
WORLD IN UNDER
46
DAYS

GIVE IT A TRY...
OUTDOOR PURSUITS

Do you know where your nearest activity centre is? Many organise outdoor training in water sports, like sailing and canoeing! Get your family and friends to plan a trip to seek out more information on how you can try out some new sports!

MARCO POLO

XTREME FACT

When it comes to championing the act of travelling and seeking out new places and cultures, Venetian Marco Polo (born September 15, 1254, and died January 9, 1324) was a bit of a legend! His extensive experiences in Asia became a vital source of knowledge to the Western world.

OUR TOP 10 UNOFFICIAL

MOST PROLIFIC PRE-20TH CENTURY EXPLORERS

	EXPLORER	COUNTRY	EXPLORED/FAMOUS FOR	CENTURY
1	Xu Fu	China	Eastern oceans	3rd BC
2	St. Brendan of Clonfert	Ireland	Iceland, America	6th BC
3	Freya Stark	France	Arabia	19th
4	Marco Polo	Italy	Asia, Persia, China, Indonesia	13th
5	Alexander von Humboldt	Germany	Biogeography research	18th
6	Isabella Bird	UK	Far East, Central Asia, USA	19th
7	Abel Tasman	Netherlands	Discovered New Zealand, Tasmania	17th
8	Vasco Núñez de Balboa	Spain	Pacific Ocean	16th
9	Matthew Flinders	Australia	First to circumnavigate Australia	19th
10	Vasco de Gama	Portugal	First to sail Europe to India	15th

BANQUE

DARE TO GO...

TOP 10 DEEPEST SOLO SEA DIVES

Ultra-deep scuba diving is incredibly dangerous, and only experts at the absolute top of their game have ever attempted going to depths below 650 ft...

	NAME	COUNTRY	LOCATION	DEPTH (M)	(FT)	YEAR
1	Pascal Bernabé	France	Mediterranean	330	1,083	2005
2	Nuno Gomes	South Africa	Red Sea	318	1,044	2005
3	Mark Ellyatt	UK	Andaman Sea	313	1,026	2003
4	John Bennett	UK	Philippines	310	1,010	2001
5	Krzysztof Starnawski	Poland	Red Sea	283	928	2011
6	Jim Bowden	USA	Mexico	282	925	1994
7	Gilberto M de Oliveira	Brazil	Brazil	274	898	2002
8	David Shaw	Australia	South Africa	271	888	2004
9	Sheck Exley	USA	Mexico	264	867	1989
10	Don Shirley	UK	South Africa	250	820	2005

YOU RATE! 1 to 100

ANOTHER THING!
Freediving is another way to explore the ocean. It involves using no breathing apparatus and experts just hold their breath. Depths of 328 ft (100 m) have been reached!

TOP 10 FIRST EXPEDITIONS TO CLIMB EVEREST

Mount Everest is the tallest mountain on Earth at 29,029 ft (8,848 m) high, and it's the summit which all climbers aim to conquer. Here are the first 10 expeditions to reach its giddy peak...

YOU RATE! 1 to 100

SIR EDMUND HILLARY

XTREME FACT
New Zealander Sir Edmund Hillary didn't put his feet up after conquering Everest in 1953, he went on to climb 10 more mountains in the Himalayas between 1956 and 1965! Plus, he reached the South Pole overland in 1958!

	NAME	COUNTRY	DATE
1	Sir Edmund Hillary & Tenzing Norgay	New Zealand & Nepal	May 29, 1953
2	Ernst Reiss & Fritz Luchsinger	Switzerland	May 18, 1956
3	Ernst Schmied & Juerg Marmet	Switzerland	May 23, 1956
4	Jim Whittaker & Nawang Gombu	USA & Tibet	May 1, 1963
5	Nawang Gombu & Lieutenant Commander M S Kohli	Tibet & India	May 20, 1965
6	Junko Tabei	Japan	May 16, 1975
7	Phantog	Tibet	May 27, 1975
8	Reinhold Messner & Peter Habeler	Italy & Austria	May 8, 1978
9	Wanda Rutkiewicz	Poland	Oct 16, 1978
10	Leszek Cichy & Krzysztof Wielicki	Poland	Feb 17, 1980

NEIL ARMSTRONG

XTREME FACT

This legend sadly passed away on August 25, 2012, aged 82. Neil's immortal words as he stepped onto the moon, "That's one small step for [a] man, one giant leap for mankind," were listened to by 450 million people around the world. After returning from the Apollo 11 mission, Armstrong decided not to venture into space again, but he'd more than served his planet.

FACT FLASH! 1ST MAN ON THE MOON

STAT ATTACK

NEIL ARMSTRONG

Born .... Aug 5, 1930
Died .... Aug 25, 2012
Space missions ..... Gemini 8 (Mar 16-17, 1966); Apollo 11 (Jul 16-24, 1969)
Awards .... Congressional Space Medal of Honor, Presidential Medal of Freedom
Skills............Aeronautical engineer, astronaut, naval aviator, test pilot, university professor

OUR TOP 10 UNOFFICIAL

MOST PROLIFIC MODERN EXPLORERS

	EXPLORER	COUNTRY	ACHIEVEMENT	DATE
1	Neil Armstrong	USA	First man on the Moon	Jul 20, 1969
2	Valentina Tereshkova	Russia	First woman in space	Jun 16, 1963
3	Ed Stafford	UK	Walked entire length of Amazon	Apr 2, 2008 - Aug 9, 2010
4	Jacques Cousteau	France	Developed scuba diving	1943
5	Peter Bray	UK	Crossed the Atlantic in a kayak	Jun 23, 2001 - Sep 5, 2001
6	Robert Ballard	USA	Discovered Titanic's shipwreck	Summer 1985
7	Yuri Gagarin	Russia	First man in space and to orbit Earth	Apr 12, 1961
8	Reinhold Messner	Italy	Scaled the world's 14 mountains of 8k+	1970-1986
9	Sir Edmund Hillary	New Zealand	First to climb Mount Everest	May 29, 1953
10	Robyn Davidson	Australia	First to cross the outback on camel	1977

Richard Branson attempted an around-the-world flight in The ICO Global balloon in 1998

TOP 10
FARTHEST AIR
BALLOON JOURNEYS

From the well-known hot air balloon, through to pressurized, mixed and gas balloons, some astounding distances have been clocked by the best balloonists...

RICHARD BRANSON
XTREME FACT

A classic example of an entrepreneur, Richard Branson launched a magazine aged just 16. Now, 46 years on, his Virgin Group covers everything from aircraft to cell phones. After his Transpacific ballooning success in 1991 along with Steve Fossett and Per Lindstrand, they then attempted to balloon around the world in 1998!

	CREW/COUNTRY	BALLOON NAME	TYPE	DATE	DISTANCE (KM)	(MI)
1	Bertrand Piccard, Brian Jones (Switzerland, UK)	Cameron Balloons Breitling Orbiter	Mixed	Mar 21, 1999	40,814	25,360
2	Steve Fossett (USA)	Cameron Balloons R-550	Mixed	Jul 4, 2002	33,195.1	20,626
3	Ben L Abruzzo, Rocky Aoki, Ron Clark, Larry Newman (USA)	Raven experimental	Gas	Nov 12, 1981	8,382.5	5,208
4	Per Lindstrand, Richard Branson, Steve Fossett (Sweden, UK, USA)	Colt 2500A	Hot air	Jan 15, 1991	7,671.9	4,767
5	Joseph W Kittinger, Jr. (USA)	Yost GB55	Gas	Sep 15, 1984	5,703.0	3,543
6	Richard Abruzzo, Troy Bradley (USA)	Cameron Balloons R-77	Mixed	Sep 16, 1992	5,340.2	3,318
7	Tomas Feliu Rius, Jesús González Green (Spain)	Cameron Balloons R-60	Mixed	Feb 9, 1992	5,046	3,135
8	David Hempleman-Adams (UK)	Padelt G-37	Gas	Jul 6, 2007	4,227.1	2,626
9	Julian R P Nott, Spider Anderson (UK)	Nott & Cameron, NCULD-1	Pressurized	Nov 20, 1984	2,391.5	1,485
10	Michio Kanda, Chikatsu Kakinuma (Japan)	Cameron Balloons N-210	Hot air	Jun 23, 1994	2,366.1	1,470

TOP 10

HIGHEST WIRE WALKS

If you've been to see the circus, chances are you've gasped at the tightrope walkers. However, the stars of the Big Top have NOTHING on these guys...

FACT FLASH!
HEIGHT
9,908
FT

FREDDY NOCK

XTREME FACT

Between 1998 and now, this inspiring Swiss daredevil has notched up an insane amount of world records. In August 2011 alone, he set seven brand-new records in just EIGHT DAYS. These include the longest and highest wire walk above sea level WITHOUT a balancing pole in Zugspitze, Germany, 3,264 ft (995 m) up in the air!

COMPARE-O-METER

Two more tall things for your reference!

WORLDS TALLEST BUILDING
2,000 4,000 6,000 8,000 10,000 12,000

K2 MOUNTAIN
2,000 4,000 6,000 8,000 10,000 12,000

HEIGHT OF TALLEST BUILDING
828 *m*
2,717 *ft*

HEIGHT OF K2 MOUNTAIN
8,611 *m*
28,251 *ft*

YOU RATE!
1 to 100

CHECK IT OUT!
Didier Pasquette's 2007 stunt was part of a multi-screen installation called *High Wire* by artist Catherine Yass, for the Glasgow International Festival of Contemporary Visual Arts.

	NAME	COUNTRY	WIRE WALK	HEIGHT (M)	(FT)	YEAR
1	**Freddy Nock**	**Switzerland**	**Mount Corvatsch**	**3,020**	**9,908**	**2011**
2	Ahdili Wuxiuer	China	China	1,600	5,249	2009
3	Eskil Rønningsbakken	Norway	Across Norwegian fjord	1,000	3,280	2009
4	Philippe Potit	France	Twin Towers	417	1,368	1974
5	Mustafa Danger	Morocco	Benidorm, Spain	186	610	2010
6	Didier Pasquette	France	Red Road, Glasgow	100	328	2007
=	Henri L'Estrange	Australia	Sydney Harbour	100	328	1877
8	Olivier Roustan	France	River Usk, Newport, Wales	76.2	250	2010
9	David Dimitri	Switzerland	Bahnhofplatz, Switzerland	50	164	2007
10	Jean François Gravelet-Blondin	France	Niagara Falls	47.7	157	1859

POWER PLAY

Presidents, prime ministers and royalty all wield immense power. Here's how they square up to each other...

TOP 10 DEPOSED DICTATORS

There's a very famous saying: "Power tends to corrupt, and absolute power corrupts absolutely." Here, we look at the lengths of dictators' reigns before they were overthrown by their own people...

FACT FLASH! RULE 34 YEARS

	NAME	COUNTRY	TIME IN POWER BEFORE OVERTHROWN
1	**Muammar Gaddafi**	**Libya**	**1969-2011 (42 years)**
2	António Salazar	Portugal	1932-1968 (36 years)
3	Alfredo Stroessner	Paraguay	1954-1989 (35 years)
4	President Saddam Hussein	Iraq	1969-2003 (34 years)
5	Mobutu Sese Seko	Zaire, Africa	1965-1997 (32 years)
6	Hosni Mubarak	Egypt	1981-2011 (30 years)
7	Nicolae Ceausescu	Romania	1965-1989 (24 years)
8	Slobodan Milosevic	Serbia/Yugoslavia	1989-2000 (21 years)
=	Ferdinand Marcos	Phillippines	1965-1986 (21 years)
10	Benito Mussolini	Italy	1925-1943 (18 years)

PRESIDENT SADDAM HUSSEIN

XTREME FACT

This 39 ft (12 m) statue of Saddam Hussein was made for his 65th birthday. It was torn down in April 2003 when he was ousted from power. In its place now stands a sculpture by Iraqi artist Bassem Hamad al-Dawiri that symbolizes freedom.

STAT ATTACK

MUAMMAR GADDAFI

Born .... June 7, 1942
Died .... Oct 20, 2011 (aged 69)
Political parties ..... Libyan Arab Republic, Libyan Arab Jamahiriya
Children 8

LONGEST SERVING RULERS

What's the longest you think a country's leader has ruled their nation?
The record terms are MUCH longer than you'd guess...

	NAME	COUNTRY	TIME RULED
1	Fidel Castro	Cuba	52 years 62 days
2	Kim Il-sung	North Korea	45 years 302 days
3	Chaing Kai-shek	China	45 years 57 days
4	Muammar Gaddafi	Libya	42 years 49 days
5	Omar Bongo	Gabon	41 years 155 days
6	Enver Hoxha	Albania	40 years 171 days
7	Francisco Franco	Spain	39 years 50 days
8	Gnassingbé Eyadéma	Togo	37 years 297 days
9	Paul Biya	Cameroon	37 years
10	Josip Broz Tito	Yugoslavia	36 years 157 days

YOU RATE!
1 to 100

FACT FLASH!
RULE
52
YEARS

OUR TOP 10 UNOFFICIAL

MOST BRUTAL ASSASSINATIONS

1	**Julius Caesar** **Roman dictator**	**44 BC**	**Stabbed 23 times by many of his opposers**
2	Juvénal Habyarimana President of Rwanda	Apr 6, 1994	Unknown faction shot surface-to-air missile at plane he was in
=	Cyprien Ntaryamira President of Burundi	Apr 6, 1994	Unknown faction shot surface-to-air missile at plane he was in
4	Inejiro Asanuma Leader of Japanese Socialist Party	Oct 12, 1960	Otoya Yamaguchi stabbed him with a samurai sword
5	John F. Kennedy President of USA	Nov 22, 1963	Gunshots, allegedly by Lee Harvey Oswald, but never proven
6	Medgar Evers Civil rights activist	Jun 12, 1963	Ku Klux Clan member Byron De La Beckwith shot him
7	Lee Harvey Oswald Alleged assassin of JFK	Nov 24, 1963	Jack Ruby shot him at point blank, as cameras watched
8	Orlando Letelier Chilean diplomat	Sep 21, 1976	Car bomb set by the Chilean secret police
9	Lord Louis Mountbatten British statesman	Aug 27, 1979	IRA (Irish Republican Army) planted bomb in his yacht
10	Antonio Cánovas del Castillo Prime Minister of Spain	Aug 8, 1897	Shot in a Spanish spa by Michele Angiolillo

FIDEL CASTRO

XTREME
FACT

Cuba's Fidel Castro was a very interesting political figure, simply because he had extreme support and criticism across the world. He has been described as a rich, corrupt dictator who kept the Cuban people oppressed, but he was also seen by some as a revolutionary for good and an ambassador for human rights.

ANOTHER THING!

Fidel Castro retired in 2008, and he appointed his brother Raúl Castro to take over his position.

POWER PLAY

TOP 10 YOUNGEST RULERS

Before you have a look at this chart, have a guess at the youngest age a king or queen has ever been crowned. You won't believe this crazy list...

	NAME	COUNTRY	AGE WHEN CROWNED	YEAR
1	Shah Shapur II	Sassanid Empire	Before birth!	309 AD
2	Alfonso XIII	Spain	Day of birth	1886
3	John I	France	1 day	1316
4	Mary Queen of Scots	Scotland	6 days	1542
5	Tsar Ivan VI	Russia	2 months	1740
6	Emperor Shang of Han	China	100 days old	105 AD
7	Sobhuza II	Swaziland	4 months	1899
8	King Henry VI	England	8 months	1422
9	King James VI	Scotland	13 months	1567
10	Pōmare III	Tahiti	17 months	1821

YOU RATE! 1 to 100

OFF THE CHART

EMPEROR PUYI

China's last emperor took the job on in 1908, at the tender age of two years old! Puyi's kingly role only lasted until he was six, though, when revolution reigned and he was forced to abdicate!

OUR TOP 10 UNOFFICIAL MADDEST RULERS

CHECK IT OUT!

The origins of Dracula, literally! Well before Bram Stoker penned *Dracula* in 1897, Vlad III (known as "The Impaler" as he was so violent) was called "Dracula" because it meant "son of Dracul", his father being Vlad II Dracul!

	NAME	COUNTRY	YEARS RULED	EXAMPLES OF CRAZY ACTS
1	Vlad the Impaler	Transylvania	1448; 1456-62; 1476	Obsessed with torture, inspired the Dracula mythos
2	Emperor Caligula	Italy	37-41 AD	Appointed his horse as a priest and a senator
3	Joanna of Castile	Spain	1504-55	Madly obsessed with her dead husband's corpse
4	King Charles VI	France	1380-1422	Insisted his name was George and attacked his own men
5	Queen Maria I	Portugal	1777-1816	Religious maniac, she would lie and scream for hours
6	Nebuchadnezzar II	Babylon (now Iraq)	605-562 BC	Possible lycanthropy: believed he changed into a beast
7	Sultan Ibrahim I	Turkey	1640-48	Tried to feed his pet fish coins
8	Crown Prince Sado	Korea	1728-89	Stalked and murdered people at whim
9	Christian VII	Denmark	1766-1808	Hallucinations and self-mutilating
10	Emperor Justin II	Byzantine	565-78	Would bite people who worked for him

TOP 10

OLDEST MODERN ERA CRIME BOSSES

It seems as though all the stress of being a big-time crime lord doesn't necessarily lead to a short life! Some of the most notorious mobsters lived to a ripe old age...

	NAME	BORN	DIED/STATUS	AGE	STATUS/CAUSE OF DEATH
1	Joseph "Lead Pipe Joe" Todaro	1923	(At large)	90	Still alive
=	Mario Gigante	1923	(At large)	90	Still alive
=	Joseph "Joey Doves" Aiuppa	1907	1997	90	Natural causes
4	Giuseppe Farinella	1925	Serving life in prison	88	Still alive
5	Anthony "Tony Ducks" Corallo	1913	2000	87	Natural causes in prison
6	Peter "Shakes" Milano	1925	2012	86	Natural causes
=	Nicolo Rizzuto	1924	2010	86	Assassinated
8	John "No Nose" DiFronzo	1928	(At large)	85	Still alive
9	Nicodemo "Little Nicky" Scarfo	1929	Serving life in prison	84	Still alive
=	Joseph "Joey the Clown" Lombardo	1929	Serving life in prison	84	Still alive

YOU RATE!
1 to 100

ANOTHER THING!

Luigi "Baby Shanks" Manocchio is currently serving time in prison, while James "Whitey" Bulger is awaiting trial for his mob crimes.

"TONY DUCKS"
XTREME FACT

Thinking about how Anthony Corallo got his nickname? Well, disappointingly, it has nothing to do with having fine feathered friends as pets. It was actually because he was known for being able to "duck" out of getting convicted for his crimes.

CHECK IT OUT!

There's "having a guilty expression on your face" and then there's THIS photo, which screams "totally busted"! Taken on September 28, 1966, this picture shows Anthony "Tony Ducks" Corallo in the back of a police van being taken in with his fellow mobster Aniello Dellacroce (wearing hat).

DANGEROUS MINDS

Criminals can carry out unspeakable, unthinkable acts. Here's a look at some of the most dangerous people who have ever walked the Earth...

TOP 10 BIGGEST SERIAL KILLERS

It's a horrific reality of our species: some human beings become terrifying monsters who murder many people...

CHECK IT OUT!

American serial killer Gary Ridgway was also known as the Green River Killer, and he has confessed to murdering at least 71 people. He has been described as a person hugely conflicted between his dark urges and rigid religious beliefs. Ridgway is currently serving life imprisonment in Washington, USA, with no chance of ever receiving parole.

FACT FLASH! KILLED 71

LUIS GARAVITO

XTREME FACT

This scary individual is known as the world's worst serial killer. Through maps that he drew in prison, which showed where bodies were buried, it suggests that the number of people Garavito killed could be more than 400. Controversially, due to Colombian law, he may only serve a mere 22 years in prison.

	NAME	COUNTRY	KILLING YEARS	VICTIMS (PROVED)	(SPECULATED)
1	**Luis Garavito**	**Colombia**	**1990s**	**138**	**172-400+**
2	Pedro López	Colombia	1969-80	110	310-350+
3	Daniel Barbosa	Colombia	1974-86	72	150
4	Pedro Rodrigues Filho	Brazil	1967-2003	71	100+
5	Gary Ridgway	USA	1982-2000	71	71-90+
6	Yang Xinhai	China	2000-03	67	67
7	Andrei Chikatilo	Ukraine	1978-90	53	56
8	Anatoly Onoprienko	Ukraine	1989-96	52	52+
9	Alexander Pichushkin	Russia	1992-2006	48	61+
10	Ahmad Suradji	Indonesia	1986-97	42	70-80+

TOP 10 MOST WANTED CRIMINALS

The FBI (Federal Bureau of Investigation) has a top 10 of the most wanted fugitives. It offers large monetary rewards for information that directly leads to any of their arrests...

FACT FLASH!
REWARD 1 MILLION DOLLARS

	NAME	ASSOCIATED CRIME	REWARD ($)
1	Victor Manuel Gerena	Armed robbery	1,000,000
2	Eric Justin Toth	Indecent materials	100,000
=	Jason Derek Brown	First-degree murder	100,000
=	Robert William Fisher	First-degree murder, arson	100,000
=	Glen Stewart Godwin	Murder, escape	100,000
=	Semion Mogilevich	Multiple fraud and false records	100,000
=	Eduardo Ravelo	Drugs and money racketeering	100,000
=	Alexis Flores	Kidnapping, murder	100,000
=	Fidel Urbina	First-degree murder, kidnappings, assault	100,000
=	Joe Luis Saenz*	Murder, kidnapping, assault	100,000

*Captured end of 2012
Source: FBI

VICTOR MANUEL GERENA

XTREME FACT

Wanted by the FBI for multiple charges, including bank robbery and related felonies, he is still at large. Journalist Edmund Mahoney's story *Chasing Gerena* was published (in 2001) in an attempt to find Gerena, but this didn't lead to authorities locating him.

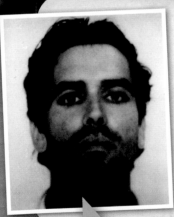

STAT ATTACK

GLEN STEWART GODWIN

Born	Jun 26, 1958
Height	6 ft (1.83 m)
Weight	200 lbs (91 kg)
Possible location	Latin America
Status	At large and considered extremely dangerous

CHECK IT OUT!

Glen Stewart Godwin's extensive criminal record includes stabbing a man 27 times and also making and detonating a homemade bomb. He escaped prison in 1991, five months after murdering a fellow inmate.

COMPARE-O-METER

Here are some other arresting sums of cash!

ORIGINAL SUPERMAN COSTUME
$80,000

COST OF A FLIGHT ON VIRGIN GALACTIC
$200,000

DANGEROUS MINDS

TOP 10

BIGGEST BANK HEISTS

Bank robbers are sometimes portrayed as bumbling idiots in TV shows and movies, but these ones knew exactly how to lift a staggering amount of money from the safes...

ANOTHER THING

Johnny Depp has portrayed infamous 1930s bank robber John Dillinger.

	BANK	ROBBER(S)	DATE	AMOUNT STOLEN ($)
1	Central Bank, Iraq	Saddam Hussein	Mar 2003	1 billion
2	Sumitomo Bank, London, UK	Belgian hacker gang	Sep 2007	300 million
3	Harry Winston, Paris	Four robbers (unknown)	Dec 2008	108 million
4	Antwerp Diamond Center, Belgium	Unknown	Feb 2003	100 million
5	Securitas Depot, Kent, UK	Unknown	Feb 2006	92.5 million
6	Banco Central, Brazil	Unknown	Aug 2005	70 million
7	Graff Diamonds, London, UK	Unknown	Aug 2009	65 million
8	Northern Bank, Northern Ireland	Unknown	Dec 2004	50 million
9	Bank of Ireland, Dublin	Unknown	Feb 2009	9 million
10	Agricultural Bank of China, Hándān, China	Ren Xiaofeng, Ma Xiangjing	Apr 2007	6.7 million

SADDAM HUSSEIN

XTREME FACT

The most notorious bank "heist" wasn't carried out by robbers... In March 2003, a panicked Saddam Hussein tasked supporters to grab him $1 billion from Iraq's Central Bank!

OFF THE CHART

JOHN DILLINGER

John Dillinger (Jun 22, 1903 to Jul 22, 1934) is one of the world's most famous bank robbers. Born in Indiana, USA, he successfully robbed 24 banks, four police stations, and even escaped jail twice. He was seen by some as deeply charismatic, but not by the long arm of the law...

CHECK IT OUT!

Terrorist Osama Bin Laden was the leader of al-Qaeda, and claimed that he was responsible for the September 11, 2001, attacks on the USA's World Trade Center. He was killed in Pakistan on May 2, 2011, by American forces.

DUMBEST CRIMINALS

	INCIDENT	LOCATION	YEAR
1	Burglar who tried to rob a house full of karate experts	Manizales (Colombia)	2008
2	Vandal wrote "Peter Addison was here" at the crime scene	Cheshire (UK)	2007
3	Claud Gipson-Reynolds stole a fire engine, then radioed for help when he got it stuck in mud	California (USA)	2004
4	Bank robber had to lift his mask up because he couldn't see through it	Berlin (Germany)	2002
5	John Pearce got stuck upside down from a window when breaking into a house	Kent (UK)	2008
6	Pal Nagy broke into the home of Olympic fencing champion Virgine Ujlaky	Budapest (Hungary)	2008
7	Man who stole expensive knives tripped and stabbed himself in the stomach	Michigan (USA)	2008
8	Man who robbed a gas station got lost and accidentally returned to it to ask directions	Vancouver (Canada)	2005
9	A 95-year-old woman stabbed Robert Horsley's hand with a screwdriver to stop a break-in	Oklahoma (USA)	2008
10	Robber passed out on champagne he stole, and police arrived to see if he was okay	Düsseldorf (Germany)	2008

TOP 10 LONGEST TIME ON FBI MOST WANTED LIST

Even with the names of suspects and their faces plastered all over databases, it can take a long, LONG time to capture some of the slipperiest criminals...

	NAME	ASSOCIATED CRIME	TIME ON "MOST WANTED" LIST
1	Victor Manuel Gerena	Armed robbery	29 years (May 14, 1984-present)
2	Donald Eugene Webb	Murder and attempted burglary	26 years (May 4, 1981-Mar 31, 2007)
3	Charles Lee Heron	Shooting two police officers	18 years (Feb 9, 1968-Jun 18, 1986)
4	Glen Stewart Godwin	Murder and robbery	17 years (Dec 17, 1996-present)
5	Frederick J. Tenuto	Mafia mob hitman	14 years (May 24, 1950-Mar 9, 1964)
=	Katherine Ann Power	Robbery and murder	14 years (Oct 17, 1970-Jun 15, 1984)
7	Leo Joseph Koury	Fraud and murder	12 years (Apr 20, 1979-Jun 16, 1991)
=	Osama Bin Laden	Terrorism	12 years (Jun 7, 1999-May 2, 2011)
=	James J. "Whitey" Bulger	Murder, drugs racketeering, extortion	12 years (Aug 19, 1999-Jun 22, 2011)
10	Wardell David Ford	Murder and robbery	1 year (Dec 20, 1989-Sep 17, 1990)

Source: FBI

BODY WORK

The human body can do many extraordinary things. Let's take a look at this natural, and sometimes SUPER-natural, biological machine...

TOP 10 TALLEST PEOPLE

If you're a fan of basketball, you'll be familiar with watching a lot of VERY tall sportsmen! These 10 people, however, dwarf them all...

FACT FLASH!
HEIGHT
8.4 FT

YOU RATE!
[ ]
1 to 100

	NAME	COUNTRY	BORN/DIED	HEIGHT (M)	(FT)
1	Robert Wadlow	USA	1918-40	2.72	8' 11"
2	John Rogan	USA	1868-1905	2.67	8' 9"
3	John F. Carroll	USA	1932-69	2.63	8' 7.5"
4	Leonid Stadnyk	Ukraine	1971-present	2.57	8' 5"
5	Väinö Myllyrinne	Finland	1909-163	2.51	8' 2.8"
=	Edouard Beaupré	Canada	1881-1904	2.51	8' 2.8"
=	Sultan Kösen	Turkey	1982-2012	2.51	8' 2.8"
8	Bernard Coyne	USA	1897-1921	2.49	8' 2"
=	Don Koehler	USA	1925-81	2.49	8' 2"
10	Zeng Jinlian*	China	1964-82	2.48	8' 1.6"

*Female (the rest are male)

LEONID STADNYK

XTREME FACT

What shoe size are you? We can guarantee they won't be anywhere near the gigantic size 64 of Leonid Stadnyk, the tallest man alive today! Georg Wessels, a German shoemaker, gave Leonid these crazy-huge sneakers at the world record holder's home in the village of Podoliantsi in the Ukraine.

COMPARE-O-METER

Here is how these tall people measure up!

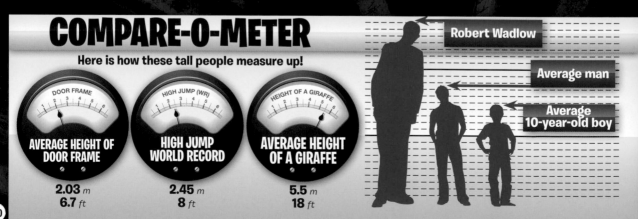

DOOR FRAME
HIGH JUMP (WR)
HEIGHT OF A GIRAFFE

AVERAGE HEIGHT OF DOOR FRAME
2.03 m
6.7 ft

HIGH JUMP WORLD RECORD
2.45 m
8 ft

AVERAGE HEIGHT OF A GIRAFFE
5.5 m
18 ft

Robert Wadlow
Average man
Average 10-year-old boy

TOP 10

HEAVIEST PEOPLE

Being morbidly obese means being 50 to 100% above your ideal body weight in relation to your height. These weights are extraordinarily dangerous...

	NAME	COUNTRY	BORN/DIED	WEIGHT (KG)	(LB)
1	**Jon Brower Minnoch**	**USA**	**1941-83**	**635**	**1,400**
2	Manuel Uribe	Mexico	1965-present	597	1,320
3	Carol Yager	USA	1960-94	545+	1,200
4	Rosalie Bradford	USA	1943-2006	544	1,200+
=	Walter Hudson	USA	1944-91	544	1,200
6	Michael Walker	USA	1934-present	538	1,187
7	Michael Hebranko	USA	1953-present	500+	1,100
8	Patrick Deuel	USA	1962-present	486	1,070
9	Robert Earl Hughes	USA	1926-58	485	1,069
10	Kenneth Brumley	USA	1968-present	469	1,030

GIVE IT A TRY...
HEIGHT CHART

Find a place in your house or a friend's with an area where you can create a height chart! It could be a bare wall that the grown-ups don't mind you writing on, or you could stick a long strip of plain paper to the wall. See how many of your friends and family's heights you can record. Then you can update the chart every year when each new T-10 book comes out!

FACT FLASH!
WEIGHT
1,320
LB

MANUEL URIBE

XTREME FACT

Mexican Manuel Uribe has struggled with his weight for many years. He used to be 1,320 lb (597 kg), but in 2012 he dropped to 440 lb (200 kg).

OUR TOP 10 UNOFFICIAL
MOST ARTISTIC BODY ART

	STYLE/PERSON	TECHNIQUE	ORIGIN
1	**Pe'a**	**Traditional tattoo**	**Independent State of Samoa**
2	Tā moko	Traditional tattoo	Māori, New Zealand
3	The Enigma	Tattoos, implants, piercings	Sideshow performer/actor from Seattle, USA
4	Koita	Traditional tattoo	Papua New Guinea
5	Spiritual markings	Traditional tattoo	Hinduism
6	Henna	Semi-permanent	Several religions including Jewish, Muslim
7	Scythian	Traditional tattoo	Scythia (Ancient Central Asia)
8	Stalking cat	Tattoos, implants, piercings	USA resident who looked like a tiger
9	Leopard man	Tattoos, implants	UK resident who looks like a leopard
10	Irezumi	Tattoo	Traditional Japanese decorative style

CHECK IT OUT!

The Maori style of tattooing is called Tā moko. Different to modern tattoo techniques using needles, the markings are achieved by the ancient process of using chisels called uhi.

TOP 10 HEAVIEST STRONGEST MEN

The World's Strongest Man competition has been going from strength to strength since it began in 1977. These are the biggest heavyweight champions...

YOU RATE!

1 to 100

	NAME	COUNTRY	LAST YEAR WON	WEIGHT (KG)	(LB)
1	Brian Shaw	USA	2011	210	462
2	Phil Pfister	USA	2006	170	375
=	Žydrūnas Savickas	Lithuania	2010	170	375
=	Don Reinhoudt	USA	1979	170	375
5	Bill Kazmaier	USA	1982	160	352
=	Ted van der Parre	Netherlands	1992	160	352
7	Magnus Samuelsson	Sweden	1998	156	344
8	Mariusz Pudzianowski	Poland	2008	152	335
9	Geoff Capes	UK	1985	150	330
10	Bruce Wilhelm	USA	1978	150	330

MARIUSZ PUDZIANOWSKI

XTREME FACT

Not only is Mariusz a five-time World's Strongest Man champion with dozens of other wins, he's a mixed martial arts expert who also has a Master's degree in International Relations! Brawn AND brains!

FACT FLASH!
WEIGHT
335
LB

COMPARE-O-METER

This is how weighty these champs are!

WASHING MACHINE

BROWN BEAR

WEIGHT OF A WASHING MACHINE
70 kg
155 lb

AVERAGE WEIGHT OF A BROWN BEAR
367.5 kg
810 lb

OFF THE CHART

MAGNÚS VER MAGNÚSSON

Who's the strongest person you know? Can they pull a car? Thought not! Here's four-time World's Strongest Man champion Magnús Ver Magnússon (287 lb/130 kg) pulling a 60,000 lb (27,216 kg) truck. If your car breaks down, Magnús is your man!

MOST AMAZING AMPUTEES

	NAME	AMPUTATED LIMB(S)	PROFESSION
1	Rick Allen	Left arm in car accident	Drummer with Def Leppard
2	Jonnie Peacock	Right leg from meningitis	Professional sprinter
3	Terry Fox	Right leg above knee from cancer	Professional athlete/runner
4	Bethany Hamilton	Left arm in shark attack	Professional surfer
5	Tom Whittaker	Right foot from car accident	Climber (scaled Mount Everest)
6	Olivia Giles	All limbs from meningitis	Founder of 500 Miles charity
7	Spencer West	Legs at the age of five	Climbed Mount Kilimanjaro
8	Chad Jukes	Right leg from Iraq conflict	Rock climber
9	Jody Cundy	Right foot at age three	World champion cyclist
10	Scott Rigsby	Both legs in a truck accident	Iron Man athlete

RICK ALLEN

XTREME FACT

It was New Year's Eve in 1984 when Def Leppard drummer Rick Allen lost his arm in a car crash. Incredibly, Rick developed a new technique and remained with the band!

TOP 10 MOST INTELLIGENT PEOPLE (HIGHEST IQ)

When you consider that an IQ (Intelligence Quotient) of above 130 represents "superior intelligence", these guys really are pure geniuses!

YOU RATE!
1 to 100

	NAME	COUNTRY	JOB	IQ
1	Kim Ung-yong	Korea	Physicist	210
2	Evangelos Katsioulis	Greece	Professor	198
3	Christopher Michael Langan	USA	Bouncer	195
4	Rick Rosner	USA	Writer	192
5	Philip Emeagwali	Nigeria	Scientist	190
=	Marilyn vos Savant	USA	Writer	190
7	Sir Andrew Wiles	UK	Mathematician	170
=	Robert Byrne	USA	Professor	170
9	Stephen Hawking	UK	Professor	160+
10	Paul Allen	USA	Microsoft co-founder	160+

CHECK IT OUT!

Professor Stephen Hawking is one of the world's most celebrated theoretical physicists. His book *A Brief History of Time* has sold more than 10 million copies! He also wowed the world at the 2012 Paralympics Opening Ceremony by giving a poignant performance with electronic duo Orbital.

UNITED WE STAND

When us human beings get organized, we really can pull off some jaw-dropping feats, both good and bad...

TOP 10 LARGEST ARMIES (BY COUNTRY)

These are the biggest military operations from around the globe. Here we're showing their size represented by active military members...

	COUNTRY	ACTIVE MILITARY MANPOWER
1	China	2,285,000
2	USA	1,452,939
3	India	1,325,000
4	Russia	1,200,000
5	North Korea	1,106,000
6	South Korea	653,000
7	Pakistan	617,000
8	Turkey	612,900
9	Iran	545,000
10	Egypt	468,500

YOU RATE! 1 to 100

CHINA

XTREME FACT

The People's Liberation Army (PLA) is the full name for China's armed forces. Every year on August 1, PLA Day is celebrated, marking the anniversary of when the army was formed in 1927.

FACT FLASH!
MANPOWER
1.1 MILLION

OFF THE CHART

BRITISH ARMY

The UK has an active military manpower of 224,500, and one of those is Prince Harry! He's known as Captain Wales when he's in military mode, and he has served in Afghanistan in the Army Air Corps.

CHECK IT OUT!

The army of North Korea is known as the Korean People's Army. It's based in the country's capital city of Pyongyang. Although North Korea ranks fifth in the list of Active Military Manpower, it is the most militarized country on Earth. There are a staggering 8,200,000 people in their reserve force alone. The age of conscription (a system where it is compulsory that you serve a period of service for your country, which is usually military in nature) is 17.

BIGGEST RIOTS

Riots are a terrifying example of what can happen when a group of people decide to act violently as one unit. These historical incidents are among the most fatal...

	NAME OF RIOT	LOCATION	DATE	NUMBER OF DEATHS
1	**Nika Riots**	**Constantinople**	**532 AD**	**30,000**
2	Arab Revolt	Palestine	1936-39	5,600
3	Direct Action Day	Calcutta	1946	4,000
4	First Intifada	Palestine	1987-93	2,326
5	Romanian Revolution	Romania	1989	1,104
6	Copper Riot	Moscow	1662	1,000
7	Bloody Sunday	St. Petersburg	1905	1,000
8	Bombay Riots	Bombay	1992-93	900
9	Bread Riots	Egypt	1977	800
10	Soweto Uprising	Soweto	1976	600

YOU RATE!
1 to 100

CHECK IT OUT!

Direct Action Day is also known as the Great Calcutta Killings (in a part of India now called Kolkata). This photo shows an example of the aftermath from the riots between Muslims and Hindus, which was related to a great deal of political and religious unrest in India.

OUR TOP 10 UNOFFICIAL
FORMIDABLE ARMIES

SPARTAN ARMY

	ARMY	FORMIDABLE QUALITIES
1	**Spartan army**	**The city of Sparta was devoted to military training**
2	Roman army	30 legions of 5,000 extremely well-organized soldiers
3	Swiss Guard	Military-trained bodyguards, ceremonial and palace guards
4	Knights Templar	Strong Catholic faith gave them a fearless edge
5	Alexander the Great's army	Utilized the most modern weapons and battle tactics
6	William Wallace's army	Passion to protect Scotland beat any military weaknesses
7	French Foreign Legion	Trained in "unit cohesion" to maintain belief in the army's task
8	Napoleon's army	Napoleon's charisma inspired his aggressive armed forces
9	Mongolian army	Clever retreat tactics revealed enemy weaknesses
10	British Empire	Its navy set out to conquer the oceans for centuries

XTREME FACT

The Spartan army is viewed by historians as one of the most formidable forces of all time. The soldiers trained obsessively and endlessly. They wouldn't have been able to function with simple day-to-day tasks, such as feeding themselves, without the aid of their helots, who were servants that lived together in family units.

FICTITIOUS FIGURES!

The fantastical world of the human imagination has created some amazing characters in books, comics and movies. Here are some of the most commercially successful we've seen so far...

TOP 10 BIGGEST HUMAN SUPERHEROES (BOX OFFICE)

Here at T-10 Towers there are HUNDREDS of comic books, DVDs, Blu-rays, and action figures all over the place. Let's find out which humans (mutated or not) have had the biggest box office success...

	CHARACTER	NUMBER OF MOVIES	TOTAL GROSS ($)
1	**Batman**	8	3,712,725,948
2	Spider-Man	4	3,235,824,753
3	Iron Man	3	2,720,313,523
4	Black Widow	2	2,135,315,343
5	The Hulk	3	2,007,676,300
6	Captain America	2	1,880,394,726
7	Wolverine	4	1,530,643,030
8	Hawkeye	1	1,511,757,910
9	Professor X	4	1,508,665,385
10	Jean Grey	3	1,155,760,014

Source: IMDB.com

YOU RATE! 1 to 100

FACT FLASH! DOLLARS GROSSED **1.5 BILLION**

WOLVERINE

XTREME FACT

Team T-10 fave Wolverine may only be the seventh most successful human superhero at the box office at the moment, but that could all change as more movies featuring Logan get made! Until then, let's take a closer look at how his total box office takings break down...

HOW HIS MOVIES DID:

X-Men Origins: Wolverine	2009	374,883,016
X-Men: The Last Stand	2006	455,260,014
X2	2003	406,400,000
X-Men	2000	294,100,000

ANOTHER THING!

In *The Amazing Spider-Man* (2012), Peter Parker has the technology to spin webs, but in the 2002-07 films the webbing is organic and produced from Parker's wrists.

OFF THE CHART

CYCLOPS, STORM, ROGUE AND ICEMAN

The mutant X-talents of Cyclops, Storm, Rogue and Ice Man actually all share 10th place with Jean Grey. They also appear in three hit *X-Men* movies that took $1,155,760,014 at the box office.

TOUGHEST MOVIE CHARACTERS

	CHARACTER	MOVIE(S)
1	**The Hulk**	The Avengers (2012), The Hulk movies (2008 & 2003)
2	Bane	The Dark Knight Rises (2012)
3	Lara Croft	Lara Croft Tomb Raider saga (2003 & 2001)
4	Roadblock	GI Joe: Retaliation (2013)
5	BA Baracus	The A-Team (2010)
6	Selina Kyle	The Dark Knight Rises (2012)
7	Atom	Real Steel (2011)
8	Storm Shadow	GI Joe movies (2013 & 2009)
9	Flash Gordon	Flash Gordon (1980)
10	Mr. Incredible	The Incredibles (2004)

TOP 10 BIGGEST DETECTIVES/AGENTS (BOX OFFICE)

Super-sleuths and government agents unite! These 10 characters have made the most impact on box office takings across the world...

YOU RATE! 1 to 100

	CHARACTER	NO. OF MOVIES	TOTAL GROSS ($)
1	**James Bond**	25	6,124,394,689
2	Commissioner Jim Gordon	8	3,712,725,948
3	Agent Phil Coulson	4	3,514,628,664
4	Felix Leiter	10	2,268,475,611
5	Ethan Hunt	4	2,086,203,230
6	Agent J	3	1,636,227,919
=	Agent K	3	1,636,227,919
8	Sherlock Holmes	37	1,081,271,445
9	Jason Bourne	3	926,774,175
10	Austin Powers	3	676,356,278

Source: IMDB.com

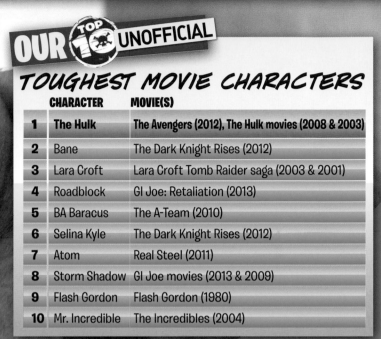

HEAD TO HEAD

IN THE BLUE CORNER... **JASON BOURNE**

IN THE RED CORNER... **SHERLOCK HOLMES**

✓ 09	Attack	04 ✗
✗ 05	Attitude	08 ✓
✗ 01	Memory	10 ✓
✗ 08	Skill	10 ✓
✗ 7	Intelligence	10 ✓

1

4

AND THE WINNER IS... SHERLOCK!

FICTITIOUS FIGURES

TOP 10

BIGGEST HUMAN VILLAINS (BOX OFFICE)

Tricky one, this list, because Mystique and Magneto weren't the villains in 2011's *X-Men: First Class*, but were baddies in the other movies. So this list just looks at villains BEING villainy...

THE JOKER

XTREME FACT

Tragically, Heath Ledger, the actor who played The Joker in *The Dark Knight*, died of an accidental overdose of medication on Jan 22, 2008, six months before the movie's release. His unforgettable performance was honoured in 2009 with an Academy Award for Best Supporting Actor.

	CHARACTER	NUMBER OF MOVIES	TITLE/YEAR	TOTAL GROSS ($)
1	Colonel Miles Quaritch	1	Avatar (2009)	2,782,275,172
2	Caledon "Cal" Hockley	1	Titanic (1997)	2,185,372,302
3	The Joker	2	The Dark Knight (2008), Batman (1989)	1,415,121,825
4	Mystique	3	X-Men: The Last Stand (2006), X2 (2003), X-Men (2000)	1,155,760,014
=	Magneto	3	X-Men: The Last Stand (2006), X2 (2003), X-Men (2000)	1,155,760,014
6	Bane	1	The Dark Knight Rises (2012)	1,081,041,287
7	Sandman	1	Spider-Man 3 (2007)	890,830,303
8	Green Goblin	1	Spider-Man (2002)	806,700,000
9	Dr. Octopus	1	Spider-Man 2 (2004)	786,077,893
10	Irina Spalko	1	Indiana Jones And The Kingdom Of The Crystal Skull (2008)	783,011,114

YOU RATE! 1 to 100

Sources: IMDB.com

OFF THE CHART

PRESIDENT SNOW

Just missing out on a place in the "Villains" Top 10 is the despicable President Snow from *The Hunger Games* (2012) (played brilliantly by movie legend Donald Sutherland). It took $644,688,212 worldwide at the box office.

STAT ATTACK

BARNABAS COLLINS

Vampire in the movie .. Dark Shadows (2012)
Played by .... Johnny Depp
Based on .... 1966-71 TV show also called Dark Shadows
Number of TV episodes ...... A jaw-dropping 1,225!

TOP 10 BIGGEST DOCTORS/ SCIENTISTS (BOX OFFICE)

CHECK IT OUT!
Harrison Ford has certainly played two of the coolest movie characters: Indiana Jones AND Han Solo from the *Star Wars* saga!

Good or bad, those who love to play around in GEEK labs have always been fun to watch on screen. If the clever character had a significant role in a movie, we've got it analyzed here...

YOU RATE!
1 to 100

	CHARACTER	NUMBER OF MOVIES	SAGA/YEAR	TOTAL GROSS ($)
1	Dr. Grace Augustine	1	Avatar (2009)	2,782,275,172
2	Dr. Curt Connors	3	The Spider-Man movies (2004-12)	2,369,643,521
3	Dr. Bruce Banner	3	The Avengers (2012), The Hulk movies (2003-08)	2,007,676,300
4	Dr. Indiana Jones	4	The Indiana Jones movies (1981-2008)	1,998,683,758
5	Dr. Alan Grant	2	The Jurassic Park movies (1995-2001)	1,283,471,927
6	Dr. John Watson	37	The Sherlock Homes movies (1943-2011)	959,845,743
7	Dr. Emmett Brown	3	The Back to the Future movies (1985-90)	957,587,347
8	Dr. Ellie Slater	1	Jurassic Park (1993)	914,691,118
=	Dr. Ian Malcolm	1	Jurassic Park (1993)	914,691,118
10	Dr. Otto Octavius	1	Spider-Man 2 (2004)	786,077,893

Sources: IMDB.com

CHECK IT OUT!
To get Johnny Depp's skin to look THAT pale for his *Dark Shadows* vampire role, the make-up artist had to pile on SEVERAL layers of special greasepaint!

OUR  **UNOFFICIAL**

COOLEST VAMPIRES

	CHARACTER	MOVIE/TV SHOW	DATE RELEASED/AIRED ON TV
1	Count Graf Orlok	Nosferatu	1922
2	Drusilla	Buffy The Vampire Slayer	1997-2003
3	Barnabas Collins	Dark Shadows	1966-71/2012
4	Count Dracula	Dracula	1931
5	Spike	Buffy The Vampire Slayer	1997-2003
6	The Vampire	The Night Stalker	1972
7	Ben Cortman	The Last Man On Earth	1964
8	Angel	Buffy The Vampire Slayer/Angel	1997-2003/1999-2004
9	Count Duckula	Count Duckula	1988-93
10	Mina Harker	The League Of Extraordinary Gentlemen	2003

ONLY HUMAN!

YOUR SHOUT!

It's time to turn things over to YOU! This is where you get to compile your ratings from the Only Human zone, plus we've thrown in some extra challenges for you, too...

YOU RATE!

T-10 HUMANS

Regardless of what the official lists are, we want to know how YOU rated your top ones. Get together with your friends and their T-10 books and compare your lists!

	NAME OF HUMAN(S)	"YOU RATE" SCORE
1		
2		
3		
4		
5		
6		
7		
8		
9		
10		

DARE TO GO...

TRUE OR FALSE...

1. It only took Loïck Peyron five weeks to skipper his sailboat around the world. ☐ T ☐ F

2. Half of the T-10 Deepest Solo Sea Dives list is made up of European divers. ☐ T ☐ F

3. Mount Everest is unbelievably 80 km (49 mi) high. ☐ T ☐ F

4. The number one highest wire walk is higher than all the rest added together. ☐ T ☐ F

BONUS QUESTION

WHAT WAS THIS MAN'S OUT-OF-THIS-WORLD ACHIEVEMENT?

....

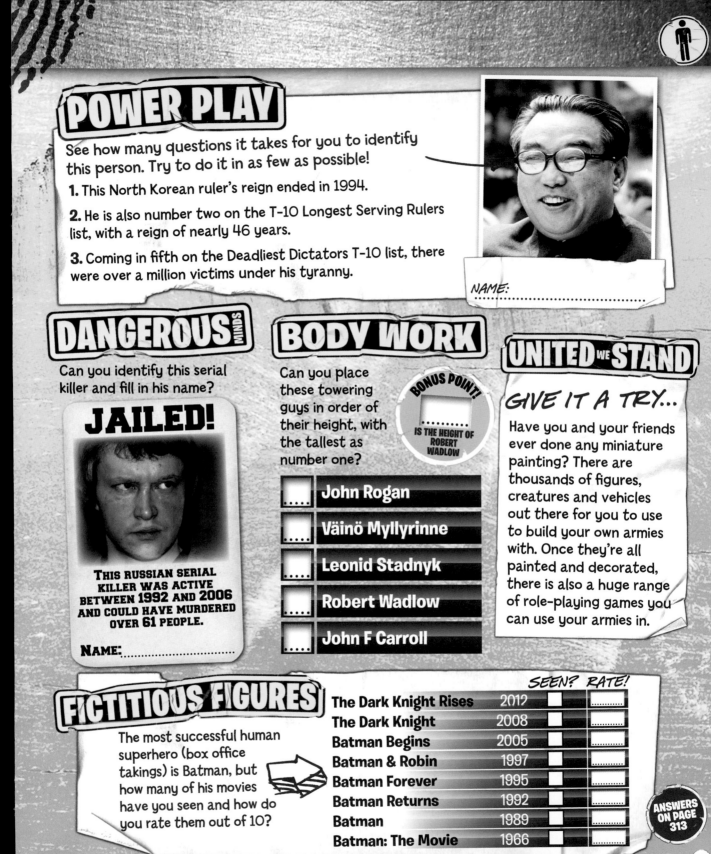

POWER PLAY

See how many questions it takes for you to identify this person. Try to do it in as few as possible!

1. This North Korean ruler's reign ended in 1994.

2. He is also number two on the T-10 Longest Serving Rulers list, with a reign of nearly 46 years.

3. Coming in fifth on the Deadliest Dictators T-10 list, there were over a million victims under his tyranny.

NAME:
....

DANGEROUS MINDS

Can you identify this serial killer and fill in his name?

JAILED!

THIS RUSSIAN SERIAL KILLER WAS ACTIVE BETWEEN 1992 AND 2006 AND COULD HAVE MURDERED OVER 61 PEOPLE.

NAME:........................

BODY WORK

Can you place these towering guys in order of their height, with the tallest as number one?

BONUS POINT!

.... IS THE HEIGHT OF ROBERT WADLOW

.....	**John Rogan**
.....	**Väinö Myllyrinne**
.....	**Leonid Stadnyk**
.....	**Robert Wadlow**
.....	**John F Carroll**

UNITED WE STAND

GIVE IT A TRY...

Have you and your friends ever done any miniature painting? There are thousands of figures, creatures and vehicles out there for you to use to build your own armies with. Once they're all painted and decorated, there is also a huge range of role-playing games you can use your armies in.

FICTITIOUS FIGURES

The most successful human superhero (box office takings) is Batman, but how many of his movies have you seen and how do you rate them out of 10?

		SEEN?	RATE!
The Dark Knight Rises	2012		
The Dark Knight	2008		
Batman Begins	2005		
Batman & Robin	1997		
Batman Forever	1995		
Batman Returns	1992		
Batman	1989		
Batman: The Movie	1966		

ANSWERS ON PAGE 313

INFINITE SPACE

Space... The final frontier. These are the pages of the T-10 Enterprise. Our mission for this section? To seek out stellar facts about outer space. To investigate the planets and the stars. To boldly go where no book for boys has gone before...

ASTRO ORBITS

Outer space is a breathtaking realm. We've learned quite a lot about it so far, but there is so much more to discover! Here are some amazing Top 10s about space that we've found for you...

TOP 10 BIGGEST MASSES IN OUR SOLAR SYSTEM

Our planet feels like a pretty big place to live, but check out how it compares to the other large masses out in space...

SUN

XTREME FACT

The boiling point of water is 212 °F (100 °C), so imagine what a splash from the Sun's core would feel like at 27,000,000 °F (15,000,000 °C)! Although it's a very special one, the Sun is still a star, one of around 100 billion... And that's just in OUR galaxy. The Sun also represents 99.8 percent of our solar system's total mass!

FACT FLASH!

332,982 TIMES BIGGER THAN EARTH

YOU RATE!

1 to 100

	OBJECT	MASS (x 10 TO THE POWER OF 21 KG)
1	Sun	1,989,100,000
2	Jupiter	1,898,600
3	Saturn	568,460
4	Neptune	102,430
5	Uranus	86,832
6	Earth	5,973.6
7	Venus	4,868.5
8	Mars	641.85
9	Mercury	330.2
10	Ganymede (a Jupiter moon)	148.2

MERCURY

XTREME FACT

Is Mercury's name related to the element? No, it's a lot cooler than that. Back in Roman times, they named this planet after Mercury, their god of travel, who had the ability to fly. As this was the fastest-moving planet the Romans could see, it's apt they named it after their fastest-moving god. Nice!

OFF THE CHART

EARTH'S MOON

Coming in at number 14 is our planet's Moon, which has a mass of 73.5×10^{22} kg. This seems quite tiny in comparison to the mind-boggling massiveness of the Sun!

OUR TOP 10 UNOFFICIAL
IMPORTANT SATELLITES

	NAME	TASK
1	Hubble Space Telescope	Outer space photos and studies
2	Galaxy 14	Digital TV signals for USA
3	GOES-12	North American weather reports
4	KH-13	USA spy satellite
5	GPS IIR11	One component of many GPS sources
6	International Space Station	Global initiative of space discovery
7	NOAA 17	Weather pattern detection
8	Landsat 7	Recording images of Earth
9	Navstar GPS	Network of satellites for GPS
10	GeoEye	Images of Earth

HUBBLE SPACE TELESCOPE

XTREME FACT

If you want to experience what it's like getting up really close to this inspiring piece of technology, don't miss the documentary film *Hubble*. It's often shown in IMAX 3D because, yes, they actually took IMAX cameras into space to film it being repaired! If you're a fan of all things to do with outer space, seek this out...

GIVE IT A TRY...
SATELLITE DESIGN

Why not try designing the next generation of space exploration satellites? Start with pen and paper, then take it to a computer screen and design your amazing satellite there!

TOP 10
PLANETS/DWARF PLANETS
NEAREST OUR SUN

We're actually pretty close to the Sun when you look at how the other planets and dwarf planets measure up...

	NAME	DISTANCE FROM THE SUN (KM)	(MI)
1	Mercury	46-70 million	28-43 million
2	Venus	108 million	67 million
3	Earth	150 million	93 million
4	Mars	230 million	142 million
5	Ceres	419 million	260 million
6	Jupiter	778 million	483 million
7	Saturn	1.4 billion	0.9 billion
8	Uranus	3 billion	1.9 billion
9	Neptune	4.5 billion	2.8 billion
10	Pluto	5.9 billion	3.7 billion

YOU RATE! 1 to 100

FACT FLASH!
93 MILLION
MILES FROM THE SUN

CHECK IT OUT!

The Gateway to Astronaut Photography of Earth (www.eol.jsc.nasa.gov) has the most comprehensive collection of photos taken of Earth from space... This includes over one million taken from the International Space Station!

TOP 10 PLANETS/DWARF PLANETS WITH THE MOST MOONS

We've only got one, but our Moon rocks! After all, it does a lot for us, including controlling all the tides. But check out how many moons our other nearby planets have...

YOU RATE!
1 to 100

	PLANET/DWARF PLANET	MOONS
1	Jupiter	67
2	Saturn	62
3	Uranus	27
4	Neptune	13
5	Pluto	5
6	Mars	2
=	Haumea	2
8	Earth	1
=	Eris	1
=	Venus	1*

The Earth orbit-crossing asteroid 2002 VE68 left experts perplexed, and became known as Venus' quasi-moon

JUPITER'S MOONS

XTREME FACT

What's fascinating about Jupiter's moons is the huge variation in size among them. The biggest, Ganymede, is a gigantic 3,273 mi (5,268 km) wide. The smallest? Five are under 1.2 mi (2 km) across, and the majority are less than 31 mi (50 km) wide. Bit of a difference, huh!

CHECK IT OUT!

Io, one of Jupiter's moons, is named after a priestess in Greek mythology. It's the fourth largest moon of our solar system at 2,263 mi (3,642 km) wide and is also considered the most volcanic mass of our system. Io was feisty, too, so quite appropriate!

TOP 10 PLANETS'/DWARF PLANETS' LONGEST DAYS

If you were to experience what a full day felt like on other planets, here's how long it would take to officially clock around from midnight to midnight...

VENUS

XTREME FACT

The Roman goddess of love and beauty was Venus, which is where this planet gets its name from. Gazing upon Venus' beauty is very easy to do as it's the most easily seen object in the night sky after the Moon.

	PLANET/DWARF PLANET	EQUIVALENT EARTH TIME
1	Venus	243 days
2	Mercury	58.65 days
3	Pluto	6.4 days
4	Eris	23.75 hours
5	Neptune	19.1 hours
6	Uranus	17.9 hours
7	Saturn	10.2 hours
8	Jupiter	9.8 hours
9	Ceres	9.1 hours
10	Haumea	3.9 hours

GIVE IT A TRY...
BUILD YOUR PLANET

Have you ever crafted anything out of papier mâché? It may sound fancy, but it's simply strips of newspaper, glue and water. Grab a grown-up to help you build up layers around a balloon to make a model planet. Let it dry, then paint your planet!

STAT ATTACK

JUPITER

Named after........Roman god of thunder and the sky, Jupiter/Jove

Magnetic field........The strongest in the solar system

Made of ....Gas and liquid, with an unknown core composition

Astronomical symbol................Looks like a lightning bolt (from the Roman god)

Life on Jupiter?....... Unlikely, but theories suggest its moons could have subterranean oceans

TOP 10 SMALLEST PLANETS/DWARF PLANETS IN OUR SOLAR SYSTEM

When we say "smallest", these are still some big masses! But compared to Earth, some of these are pretty little...

MAKEMAKE

XTREME FACT

This dwarf planet was discovered at Easter time in 2005, which influenced its name. On Easter Island (on our planet), the native Rapa Nui belief is that Makemake was the creator of humanity, and so a fitting name for the dwarf planet's Easter-time discovery.

	PLANET/ DWARF PLANET	DIAMETER (KM)	(MI)
1	Ceres	950	590
2	Makemake	1,516	941
3	Haumea	1,960	1,217
4	Pluto	2,274	1,413
5	Eris	2,500	1,553
6	Mercury	4,878	3,031
7	Mars	6,790	4,219
8	Venus	12,104	7,521
9	Earth	12,756	7,926
10	Neptune	49,528	30,775

ASTRO ORBITS

TOP 10 BIGGEST ASTEROIDS TO SHARE EARTH'S ORBIT

We definitely do NOT want any of these to ever collide with our planet...

	NAME	DIAMETER (KM)	(MI)
1	Pallas	544	338
2	Vesta	525.4	326
3	Hygeia	431	267
4	Interamnia	326	202
5	Europa	301	187
6	Davida	289	179
7	Sylvia	286	177
8	Cybele	273	169
9	Eunomia	268	166
10	Juno	258	160

YOU RATE!
1 to 100

HYGEIA

XTREME FACT

This, the fourth largest asteroid out there orbiting the Sun, was discovered by a very smart Italian astronomer back in April 12, 1849. Annibale de Gasparis was that man, and he went on to discover a total of NINE asteroids over the next 16 years, AND got himself awarded the Gold Medal of the Royal Astronomical Society!

FACT FLASH!
DIAMETER
267 MI

CHECK IT OUT!

This is a superb artist's impression of NASA's robotic Dawn checking out asteroid Vesta, as well as dwarf planet Ceres. Dawn's mission if she chooses to accept it? To use its technology to study the differences between Vesta and Ceres, and report them back to Earth... All remotely, of course, as Dawn is quite far away!

ANOTHER THING!

In 2013, NASA's Dawn completed its study of asteroid Vesta, and is winging its way to dwarf planet Ceres. It will arrive there in early 2015.

COMPARE-O-METER

Here are some other very wide widths!

WIDTH OF IRELAND
304 km
189 mi

DIAMETER OF THE MOON
3,476 km
2,160 mi

MARS SCIENCE LABORATORY

XTREME FACT

The Mars Science Laboratory mission costs a massive $2.5 billion, and this is an extremely important mission. The data acquired by the machines exploring Mars will help us plan for a manned trip to the planet in the future.

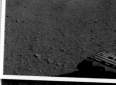

A photo taken by robot rover Curiosity

CHECK IT OUT!

As one of Mars' Science Laboratory, the robot rover Curiosity touched its wheels down onto the Martian surface on August 6, 2012, and it means business! It has 10 times the scientific tech as its predecessors Spirit (landed January 4, 2004, and stopped working March 22, 2010) and Opportunity (landed January 25, 2004, and is still active on Mars).

FACT FLASH!
CURRENTLY ON MARS FROM AUGUST 6, 2012

SHUFFLE UP

Do you have your own preference when it comes to the technology we've left on other rocks? Detail YOUR ranking system here!

1 ....
2 ....
3 ....
4 ....
5 ....
6 ....
7 ....
8 ....
9 ....
10 ....

CHECK IT OUT!

Apollo 15 was the first rocket to carry a lunar rover, so astronauts could drive around and collect more samples. It's still up there!

OUR TOP 10 UNOFFICIAL

COOLEST MAN-MADE THINGS LEFT ON OTHER PLANETS & MOONS

	OBJECT	LEFT ON
1	**Mars Science Laboratory**	**Mars**
2	Venera 14 Probe	Venus
3	Luna 23	Earth's Moon
4	SELENE	Earth's Moon
5	Huygens Probe	Titan
6	Apollo Lunar 15 Rover	Earth's Moon
7	Rover Opportunity	Mars
8	Vega 1 Descent Craft	Venus
9	Centaur	Earth's Moon
10	Viking 1 Lander	Mars

ASTRO ORBITS

TOP 10 FASTEST PLANETS/DWARF PLANETS TO ORBIT OUR SUN

We know that our calendar year in a non-leap year is 365 days (the time it takes Earth to go around the Sun once), but how do the other planets and dwarf planets compare?

	MASS	DAYS FOR ONE ORBIT OF THE SUN
1	Mercury	87.967
2	Venus	224.70
3	Earth	365.26
4	Mars	686.97
5	Ceres	1,679.67
6	Jupiter	4,332.59
7	Saturn	10,759.22
8	Uranus	30,799.10
9	Neptune	60,190.03
10	Pluto	90,613.31

YOU RATE! 1 to 100

MERCURY XTREME FACT

Mercury isn't just the fastest-moving planet around the Sun, it's also the smallest at 3,032 mi (4,880 km) in diameter.

FACT FLASH!
DAYS IN A MARS YEAR
686.9

MARS XTREME FACT

Mankind has been fascinated with Mars more than any other planet out there in our solar system. There have been countless works of fiction, from books and comics to movies and songs, that have seen our imaginations embracing the ideas of alien beings and UFOs journeying from Mars to Earth. Methane, a gas produced by living organisms, has been detected there, and scientists are now striving to find out if there is life (even if it's only microbes) on Mars!

OFF THE CHART

The dwarf planet Eris

HAUMEA, MAKEMAKE & ERIS

The other three dwarf planets in our solar system take a lot longer to complete one orbit of the Sun: Haumea takes 103,468 days, Makemake 113,183, and Eris takes a massive 204,870 days!

STAT ATTACK

MARS

Named after....... The Roman god of war
Orbital speed....... 14.9 mi/s (24.1 km/s)
Temperature ....-225-95 °F (-143-35 °C)
First calculations......Tycho Brahe (1576)
Moons ....Deimos, Phobos

CHECK IT OUT!

What you can see in this image is a canyon system that was created by flowing water at some point in Mars' history. NASA's robot rover Curiosity continues the hunt to see if there is any water hidden on Mars.

TOP 10 FIRST COUNTRIES TO LAUNCH ORBITAL SATELLITES

Satellites are common these days, but not many countries have launched one. These are the firsts for these countries...

YOU RATE! 1 to 100

	COUNTRY	SATELLITE	DATE
1	Soviet Union	Sputnik 1	Oct 4, 1957
2	USA	Explorer 1	Feb 1, 1958
3	France	Astérix	Nov 26, 1965
4	Japan	Ōsumi	Feb 11, 1970
5	China	Dong Fang Hong 1	Apr 24, 1970
6	UK	Prospero X-3	Oct 28, 1971
7	India	Rohini 1	Jul 18, 1980
8	Israel	Ofeq 1	Sep 19, 1988
9	Ukraine	Strela-3	Sep 28, 1991
10	Iran	Omid	Feb 2, 2009

SPUTNIK 1 XTREME FACT

Sputnik 1 was a very important satellite: the then Soviet Union (now Russia) scored the first win in its space race with the USA, getting the first satellite launched by mankind into space! It was sent up to study the Earth's atmosphere. It clocked up an amazing 37,000,000 mi (60,000,000 km) during its three months in orbit, before burning up on re-entry towards Earth.

OUR TOP 10 UNOFFICIAL CRAZY SPACE DEBRIS

Check our favourite examples of space junk and the years they became debris...

1	Vanguard 1 research satellite	1964
2	Ed White's space glove	1965
3	Cerise satellite	1995
4	Rossi X-ray Timing Explorer	1995
5	Heidemarie Stefanyshyn-Piper's tool bag	2008
6	Sunita Williams' camera	2007
7	UARS satellite	2006
8	Mars Global Surveyor	2006
9	Mir space station	2001
10	Mariner 9 orbiter	1971

CHECK IT OUT!

Upper Atmosphere Research Satellite (UARS) is a huge 6.6 tonne (6,600kg) satellite, which was deployed from the space shuttle Discovery in 1991. It was then decommissioned in December 2005.

GALAXY WATCH

From unlocking the secrets of black holes to amazing revelations about the Universe, let's take a closer look at what those space geniuses have been up to...

OUR **TOP 10** UNOFFICIAL

MYSTERIES OF THE UNIVERSE

1	**Dark matter and dark energy: what exactly is it?**
2	NASA UFO sightings/extraterrestrial lifeforms: is there anybody else out there?
3	Multiverse: are there parallel universes to ours?
4	Black holes: how can galaxies survive with these energy-sucking forces in them?
5	Do rock formations on Mars indicate a connection to Earth?
6	How did the Universe begin, and how will it end?
7	Are the photos/footage of ancient ruins on the Moon real or fabricated?
8	White holes: the opposite of black holes, they release matter/energy, but how?
9	Spiral shape of galaxies: why do some have this elegant, swirly form?
10	Sounds from space: where did the eerie sounds come from, detected in December 2000?

EXTRATERRESTRIAL LIFE FORMS

XTREME FACT

Alleged encounters with aliens date back to 1897! In April of that year, in Aurora, Texas, it is claimed a craft crashed and that an alien is buried in the local cemetery!

SHUFFLE UP

What would YOU have at Number One? Now you've seen this Top 10, why not list them in the order that blows you and your friends' minds the most!

1	
2	
3	
4	
5	
6	
7	
8	
9	
10	

FACT FLASH!

REPORTED UFO SIGHTINGS EACH YEAR
5,000

CHECK IT OUT!

This is the Andromeda Galaxy, part of the Andromeda constellation, and it's 2.5 million light-years away from us! It is one of the brightest of its kind and you can actually see it pretty clearly without the aid of a powerful telescope.

Know of any other strange space phenomena? Add 'em in... It's YOUR list!

TOP 10 MOST IMPORTANT ASTRONOMICAL EVENTS

In order of their historical discovery/development, here are the most significant space-related events that have helped shape our understanding of the Universe...

	EVENT	DATE
1	Greek astronomer Aristarchus suggests the Earth goes around the Sun	280 BC
2	Greek scientist Eratosthenes calculates the circumference of the Earth	240 BC
3	Hipparchus, another smart Greek astronomer creates the first ever star map, with 850 stars logged	130 BC
4	Greek astronomer Ptolemy's theory of a geocentric universe (Earth is the centre of everything)	140 AD
5	Astronomers in China witness a supernova in Taurus	1054
6	First observatory constructed in Cairo, Egypt	1120
7	Persian astronomer Nasir al-Din al-Tusi has an observatory constructed for him in Iran	1259
8	Observatory built in Asia for astronomer Ulugh Beg	1420
9	Polish astronomer Nicolaus Copernicus assumes a heliocentric view of the universe (that the Sun is the centre)	1543
10	German celestial cartographer Johann Bayer gives stars Greek letters, a system we still use	1603

TOP 10 LARGEST TELESCOPES

As a reference, an average door is about 6.6 ft (2 m) tall. Check out the sizes of the apertures (the opening which light travels into) on the biggest operational optical-reflecting telescopes...

	NAME	DATE	LOCATION	APERTURE
1	Large Binocular Telescope	2004	Arizona (USA)	11.9
2	Gran Telescopio Canarias	2009	Canary Islands (Spain)	10.4
3	Keck 1	1993	Hawaii (USA)	10
=	Keck 2	1996	Hawaii (USA)	10
5	Southern African Large Telescope	2005	Northern Cape (S Africa)	9.2
=	Hobby-Eberly Telescope	1997	Texas (USA)	9.2
7	Subaru	1999	Hawaii (USA)	8.2
=	VLT UT1 (Antu)	1998	Antofagasta Region (Chile)	8.2
=	VLT UT2 (Kueyen)	1999	Antofagasta Region (Chile)	8.2
=	VLT UT3 (Melipal)	2000	Antofagasta Region (Chile)	8.2

CHECK IT OUT!

Although the Large Binocular Telescope is dedicated to looking out into space, the "LBT" has become a star in its own right. The Discovery Channel, National Geographic and the BBC have all featured the groundbreaking telescope on various documentaries. You can check out the telescope yourself by visiting www.lbto.org.

TOP 10 MOST RECENT TOTAL SOLAR & LUNAR ECLIPSES

Which is which? A solar eclipse is when the Sun is obscured by the Moon, and a lunar one is when the Moon is in the Earth's shadow and looks darkened. Here are the most recent total eclipses...

	DATE	TYPE	DURATION
1	Nov 13, 2012	Solar	4 mins 2 secs
2	Dec 10, 2011	Lunar	14 mins 32 secs
3	Jun 15, 2011	Lunar	20 mins 13 secs
4	Dec 21, 2010	Lunar	8 mins 17 secs
5	Jul 11, 2010	Solar	5 mins 20 secs
6	Jul 22, 2009	Solar	6 mins 39 secs
7	Aug 1, 2008	Solar	2 mins 27 secs
8	Feb 21, 2008	Lunar	3 mins 26 secs
9	Aug 28, 2007	Lunar	10 mins 37 secs
10	Mar 3, 2007	Lunar	23 mins 21 secs

CHECK IT OUT!

Why do eclipses occur? Well, put in simple terms, it's just a coincidental combination of time and the orbital axis of planets and moons. With our Moon orbiting the Earth, and our planet orbiting the Sun, there are those fluke moments where the Moon is in exactly the right position between us and the Sun to "block" it out for a period of time.

TOP 10 BIGGEST CONSTELLATIONS

A constellation is an area in the sky which contains many, MANY stars. Some of those are bright enough for us to see patterns. These are the most vast...

HYDRA

XTREME FACT

Hydra isn't just the biggest constellation in terms of sky space, it's also the longest, hence it being named after a giant sea serpent!

YOU RATE!
1 to 100

	NAME	ALSO KNOWN AS	AREA OF SKY (SQ. DEG*)
1	Hydra	The Sea Serpent	1,302.844
2	Virgo	The Virgin	1,294.428
3	Ursa Major	The Great Bear	1,279.660
4	Cetus	The Whale/Sea Monster	1,231.411
5	Hercules	The Hero Hercules	1,225.148
6	Eridanus	The River Eridanus	1,137.919
7	Pegasus	The Winged Horse	1,120.794
8	Draco	The Dragon	1,082.952
9	Centaurus	The Centaur	1,060.422
10	Aquarius	The Water Bearer	979.854

EXTRA! * A "steradian" is the unit of a solid angle. You know the angles on your protractor? Well, the steradian is used to measure angles in three-dimensional space. See the column of "square degrees" on the right? They express the size of the area that the constellation takes up.

BEEN & SEEN

Which of these constellations have you seen? Get a star chart or star book and get stargazing, then tick them off as you spot each one!

- [ ] ORION
- [ ] THE BIG DIPPER (PART OF THE GREAT BEAR)
- [ ] THE GREAT DOG
- [ ] THE SWAN
- [ ] GEMINI
- [ ] ANDROMEDA
- [ ] THE LION
- [ ] THE BULL
- [ ] THE CRAB
- [ ] THE FISHES

OUR TOP 10 UNOFFICIAL

MIND-BLOWING SPACE QUOTES

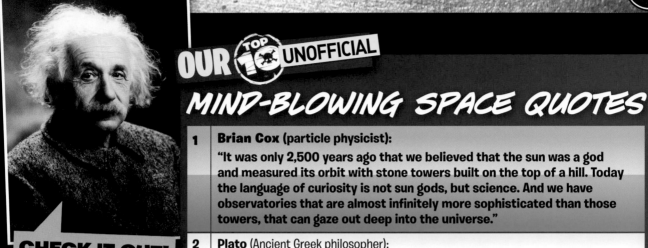

1 Brian Cox (particle physicist):
"It was only 2,500 years ago that we believed that the sun was a god and measured its orbit with stone towers built on the top of a hill. Today the language of curiosity is not sun gods, but science. And we have observatories that are almost infinitely more sophisticated than those towers, that can gaze out deep into the universe."

2 Plato (Ancient Greek philosopher):
"Astronomy compels the soul to look upward, and leads us from this world to another."

3 Yuri Gagarin (first man in space):
"To be the first to enter the cosmos, to engage, single-handed, in an unprecedented duel with nature... Could one dream of anything more?"

4 Carl Sagan (astrophysicist):
"Since, in the long run, every planetary civilization will be endangered by impacts from space, every surviving civilization is obliged to become spacefaring, not because of exploratory or romantic zeal, but for the most practical reason imaginable: staying alive... If our long-term survival is at stake, we have a basic responsibility to our species to venture to other worlds."

5 Neil Armstrong (first man on the Moon):
"That's one small step for [a] man, one giant leap for mankind."

6 Frank Borman (commander of Apollo 8):
"The view of the Earth from the Moon fascinated me... a small disk, 240,000 miles away. Raging nationalistic interests, famines, wars, pestilence, don't show from that distance."

7 Konstantin Tsiolkovsky (one of the founding fathers of rocketry and astronautics):
"The Earth is the cradle of humankind, but one cannot live in the cradle forever."

8 Stephen Hawking (theoretical physicist):
"I don't think the human race will survive the next thousand years, unless we spread into space. There are too many accidents that can befall life on a single planet. But I'm an optimist. We will reach out to the stars."

9 Albert Einstein (theoretical physicist):
"Only two things are infinite: the Universe and human stupidity; and I'm not sure about the Universe."

10 Pope Pius XII (former Pope of the Vatican):
"God has no intention of setting a limit to the efforts of man to conquer space."

MEGA ROCKS

Astronomical asteroids and mega meteoroids whizzing through space are considered potential threats to the fate of our planet, so we should definitely take a look at them!

TOP 10 CLOSEST ASTEROID MISSES

Lots of rocks zoom past our orbit, ranging from meteoroids as small as 3.3 ft (1 m) wide, to massive 3,281 ft (1,000 m) asteroids! Here are the biggest asteroids that have gotten closest to our planet...

	NAME	DIAMETER (M)	DATE	PROXIMITY (KM)	(MI)
1	2002 JE	200	Apr 11, 1971	150,000	93,210
2	(152680) 1998 KJ	500	Dec 31, 1914	232,000	144,164
3	2010 XC	200	Dec 26/27, 1976	30 0,000	186,420
4	2005 YU55	400	Nov 8, 2011	324,900	201,892
5	2004 XP14	500	Jul 3, 2006	432,430	268,712
6	2007 TU24	250	Jan 29, 2008	554,209	344,385
7	69230 Hermes	300	Apr 26, 1942	634,520	394,290
8	4581 Asclepius	300	Mar 22, 1989	684,000	425,037
9	69230 Hermes	300	Oct 30, 1937	739,000	459,214
10	2012 LZ1	1,000	Jun 14, 2012	5,400,000	3,355,560

2011 CQ1 METEOROID

OFF THE CHART

This chunk of space rock was only a little dude at 3.3 ft (1 m) wide, but the meteoroid catchily named "2011 GQ" was actually the closest chunk of rock to ever fly past Earth. On Feb 4, 2011, it zoomed by just 3,405 mi (5,480 km) away from our planet. Close enough, thank you very much!

COMPARE-O-METER

But just how close did these asteroids get to Earth? Here are some useful distance stats:

EARTH TO EDGE OF SPACE
100 km
62 mi

EARTH TO INTERNATIONAL SPACE STATION
354 km
220 mi

Artist's impression of an asteroid

CHECK IT OUT!

Just how many asteroids do you think are up there in outer space? Most of the ones we know about are between Jupiter and Mars, where there are approximately 1.9 million, alone!

LARGEST METEORITES FOUND ON EARTH

A meteorite is the name we give an object that comes from space and is found intact after smashing into Earth. These are the big boys...

YOU RATE!
1 to 100

	NAME	LOCATION	ESTIMATED WEIGHT (T)
1	Hoba	Namibia	60
2	El Chaco	Argentina	37
3	Ahnighito	Greenland	31
4	Sikhote-Alin	Siberia	28
5	Bacubirito	Mexico	22
6	Agpalilik	Greenland	20
=	Armanti	W Mongolia	20
8	Mbosi	Tanzania	16
9	Willamette	USA	15.5
10	Chupaderos	Mexico	14

HOBA
XTREME FACT

The Hoba meteorite is estimated to have crashed onto our planet in excess of 80,000 years ago! A feature of steps has been built around it, because its 60-tonne weight can't be moved easily!

AGPALILIK
XTREME FACT

This meteorite was discovered in Savissivik, Greenland, in 1894. It's estimated to have smashed into the Earth's surface 10,000 years ago.

OUR TOP 10 UNOFFICIAL

MOST SPECTACULAR METEOR SHOWERS

	NAME
1	Perseids
2	Leonids
3	Alpha Centaurids
4	Alpha Capricornids
5	Southern Taurids
6	Northern Taurids
7	Quadrantids
8	Lyrids
9	Alpha Monocerotids
10	Eta Aquariids

CHECK IT OUT!
Photo of Perseids meteor shower taken over the town of Radium Springs, New Mexico...

VOYAGES OF DISCOVERY

Space is not only the final frontier but extraordinarily VAST! This is why mankind has been doing its best to explore that intriguing inky darkness...

TOP 10 FARTHEST A MAN-MADE MACHINE HAS VENTURED

We're doing extremely well with getting mechanical devices to study outer space! Check out how far these man-less explorers have reached so far...

	PROBE	DISTANCE (AU*)
1	**Voyager 1**	**123**
2	Voyager 2	101.7
3	Pioneer 11	86
4	Pioneer 10	80
5	New Horizons	26.2
=	STAR-48 Booster (New Horizons 3rd stage)	26.2
=	Centaur (New Horizons 2nd stage)	26.2
8	Juno	18.7**
9	Opportunity	0.5
10	Curiosity	0.5

**Once Juno reach Jupiter

*AU (Astronomical Unit) = 92,955,807.273 miles.

YOU RATE!
1 to 100

PIONEER 10

XTREME FACT

Aside from its mission to explore space, Pioneer 10 has a plaque designed to be a friendly greeting to any extraterrestrial life forms that may come across it. It also shows where Earth is!

CHECK IT OUT!

This might look like a movie special effect, but it is an actual photo of Callisto, one of Jupiter's moons, taken by Voyager 1. You can tell from this image that Callisto's surface is covered with craters... which have the potential of sheltering microscopic life forms.

COMPARE-O-METER

See how these probes' distances compare with orbiting masses...

EARTH TO THE MOON	EARTH TO THE SUN	EARTH TO MARS
AVERAGE DISTANCE TO THE MOON	**AVERAGE DISTANCE TO THE SUN**	**AVERAGE DISTANCE TO MARS**
384,400 km	**150,000,000** km	**225,000,000** km
238,855 mi	**93,205,678** mi	**139,808,517** mi

FIRST LIVING THINGS SENT INTO SPACE

A long time before we were brave enough to send a human being into space, lots of tests were carried out with all manner of other living organisms...

HAM THE CHIMP

XTREME FACT

Ham the chimpanzee became a megastar for his mission. He was trained to operate simple levers inside the craft, which helped scientists prove that humans could do the same thing in space. Monkey magic!

YOU RATE! 1 to 100

	ORGANISM	ROCKET	DATE
1	Fruit flies	V2	Feb 20, 1947
2	Moss	V2	Various, 1947
3	Rhesus monkey (Albert II)	V2	Jun 14, 1949
4	Mouse	V2	Aug 31, 1950
5	Dogs (Tsygan & Dezik)	R-1 IIIA-1	Jul 22, 1951
6	Dog (Laika)	Sputnik 2	Nov 3, 1957
7	Squirrel monkey (Gordo)	Jupiter IRBM AM-13	Dec 13, 1958
8	Rabbit (Marfusa)	R2	Jul 2, 1959
9	Dogs (Belka & Strelka)	Sputnik 5	Aug 19 1960
10	Chimpanzee (Ham)	Mercury-Redstone	Jan 31, 1961

ZARMINA

XTREME FACT

What's in a name? Well, the International Astronomical Union (a collection of PhD-level and above astronomers) have classified this Earth-like planet as Gliese 581 g. However, it was discovered by a team led by Steven S. Vogt, who named the planet Zarmina after his wife's name, and its nickname is now widely used.

FACT FLASH! LIGHT YEARS FROM EARTH **620**

CHECK IT OUT!

The discovery of this planet that could harbour life is incredibly new and exciting! Kepler-22 b's existence was only confirmed on December 5, 2011, and was discovered by NASA's Kepler Space Telescope. Considering this telescope's mission was to discover planets similar to Earth, we reckon it's doing pretty well! It's not close enough for us to easily visit, though... 6,000 TRILLION km away to be precise!

OUR TOP 10 UNOFFICIAL

MOST HABITABLE PLANETS

	PLANET	DISTANCE FROM EARTH (LIGHT YEARS)
1	Gliese 581 g aka Zarmina	20.3 ± 0.3
2	Gliese 667C c	22 ± 1
3	Kepler-22 b	620
4	HD 85512 b	36
5	Gliese 581 d	20.3 ± 0.3
6	Gliese 667 A	22 ± 1
7	Gliese 667 B	22 ± 1
8	KOI-494.01	1250
9	KOI-812.03	1394
10	KOI-2020.01	1116

VOYAGES OF DISCOVERY

TOP 10 FIRST ROCKETS IN SPACE

There have been hundreds of rocket-powered probes, satellites and craft launched into space, but these were the first 10 rockets...

	NAME	LAUNCH DATE
1	V2	Feb 20, 1947
2	Sputnik 2	Nov 3, 1957
3	USAF Explorer	Jan 31, 1958
4	Jupiter IRBM AM-13	Dec 13, 1958
5	Luna 1	Jan 2, 1959
6	Luna 2	Sept 14, 1959
7	Luna 3	Oct 4, 1959
8	R2	July 2, 1959
9	Mercury-Redstone	Jan 31, 1961
10	Vostok 3A	Apr 12, 1961

YOU RATE! [ ] 1 to 100

CHECK IT OUT!
Controversially, Sputnik 2 (and its canine passenger, Laika) were never intended to return to Earth after the November 3, 1957 takeoff. Many years later, one of the mission's Russian scientists, Oleg Gazenko, admitted he regretted what they had done, as the data collected did not justify Laika's death.

OFF THE CHART

APOLLO 13
Seemingly ill-fated by its number, a couple of days into the Apollo 13 mission in 1970, one of their oxygen tanks ruptured. This meant the planned lunar landing had to be scrapped, and an elaborate strategy was executed to get the crew safely back to Earth.

CHECK IT OUT!
If you think you'll have to wait until you're very old to experience being on a spacecraft, think again! Virgin Galactic plans to have five of these amazing SpaceShipTwo craft ready to take passengers on a suborbital flight (not into outer space, but pretty close) by the end of 2013. Got a spare $200,000? Book yourself a ticket now!

BIGGEST SPACE PROGRAMS

Space adventures are very, VERY expensive! Here are the biggest, most-funded space agencies currently dedicated to reaching the stars...

	AGENCY	COUNTRY	BUDGET ($ MILLIONS)
1	NASA (National Aeronautics & Space Administration)	USA	17,700
2	ESA (European Space Agency)	(European syndication)	5,430
3	ROSCOSMOS (Russian Federal Space Agency)	Russia	3,800
4	CNES (National Centre of Space Research)	France	2,822
5	JAXA (Japan Aerospace Exploration Agency)	Japan	2,460
6	DLR (German Aerospace Centre)	Germany	2,000
7	ISRO (Indian Space Research Organization)	India	1,320
8	CNSA (China National Space Administration)	China	1,300
9	ASI (Italian Space Agency)	Italy	1,000
10	ISA (Iranian Space Agency)	Iran	500

NASA XTREME FACT

Formed 55 years ago, NASA (National Aeronautics and Space Administration) employs over 18,000 people in the US!

FACT FLASH!
YEAR OF THE FIRST SCHEDULED SUBORBITAL FLIGHT
2013

OUR TOP 10 UNOFFICIAL

FUTURE SPACE PROJECTS

	PROJECT TITLE	INTENTIONS	YEAR
1	Euclid	Investigate dark matter and dark energy	2020
2	Virgin Galactic	First commercial space flight	2013
3	Sentinel	Multi-satellite project for global monitoring	2013
4	Aurora	Several, including a sample from Mars returned to Earth	2016
5	Solar Orbiter	To observe and study previously unobservable areas of the Sun	2017
6	PLATO	Investigate characteristics of extrasolar planets	2017
7	Lunar Lander	Robot vehicle to go to the Moon	2018
8	EDDE	Collect space debris for reuse or controlled re-entry	2017
9	EarthCARE	Investigate processes affecting Earth's climate	2016
10	Titan Saturn System Mission	To explore Saturn and its moons	2020

SCI-FI STATION

Outer space is so awesome that the worlds of movies, books and video games have all created amazing tales about it. Here are some of the most successful...

TOP 10

BIGGEST "ALIENS INVADING EARTH" MOVIES

There have been plenty of alien invasions on the big screen over the years. Here are the most successful 10...

FACT FLASH!
GROSSED
1.48 BILLION DOLLARS

TRANSFORMERS: DARK OF THE MOON

XTREME FACT
The digital effect of 32 ft (10 m) Optimus Prime in the movies has 10,018 components, all hand-built inside a computer. In 2010 in China, a lifesize replica of Prime was unveiled... Made of 10,018 bits of junk! Geek-tastic!

MEN IN BLACK

XTREME FACT
Men In Black originates from a 1990 comic created by American writer Lowell Cunningham and illustrated by Canadian Sandy Carruthers.

YOU RATE!
1 to 100

	MOVIE	YEAR	WORLDWIDE GROSS ($)
1	**The Avengers**	2012	1,511,757,910
2	Transformers: Dark Of The Moon	2011	1,123,746,996
3	Transformers: Revenge Of The Fallen	2009	836,303,693
4	Independence Day	1996	817,400,891
5	Transformers	2007	709,709,780
6	War Of The Worlds	2005	591,745,540
7	Men In Black	1997	589,390,539
8	Thor	2011	449,326,618
9	Men In Black II	2002	441,818,803
10	Signs	2002	408,247,917

Source: IMDB.com

TOP 10 LONGEST RUNNING
TV SHOWS SET IN SPACE

Likewise, the small screen has always been a place for space adventures. Here are the 10 that have crafted the most episodes...

YOU RATE!
1 to 100

	SHOW	YEARS ON AIR	EPISODES
1	**Space Patrol**	**1950-55**	**1,110**
2	Doctor Who	1963-84; 1985-89; 2005-present	784
3	Stargate SG-1	1997-2007	214
4	Mystery Science Theater 3000	1988-99	197
5	Star Trek: The Next Generation	1987-94	178
6	Star Trek: Deep Space Nine	1993-99	176
7	Star Trek: Voyager	1995-2001	172
8	Futurama	1999-2003; 2008-present	136
9	Thundercats	1985-89	130
10	Voltron	1984-85	124

DOCTOR WHO
XTREME FACT

Including the current Doctor (Matt Smith), there have so far been 11 incarnations of the Doctor. The fourth one, played by Tom Baker between 1974-81, clocked up 172 episodes!

HEAD TO HEAD

IN THE BLUE CORNER...   IN THE RED CORNER...

OPTIMUS PRIME		THE DOCTOR
✓ 10	WEAPONS	05 ✗
✗ 8	INTELLIGENCE	10 ✓
✗ 9	SPACE TRAVEL	10 ✓
✓ 10	SIZE	04 ✗
✓ 10	TEAMWORK	08 ✗

3   AND THE WINNER IS... PRIME!   **2**

OUR TOP 10 UNOFFICIAL
DEADLIEST MOVIE ALIENS

ANOTHER THING!

We know Loki from *The Avengers* was a very dangerous and devious alien, BUT he wasn't as scary looking as the Chitauri's space eel!

	ALIEN(S)	MOVIE	YEAR
1	**Galactus**	**Fantastic Four: Rise Of The Silver Surfer**	**2007**
2	Chitauri's space eel	The Avengers	2012
3	Tripod aliens	War Of The Worlds	2005
4	Pod people	Invasion Of The Body Snatchers	1956
5	Frost Giants	Thor	2011
6	Triffids	The Day Of The Triffids	1962
7	Devastator	Transformers: Revenge Of The Fallen	2009
8	Alien attackers	Cowboys & Aliens	2011
9	Armoured aliens	Battleship	2012
10	Aliens	Battle Los Angeles	2011

TOP 10 BIGGEST SPACE COMPUTER GAME FRANCHISES

Video games across all of the consoles have ventured into space for battles and adventures since the first ever arcade machine. These are the super-successful ones...

YOU RATE!
1 to 100

STAR WARS

XTREME FACT

Not only has the *Star Wars* franchise sold millions of units in movies and toys, it's also spawned over 100 games! 1982 saw the first adaptation of *The Empire Strikes Back* arrive on home consoles, and the latest *Kinect Star Wars* adventure on the Xbox 360 has already sold over one million copies.

FACT FLASH!
GROSS SALES
38 MILLION

	GAME FRANCHISE	FIRST GAME	GROSS SALES
1	Lego	1997	50,000,000
2	Star Wars	1983	38,000,000
3	Gundam	1984	30,904,400
4	Mega Man	1987	29,000,000
5	Ratchet & Clank	2002	25,000,000
6	Metroid	1986	14,000,000
7	Star Fox	1993	11,500,000
8	Oddworld	1997	5,000,000
9	Asteroids	1979	3,800,000
10	Space Invaders	1980	2,000,000

CHECK IT OUT!

Team T-10 cannot get enough of the Lego video game adventures! How many have you and your friends played? We love the *Indiana Jones* and *Batman* ones the most. Did you know there have been 42 official Lego games released since 1997, and 60 million copies sold? You do now! Software geniuses Traveller's Tales are behind lots of Lego and *Sonic The Hedgehog* games, and they develop titles for Pixar, too!

COMPARE-O-METER

Game sales versus population figures!

POPULATION OF AUS

POPULATION OF FRA

POPULATION OF AUSTRALIA
22,620,600

POPULATION OF FRANCE
65,436,552

OUR TOP 10 UNOFFICIAL
STRONGEST UFO ENCOUNTER CLAIMS

	INCIDENT	SIGHTING	DATE
1	**US spy-plane encounter**	**UFO tailgated crew in Oregon, USA**	**17 Jul, 1957**
2	Tehran, Iran	Bright orb seen 70 mi (113 km) away	Sep 19, 1976
3	Rendlesham forest, UK	Crafts and lights observed	Dec 26-28, 1980
4	Paul Trent's photos, USA	Two photos of a UFO proved genuine	May 11, 1950
5	Kelly Johnson, Agoura, USA	200 ft (61 m) long single-wing UFO	Dec 16, 1953
6	Shag Harbour, Nova Scotia	Underwater UFO tracked	Oct 4, 1967
7	Malmstrom Air Force Base, USA	Several large red UFOs; missiles shut down	Mar 16, 1967
8	Yukon, Canada	1 mi (1.6 km) wide UFO	Dec 11, 1996
9	Skylab III	800 ft (244 m) wide UFO in space	Sep 20, 1973
10	Nuremberg incident, Germany	Dozens of sky orbs and discs	Apr 14, 1561

OFF THE CHART

BULAWAYO, SOUTHERN RHODESIA

The 1950s saw an increasing amount of UFO sightings, including this one on December 29, 1953 in Bulawayo (now Zimbabwe). The region has quite a history of UFOs and ghostly supernatural happenings.

TOP 10
BESTSELLING PUBLISHED SPACE STORIES (FICTION)

Authors have been fascinated with the outer limits for hundreds of years. These are the most successful books that feature space and/or celestial realms beyond our planet...

	BOOK	AUTHOR	YEAR	SALES (MILLIONS)
1	**The Little Prince**	**Antoine de Saint-Exupéry**	**1943**	**200+**
2	Jonathan Livingston Seagull	Richard Bach	1970	40
3	The Foundation Trilogy	Isaac Asimov	1951-53	20
4	The Neverending Story	Michael Ende	1979	16
5	The Hitchhiker's Guide To The Galaxy	Douglas Adams	1979	14
6	Dune	Frank Herbert	1965	12
7	Divine Comedy	Dante Alighieri	1321	11-12
8	A Wrinkle In Time	Madeleine L'Engle	1962	10
9	Deception Point	Dan Brown	2001	2+
10	Spawn #1	Todd McFarlane	1992	1.7

YOU RATE! 1 to 100

OFF THE CHART

SUPERMAN

Do you love Superman? Bet you don't love him as much as the fan who paid $1 million for a copy of *Action Comics* #1 (1938), the comic (above) he first appeared in!

OUR TOP 10 UNOFFICIAL

COOLEST SCI-FI SPACE PILOTS & CAPTAINS

	NAME	MOVIE/TV SHOW
1	**Turanga Leela**	**Futurama**
2	Malcolm Reynolds	Firefly
3	Han Solo	Star Wars
4	Kara "Starbuck" Thrace	Battlestar Galactica
5	The Doctor	Doctor Who
6	Jean-Luc Picard	Star Trek: The Next Generation
7	Zapp Brannigan	Futurama
8	James T. Kirk	Star Trek
9	Luke Skywalker	Star Wars
10	Tuck Pendleton	Inner Space

CHECK IT OUT!

Trek trivia incoming! Chris Pine (above) played a young version of Captain James T. Kirk (replacing the legendary William Shatner) in *Star Trek* (2009), and returned to the role in 2013. Secondly, did you know the world of comics crafted a prequel? *Star Trek: Countdown* revealed more about villain Nero's past. Finally, the budget for the sequel *Star Trek Into Darkness* (2013)? $185 million... In movie terms, that's not outrageous when you consider *Pirates Of The Caribbean: At World's End* cost $300 million!

OUR TOP 10 UNOFFICIAL

BIGGEST MOVIE SPACECRAFT

	NAME	MOVIE	YEAR
1	**Death Star**	**Stars Wars Episode IV: A New Hope**	**1977**
2	Star Destroyer	Stars Wars Episode IV: A New Hope	1977
3	Space Station 5	2001: A Space Odyssey	1968
4	Borg Cube	Star Trek: First Contact	1996
5	USS Cygnus	The Black Hole	1979
6	Invading mothership	Independence Day	1996
7	Axiom	WALL·E	2008
8	Narada	Star Trek	2009
9	Gallaxhar's craft	Monsters Vs Aliens	2009
10	Titan	Titan AE	2000

STAR DESTROYER

XTREME FACT

Star Wars' Imperial Star Destroyers were the flagship vessels of the Imperial fleet, the bad guys. This colossal craft was packed with fire power, including laser cannons and tractor beams, and intended to do serious damage.

AVATAR

XTREME FACT

Guess what inspired writer/director James Cameron to attempt *Avatar*'s complicated CGI (Computer Generated Imagery) characters? He saw Gollum in *The Lord Of The Rings* films and realized technology was advanced enough!

FACT FLASH!
GROSSED
2.7
BILLION
DOLLARS

YOU RATE!
1 to 100

STARS WARS
EPISODE III

XTREME FACT

The first three *Star Wars* episodes are known for their heavy use of CGI, and in *Revenge Of The Sith* (starring Hayden Christensen, above) the digital artists achieved some amazing sights. For one, however real they look, every aspect of all the Clone Troopers is 100 percent CGI!

TOP 10 BIGGEST SPACE MOVIE MISSIONS

It's no surprise that the *Stars Wars* franchise dominates this list, but did you expect to see any of the other entries here?

	MOVIE	YEAR	WORLDWIDE GROSS ($)
1	**Avatar**	**2009**	**2,782,275,172**
2	Star Wars Episode I: The Phantom Menace	1999	1,027,044,677
3	Star Wars Episode III: Revenge Of The Sith	2005	848,754,768
4	Star Wars Episode IV: A New Hope	1977	775,398,007
5	Star Wars Episode II: Attack Of The Clones	2002	649,398,328
6	Armageddon	1998	553,709,788
7	Star Wars Episode V: The Empire Strikes Back	1980	538,375,067
8	WALL·E	2008	521,311,860
9	Star Wars Episode VI: Return Of The Jedi	1983	475,106,177
10	Apollo 13	1995	355,237,933

Source: IMDB.com

INFINITE SPACE

YOUR SHOUT!

Check out these questions. Can you answer them without looking back through the book?

Let's take a break from Team T-10 bringing you all the space news and facts, and spin it around so that YOU are in command of these pages...

T-10 SPACE STUFF

Travel back in time to when you rated elements of the Infinite Space zone, and list all of YOUR top ones here!

	NAME	"YOU RATE" SCORE
1		
2		
3		
4		
5		
6		
7		
8		
9		
10		

ASTRO ORBITS

Do you know which colossal planet these giant swirling forms belongs to?

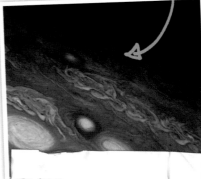

PLANET: ....

WHICH PLANET?

Named after....... The Roman god of war
Orbital speed....... 14.9 mi/s (24.1 km/s)
Temperature ....-225-95 °F (-143-35 °C)
First calculations......Tycho Brahe (1576)
Moons .... Deimos, Phobos

PLANET:..................

MEGA ROCKS

Can you name the largest meteorite to have been found on Earth?

....

BONUS POINT!

....TONNES IS THE WEIGHT OF THIS METEORITE

GALAXY WATCH

Remember the section on the Largest Telescopes? Rank these in order of size, one being the biggest and five being the smallest...

..... **SUBARU**

..... **LARGE BINOCULAR**

..... **HOBBY-EBERLY**

..... **VLT UT1 (ANTU)**

..... **KECK 2**

VOYAGES OF DISCOVERY

Gliese 581 g, aka Zarmina, is arguably the most habitable planet after Earth. But at 20.3 light years away, it's gonna take a megacraft to make it there. Why not try designing yours here?

Divide 1,000 points across these 10 stats. How you spread the points is up to you... You could have a super-sleek futuristic ship or a heavyweight industrial juggernaut!

SIZE ....

SPEED ....

WEIGHT ....

MANOEUVRABILITY/AGILITY .....

WEAPONS ABILITY ....

ARMOUR ....

CREW MEMBERS ....

COLONY MEMBERS ....

SHUTTLECRAFT ....

WARP LEVEL ....

NOW DESIGN YOUR CRAFT BASED ON THE ATTRIBUTES YOU'VE LISTED ABOVE!

TOTAL: 1,000

SCI-FI STATION

Can you name these space characters AND a movie that they appear in?

A
NAME:
....
MOVIE:
....

B
NAME:
....
MOVIE:
....

C
NAME:
....
MOVIE:
....

D
NAME:
....
MOVIE:
....

ANSWERS ON PAGE 313

YOUR ROUND UP... SHOUT!

Here it is... we've reached the end of your T-10 journey! To wrap things up, it's time for the ultimate test of your T-10 knowledge...

YOU RATE!

T-10 OF EVERYTHING!

Combine them all! Here is where you round up all of the number ones of the previous Your Shout zones. What will be your T-10?

	NAME	"YOU RATE" SCORE
1		
2		
3		
4		
5		
6		
7		
8		
9		
10		

HIGH-OCTANE MACHINES

TRUE OR FALSE...

1. Kawasaki occupy four spots in the Top 10 Fastest Production Motorbikes list. ☐ T ☐ F

2. The number of T-28 tanks in America's arsenal is over 1,000. ☐ T ☐ F

3. The Bugatti Veyron 16.4 appears on the Top 10 Most Powerful Car Engines list. ☐ T ☐ F

ANIMAL KINGDOM

Can you name the insect that these savage looking horns belongs to?

NAME: ....

GAMING GALAXY

NAME THAT GAME?

1. This mega-famous gaming franchise was turned into a movie in 1993 that went on to gross $20,915,465 worldwide.

2. This game appears in the Number Two spot of the Top 10 Biggest Selling Console Games with a whopping 79,300,000 copies sold.

3. The star of this game and his brother, Luigi, went on their very first adventure back in 1985.

GAME: ....

SPORT ZONE

Put a tick in the box next to the name of this 23 times X Games medal winner?

- **TONY HAWK**
- **DAVE MIRRA**
- **CAREY HART**
- **SHAUN WHITE**
- **RYAN SHECKLER**

FORCES OF NATURE

WHICH WATERFALL?

Place..............................Bolívar State, Venezuela

Location type................Dense jungle within Canaima National Park

Named after.........Pilot Jimmie Angel who flew over it

Drops.......................................47

Highest drop............2,648 ft (807 m)

NAME: ....

MUSIC MASH-UP

WHO'S THAT GROUP?

This pop group occupy five of the Top 10 Official Music Videos With The Most YouTube "Likes", and 2013 took in 116 live shows across the world. They seem to be going in the right direction!

....

EPIC STRUCTURES

See if you can name the mega-castle pictured here where parts of The Dark Knight Rises were shot:

CASTLE: ....

MOVIE SHOWTIME

Can you name the movie that this little menace is in?

MOVIE: ....

ONLY HUMAN

MATH PROBLEM

Add together the amount of time each of the Top 10 Longest Serving Rulers has reigned. See if you and your friends can guess the figure first and then see who was closest.

....

INFINITE SPACE

Can you name this Russian orbital satellite?

NAME: ....

ANSWERS ON PAGE 313

YOUR SHOUT! ANSWERS

HIGH-OCTANE MACHINES

PAGES 34-35

EXTREME SPEED
True or False
1. True
2. True
3. False

Logo: Lamborghini

BIGGER THE BETTER
Whose Tracks?
Crawler-Transporter

HIGH PERFORMANCE
SSC Ultimate Aero
2004 Lotec Sirius
Zenvo ST1
2006 Bristol Fighter T
Koenigsegg CCXR

CASH MACHINES
Name The Country?
China

ARMED & DANGEROUS
Which Battleship?
Yamato

TOP SECRET
Movie: The Green Hornet

ANIMAL KINGDOM

PAGES 72-73

OUT FOR BLOOD
Whose Jaw?
Hyena

True or False
1. True
2. False
3. True

MOST HUNTED

Any three of these:
- Panda
- Greater One-Horned Rhino
- Tiger
- Black Rhinoceros
- Snow Leopard
- Nigeria-Cameroon Chimpanzee
- Sumatran Orangutan
- Clouded Leopard
- Southern White Rhinoceros

RAPID MOVEMENT
1. Peregrine Falcon
2. Cheetah
3. Sailfish
4. Ostrich
5. Swordfish

SIZING THINGS UP
Tooth: Lion

Which Animal?
Warthog

MILLIONS OF YEARS AGO...
Reptile: Liopleurodon

GAMING GALAXY

PAGES 98-99

GOLD COINS
Game: FIFA Soccer 12

Bonus Point
6.13 *million copies sold on the PS3*

DOWNLOAD FOCUS
1. Angry Birds
2. Tetris
3. The Sims FreePlay
4. Smurfs' Village
5. Bejeweled

TOTAL PLATFORMS
A. Device: **Nintendo DS**
   Made By: **Nintendo**
B. Device: **Wii**
   Made By: **Nintendo**
C. Device: **PlayStation 3**
   Made By: **Sony**

SPORT ZONE

PAGES 144-145

JUST FOR KICKS
Which Sport?
Soccer

LEAP OF FAITH
Which Sportsman?
Kobe Bryant

IN FULL SWING
1. Golf
2. Ice hockey
3. Cricket

THROW DOWN
Name: Muhammad Ali

MUSCLE MOVEMENT
Sprinter: **Jonnie Peacock**

EXTREME DANGER
Total Medals: **157**

THE A-TEAMS
True or False
1. True
2. False

YOU'RE ON YOUR OWN
Who's That Star?
Valentino Rossi

FORCES OF NATURE

PAGES 166-167

LAND DEMOLITION
Name The Year?
1972

True or False
1. False
2. True
3. False

SAVAGE OCEANS
Ship: Costa Concordia

HEAVEN-SENT
A. London
B. Pretoria
C. New York

AROUND THE WORLD
Top 3 Highest Waterfalls
1. Angel Falls
2. Tugela Falls
3. Cataratas las Tres Hermanas

Top 3 Highest Mountains
1. Mount Everest
2. K2
3. Kangchenjunga

MUSIC MASH-UP

PAGES 198-199

CHART TOPPERS
Guess Whose Frizz?
LMFAO

True or False
1. False
2. False
3. True

FAN FORUM
Artist: Miley Cyrus

PRICE TAG
A. Katy Perry
B. Lady Gaga

ON STAGE
Top 3 Biggest Tour Attendances
1. U2
2. The Rolling Stones
3. Pink Floyd

Top 3 Longest Tours
1. Cher
2. Lady Gaga
3. Pink Floyd

EPIC STRUCTURES

PAGES 226-227

SKYSCRAPING
1 - D
2 - B
3 - A
4 - C

True or False
False

MASS APPEAL
Close Up!
Gomateshwara

GREAT LENGTHS

1. The Great Wall Of China
2. Danyang-Kunshan Grand Bridge
3. Thirlmere Aqueduct
4. Bamda/Bangda
5. Steel Dragon 2000

Bonus Point
2,479 *is the length of Steel Dragon 2000*

DESIGNED TO DELIVER

Stadiums with capacity exceeding 200,000:
Tokyo Racecourse
Nürburgring
Texas Motor Speedway

BIZARRE BUILDS

Quick-fire Questions
1. It is upside-down
2. Catacombs of Paris
3. Trojan Nuclear Plant Cooling Tower
4. 2

MOVIE SHOWTIME

PAGES 252-253

BLOCKBUSTERS

True or False
1. False
2. False
3. True

Name: **Ivan Vanko** *or* **Whiplash**

BEFORE THE BIG SCREEN

1. GI Joe
2. Battleship
3. He-Man
4. Transformers
5. She-Ra

Comic: **Batman**

Bonus Point
8 *movies have been made of this comic*

THE MAKING OF...

A. Name: **Doug Jones**
   Movie: **Hellboy movies**
B. Name: **Mike Myers**
   Movie: **Austin Powers 2**

STAR TALENT

Who's That Star?
Sean Connery

ONLY HUMAN

PAGES 280-281

DARE TO GO

True or False
1. False
2. True
3. False
4. False

Bonus Point
He was the first man on the moon

POWER PLAY

Name: **President Kim Il-sung**

DANGEROUS MINDS

Name: **Alexander Pichushkin**

BODY WORK

1. Robert Wadlow
2. John Rogan
3. John F. Carroll
4. Leonid Stadnyk
5. Väinö Myllyrinne

Bonus Point
2.72m *is the height of Robert Wadlow*

INFINITE SPACE

PAGES 308-309

ASTRO ORBITS

Planet: **Jupiter**

Which Planet?
Mars

MEGA ROCKS

Meteorite: **Hoba**

Bonus Point
60 *tonnes is the weight of this meteorite*

GALAXY WATCH

1. Large Binocular
2. Keck 2
3. Hobby-Eberly
4. Subaru
5. VLT UT1 (Antu)

SCI-FI STATION

A. Name: **Colonel Miles Quaritch**
   Movie: **Avatar**
B. Name: **Yoda**
   Movie: **Star Wars**
C. Name: **Spock**
   Movie: **Star Trek**
D. Name: **Thor**
   Movie: **The Avengers**

ROUND UP... YOUR SHOUT!

PAGES 310-311

HIGH-OCTANE MACHINES

True or False
1. True
2. False
3. True

ANIMAL KINGDOM

Name: **Rhinoceros Beetle**

GAMING GALAXY

Game: **Super Mario Bros**

SPORT ZONE

Picture: **Shaun White**

FORCES OF NATURE

Which Waterfall?
Angel Falls

MUSIC MASH-UP

Who's That Group?
One Direction

EPIC STRUCTURES

Castle: **Mehrangarh Fort**

MOVIE SHOWTIME

Movie: **Star Wars: Episode I - The Phantom Menace**

ONLY HUMAN

Math Problem
417 years 205 days

INFINITE SPACE

Name: **Sputnik 1**

313

INDEX BY CATEGORY

HIGH-OCTANE MACHINES

fastest in the air 10
fastest on land 11
fastest production cars 12
movie vehicles (unofficial) 13
fastest production motorbikes 13
heaviest land transporters 14
biggest passenger carriers (unofficial) 15
giant machine disasters (unofficial) 15
planes with the largest wingspan 16
smallest man-driven machines (unofficial) 17
most powerful car engines 18
most streamlined cars 19
highest passenger numbers 20
coolest amphibious vehicles (unofficial) 21
most expensive railway systems 22
most expensive private boats 23
most expensive planes to build 24
most expensive production cars 24
billionaire owners & their hardware (unofficial) 25
biggest tanks 26
battling movie robots (unofficial) 27
missiles with the longest range 28
largest battleships 29
worst nuclear submarine disasters 30
fastest unmanned stealth aircraft 31
alien craft discovery claims (unofficial) 32
secret military intelligence projects (unofficial) 32
movie secret agent/detective vehicles 33

ANIMAL KINGDOM

most deadly 38
mythical monsters (unofficial) 39
most poisonous 40
longest snakes 40
night hunters (unofficial) 41
largest spiders 41
powerful jaws 42
most shark attacks 42
most bizarre ways to kill (unofficial) 43
pack hunters 44
largest big cats 45
killer battles (unofficial) 45
largest defence weapons 46
fastest land prey 47
best defence methods (unofficial) 47
priority species 48
endangered mammals 49
fastest of all 50
speedy reactions (unofficial) 51
fastest ocean creatures 52
longest journeys 53
fastest animals on four legs 54
fastest animals on two legs 55
dangerous journeys (unofficial) 55
heaviest on land 56
biggest movie beasts (unofficial) 57
tallest of all 57
widest wingspans 58

largest insects 58
tallest dogs kept as pets 59
largest teeth 60
strongest animals (unofficial) 61
biggest bears 61
oldest surviving species 62
hardest to destroy (unofficial) 63
back from the dead 63
sonic super-animals 64
unbelievable senses (unofficial) 65
most evolved sci-fi characters (unofficial) 65
PREHISTORIC:
largest carnivores of them all 66
biggest dinosaur movies (unofficial) 67
biggest in the air 68
largest ocean reptiles 68
longest herbivores on land 69
deadliest weapons (unofficial) 70
biggest fish 71
coolest beasts unearthed (unofficial) 71

GAMING GALAXY

most expensive games to develop 76
development breakthrough 77
largest video games developing countries 78
best character designs (unofficial) 79
biggest selling console games 80
biggest arcade games 81
biggest selling PS3 games 82
biggest selling Wii games 83
biggest selling Xbox 360 games 83
biggest selling game brands 84
longest running game brands 85
coolest games brands (unofficial) 85
downloaded mobile games 86
bestselling modern mobile gaming devices ... 87
biggest free iphone apps 88
biggest free ipad apps 89
biggest movies based on video games 90
comic books based on games (unofficial) 91
biggest gaming conventions 92
most bizarre games merchandise ever created (unofficial) 93
bestselling gaming platforms 94
first ever gaming consoles 95
bestselling home consoles 96
bestselling handheld platforms 97

SPORT ZONE

largest attendance to sports that kick 102
most important kicks in sport (unofficial) 103
most damaging kick sports (unofficial) 104
fastest shots in soccer 105
most accurate NFL kickers 106
illegal kicks in sport (unofficial) 107
greatest UFC hall of famers 107
sports with the highest jumps 108
sports with the longest jumps 109
most important leaps in sporting history (unofficial) 109
greatest NBA slam dunk contest participants 110

sports with the most dangerous jumps (unofficial) 111
sports with the fastest swings 112
most important swings in sport (unofficial) ... 113
fastest tennis serves 114
farthest golf drives (in long drive) 115
oddest racket sports (unofficial) 115
largest attendance to sports with a swing 116
weirdest swingin' sports (unofficial) 117
sports with the farthest throws 118
most important throws in sport (unofficial) ... 119
fastest baseball pitchers 120
most spectacular basketball shots (unofficial) 121
sports that propel the fastest 122
fastest sprinters 123
fastest on water (unassisted by motors) 124
sporting tricksters (unofficial) 125
fastest on land (unassisted by motors) 125
fastest machines in sport 126
greatest racing drivers (unofficial) 127
highest scoring monster jam freestyle winners 128
craziest motorsports 129
most decorated X Games competitors 130
snowboarding masters & their tricks (unofficial) 131
most decorated X Games skateboarders 132
highest air sports 133
most dangerous sports 134
greatest boxers who retired undefeated 134
taking it further (unofficial) 135
ultimate sporting daredevils (unofficial) 135
teams with the largest stadium 136
teams with the coolest nicknames (unofficial) 137
most successful Olympic nations 138
nations that have never won an Olympic medal 138
most popular teams on facebook 139
most popular solo sports stars 140
most successful Olympians 141
most successful MMA fighters 142
sports stars in movies (unofficial) 143

FORCES OF NATURE

biggest earthquakes 148
oddest natural disasters (unofficial) 149
most fatal avalanches 149
biggest volcanic eruptions 150
natural disaster movies 151
tallest tsunami 152
deadliest floods 153
strangest aquatic mysteries (unofficial) 153
largest ships sunk by nature 154
cities most at risk of flooding 155
deadliest tornadoes 156
fastest cyclonic storms, hurricanes & typhoons 156
amazing lightning pictures (unofficial) 157
most destructive hailstorms 158
weirdest objects to fall from the sky (unofficial) 159
highest waterfalls 160
highest mountains 161
deepest lakes 161
coldest places 162
hottest places 162

recurring phenomena (unofficial)....................163
longest rivers 164
amazing rock forms (unofficial) 164
largest craters..165

MUSIC MASH-UP

most downloaded songs ever 170
most popular music genre 171
biggest selling digital albums 2012.................173
biggest selling artists of 2012........................174
biggest selling digital songs 2012...................175
most streamed artists 2012...........................176
most streamed song 2012...............................177
most "Likes" on their official Facebook page......178
social networking-related music sites (unofficial).....179
artists with the most web searches 2012...180
coolest official artist/group websites (unofficial) ...181
official music videos with the most Youtube "likes"....182
official music videos with the most Youtube views......183
solo artists with the most followers on Twitter......184
groups/bands with the most followers on Twitter......185
highest earning solo artists in 2012...............186
highest earning bands/groups in 2012 187
most expensive music videos..........................188
most epic music videos (unofficial) 189
artist/group with the highest grossing tours ...190
actors that are also singers/musicians (unofficial)...191
biggest tour attendance.................................192
most amazing set/stage production (unofficial)......193
groups with more than five members (unofficial) 193
longest concerts (running time) 194
longest tours (amount of shows) 195
strangest places bands have played live (unofficial) 195
largest festivals 196
standout festival sets (unofficial)...................197

EPIC STRUCTURES

tallest buildings 202
tallest roller coasters 204
tallest ferris wheels.....................................204
giant attractions (unofficial)..........................205
highest water slide drops...............................205
tallest dams 206
tallest bridges 207
tallest lighthouses 207
awesome non-land structures (unofficial)......208
biggest buildings 209
biggest cities 210
underground spaces (unofficial) 210
biggest stone monoliths 211
longest tunnels 212
longest bridges 213
most terrifying bridges (unofficial)................213
longest roller coasters 214
longest walls 215
longest airport runways 216
craziest movie races (unofficial)....................217
longest race car circuits 217
biggest castles 218

biggest airports 219
coolest tree houses (unofficial)......................219
biggest indoor arenas..................................220
biggest stadiums...220
most visited theme parks 221
spiritual structures (unofficial)......................221
strangest buildings (unofficial)......................222
tallest demolished structures 223
tallest abandoned structures 224
most haunted places (unofficial) 225

MOVIE SHOWTIME

biggest movies of all time 230
superhero movies 231
animated movies 232
movie villains (unofficial)..............................232
most movies in a franchise 233
Blu-Ray & DVD sales....................................234
best movie-going snacks (unofficial) 235
sci-fi/fantasy movies....................................236
comedy (live-action) movies.........................237
weirdest movie merchandise (unofficial) 237
biggest toys before the movie........................238
longest-running comic books with movies....239
biggest novels with movies...........................240
biggest animated TV shows with movies......240
biggest live-action TV shows with movies......241
movies based on historic events/ people's lives......242
biggest pop music documentaries..................243
coolest locations movies have been filmed (unofficial) ..243
most complex make-up (unofficial) 244
iconic costumes (unofficial) 244
biggest movie budgets.................................245
most expensive movies with special effects ...246
insane movie explosions! (unofficial) 247
biggest movie studios...................................247
most bankable movie stars............................248
best actor/actress academy award winners....249
most recurring roles.....................................250
tallest actors of all time 251
unrecognisable stars (unofficial) 251

ONLY HUMAN

fastest around the world by sailboat (eastbound)....256
most prolific pre-20th century explorers (unofficial)....257
deepest solo sea dives..................................258
first expeditions to climb everest...................258
most prolific modern explorers (unofficial)......259
furthest air balloon journeys..........................260
highest wire walks.......................................261
deadliest dictators.......................................262
longest serving rulers...................................263
most brutal assassinations (unofficial)........263
youngest rulers 264
maddest rulers (unofficial)............................264
oldest modern era crime bosses....................265
biggest serial killers....................................266
most wanted criminals..................................267
biggest bank heists......................................268

dumbest criminals (unofficial) 269
longest time on FBI most wanted list..........269
tallest people 270
heaviest people 271
most artistic body art (unofficial) 271
heaviest strongest men 272
most amazing amputees (unofficial)............273
most intelligent people (highest IQ) 273
largest armies (by country)...........................274
biggest riots...275
formidable armies (unofficial)........................275
biggest human superheroes (box office) 276
toughest movie characters (unofficial)........277
biggest detectives/agents (box office)........277
biggest human villains (box office) 278
biggest doctor/scientists (box office).........279
coolest vampires (unofficial)..........................279

INFINITE SPACE

biggest masses in our solar system..............284
important satellites (unofficial)......................285
planets/dwarf planets nearest our sun........285
planets/dwarf planets with the most moons ...286
planets'/dwarf planets' longest days 286
smallest planets/dwarf planets in our solar system ...287
biggest asteroids to share earth's orbit........288
coolest man-made things left on other planets & moons...289
fastest masses to orbit our sun....................290
first countries to launch orbital satellites...291
crazy space debris (unofficial)......................291
mysteries of the universe (unofficial)...........292
most Important astronomical events 293
largest telescopes 293
most recent total solar & lunar eclipses 294
biggest constellations..................................294
mind-blowing space quotes..........................295
closest asteroid misses................................296
largest meteorites found on earth 297
largest comets..297
most spectacular meteor showers (unofficial)....297
furthest a man-made machine has ventured ...298
first living things sent into space..................299
most habitable planets (unofficial) 299
first rockets in space...................................300
biggest space programs 301
future space projects (unofficial) 301
biggest "aliens invading earth" movies.........302
longest running TV shows set in space........303
deadliest movie aliens (unofficial) 303
biggest space computer game franchises...304
strongest UFO encounter claims (unofficial)...305
bestselling published space stories (fiction)....305
coolest sci-fi space pilots & captains (unofficial) .. 306
biggest movie spacecraft (unofficial)..........306
biggest space movie missions.......................307

INDEX A-Z

A

ACTORS
actors that are also singers/musicians (unofficial) 191
Best Actor/Actress Academy Award winners 249
most bankable movie stars 248
most recurring roles 250
tallest actors of all time 251
unrecognisable stars (unofficial) 251

AIRPORTS
biggest airports 219
longest airport runways 216

ALIENS
biggest "aliens invading earth" movies 302
deadliest movie aliens (unofficial) 303

AMERICAN FOOTBALL
most accurate NFL kickers 106

AMPUTEES
most amazing amputees (unofficial) 273

ANIMALS
back from the dead 63
best defence methods (unofficial) 47
biggest bears 61
dangerous journeys (unofficial) 55
endangered mammals 49
fastest animals on four legs 54
fastest animals on two legs 55
fastest land prey 47
fastest ocean creatures 52
fastest of all 50
hardest to destroy (unofficial) 63
heaviest on land 56
killer battles (unofficial) 45
largest big cats 45
largest defence weapons 46
largest insects 58
largest spiders 41
largest teeth 60
longest journeys 53
longest snakes 40
most bizarre ways to kill (unofficial) 43
most deadly 38
most poisonous 40
most shark attacks 42
night hunters (unofficial) 41
oldest surviving species 62
pack hunters 44
powerful jaws 42
priority species 48
sonic super-animals 64
speedy reactions (unofficial) 51
strongest animals (unofficial) 61
tallest dogs kept as pets 59
tallest of all 57
unbelievable senses (unofficial) 65
widest wingspans 58

APPS
biggest free iPad apps 89
biggest free iPhone apps 88

ARMIES
formidable armies (unofficial) 275
largest armies (by country) 274

ASTEROIDS
biggest asteroids to share earth's orbit 288
closest asteroid misses 296

ATHLETICS
fastest sprinters 123

ATTRACTIONS
giant attractions (unofficial) 205

AVALANCHES
most fatal avalanches 149

AWARDS
best actor/actress Academy Award winners 249
most decorated X Games competitors 130
most successful Olympic nations 138
most successful Olympians 141
nations that have never won an Olympic medal 138

B

BASEBALL
fastest baseball pitchers 120

BASKETBALL
greatest NBA slam dunk contest participants 110
most spectacular basketball shots (unofficial) 121

BEARS
biggest bears 61

BIRDS
widest wingspans 58

BLU-RAY & DVDS
Blu-Ray & DVD sales 234

BODY ART
most artistic body art (unofficial) 271

BOOKS
bestselling published space stories (fiction) 305
biggest novels with movies 240

BRIDGES
longest bridges 213
most terrifying bridges (unofficial) 213
tallest bridges 207

BUILDINGS
awesome non-land structures (unofficial) 208
biggest buildings 209
biggest castles 218
coolest tree houses (unofficial) 219
most haunted places (unofficial) 225
spiritual structures (unofficial) 221
strangest buildings (unofficial) 222
tallest abandoned structures 224
tallest buildings 202
tallest demolished structures 223
underground spaces (unofficial) 210

C

CARS
coolest amphibious vehicles (unofficial) 21
fastest on land 11
fastest production cars 12
most expensive production cars 24
most powerful car engines 18
most streamlined cars 19
movie secret agent/detective vehicles 33
smallest man-driven machines (unofficial) 17

CASTLES
biggest castles 218

CATS
largest big cats 45

CITIES
biggest cities 210

CRIME
biggest bank heists 268
biggest serial killers 266
dumbest criminals (unofficial) 269
longest time on FBI most wanted list 269
most wanted criminals 267
oldest modern era crime bosses 265

COMIC BOOKS
comic books based on games (unofficial) 91
longest-running comic books with movies 239

CONCERTS
artist/group with the highest grossing tours 190
biggest tour attendance 192
longest concerts (running time) 194
longest tours (amount of shows) 195
most amazing set/stage production (unofficial) 193
strangest places bands have played live (unofficial) 195

D

DAMS
tallest dams 206

DINOSAURS
biggest dinosaur movies (unofficial) 67

biggest fish 71
biggest in the air 68
coolest beasts unearthed (unofficial) 71
deadliest weapons (unofficial) 70
largest carnivores of them all 66
largest ocean reptiles 68
longest herbivores on land 69

DISASTERS
biggest volcanic eruptions 150
deadliest floods 153
deadliest tornadoes 156
fastest cyclonic storms, hurricanes & typhoons 157
largest ships sunk by nature 154
most fatal avalanches 149
oddest natural disasters (unofficial) 149
tallest tsunami 152

DIVING
deepest solo sea dives 258

DOGS
tallest dogs kept as pets 59

DOWNLOADS
biggest selling artists of 2012 174
biggest selling digital albums 2012 173
biggest selling digital songs 2012 175
downloaded mobile games 86
most downloaded songs ever 170

E

EARTHQUAKES
biggest earthquakes 148

ENDANGERED
back from the dead 63
endangered mammals 49
priority species 48

EXPLORERS & EXPLORATION
biggest space programs 301
farthest a man-made machine has ventured 298
first expeditions to climb everest 258
first living things sent into space 299
first rockets in space 300
future space projects (unofficial) 301
most prolific modern explorers (unofficial) 259
most prolific pre-20th century explorers (unofficial) 257

EXTREME SPORTS
craziest motorsports 129
greatest boxers who retired undefeated 134
highest air sports 133
most dangerous sports 134
most decorated X Games competitors 130
most decorated X Games skateboarders 132

snowboarding masters & their tricks (unofficial) 131
taking it further (unofficial) 135
ultimate sporting daredevils (unofficial) 135

F

FACEBOOK
(music artists) most "Likes" on their official Facebook page 178
most popular solo sports stars 140
most popular (sports) teams on facebook 139

FERRIS WHEELS
tallest ferris wheels 204

FESTIVALS
largest festivals 196
standout festival sets (unofficial) 197

FISH
biggest fish (prehistoric) 71
fastest ocean creatures 52

FLOODS
cities most at risk of flooding 155
deadliest floods 153
tallest tsunami 152

G

GAMING
best character designs (unofficial) 79
bestselling gaming platforms 94
bestselling handheld platforms 97
bestselling home consoles 96
bestselling modern mobile gaming devices 87
biggest arcade games 81
biggest gaming conventions 92
biggest movies based on video games 90
biggest selling console games 80
biggest selling game brands 84
biggest selling PS3 games 82
biggest selling Wii games 83
biggest selling Xbox 360 games 83
biggest space computer game franchises 304
comic books based on games (unofficial) 91
coolest games brands (unofficial) 85
development breakthrough 77
downloaded mobile games 86
first ever gaming consoles 95
largest video games developing countries 78
longest running game brands 85
most bizarre games merchandise ever created (unofficial) 93
most expensive games to develop 76

GOLF
farthest golf drives (in long drive) 115

H

HAILSTORMS
most destructive hailstorms 158
weirdest objects to fall from the sky (unofficial) 159

HOT AIR BALLOONING
farthest air balloon journeys 260

I

INSECTS
largest insects 58

L

LAKES
deepest lakes 161

LIGHTHOUSES
tallest lighthouses 207

LIGHTNING
amazing lightning pictures (unofficial) 157

M

MARTIAL ARTS
greatest UFC hall of famers 107
most successful MMA fighters 142

MERCHANDISE
most bizarre games merchandise ever created (unofficial) 93
weirdest movie merchandise (unofficial) 237

METEORS & METEORITES
largest comets 297
largest meteorites found on earth 297
most spectacular meteor showers (unofficial) 297

MILITARY
biggest castles 218
biggest tanks 26
largest battleships 29
missiles with the longest range 28
secret military intelligence projects (unofficial) 32
worst nuclear submarine disasters 30

MONOLITHS
biggest stone monoliths 211

MONSTERS & BEASTS
biggest movie beasts (unofficial) 57
mythical monsters (unofficial) 39

MOTORBIKES
fastest production motorbikes 13
smallest man-driven machines (unofficial) 17

MOTOR RACING
craziest motorsports 129
fastest machines in sport 126
highest scoring monster jam freestyle winners 128

longest race car circuits 217
greatest racing drivers (unofficial) 127

MOUNTAINS
highest mountains 161

MOVIES
animated movies 232
battling movie robots (unofficial) 27
best actor/actress Academy Award winners 249
best movie-going snacks (unofficial) 235
biggest "aliens invading earth" movies 302
biggest animated TV shows with movies 240
biggest detectives/agents (box office) 277
biggest dinosaur movies (unofficial) 67
biggest doctor/scientists (box office) 279
biggest human superheroes (box office) 276
biggest human villains (box office) 278
biggest live-action TV shows with movies 241
biggest movies based on video games 90
biggest movie beasts (unofficial) 57
biggest movie budgets 245
biggest movies of all time 230
biggest movie spacecraft (unofficial) 306
biggest movie studios 247
biggest novels with movies 240
biggest pop music documentaries 243
biggest space movie missions 307
biggest toys before the movie 238
comedy (live-action) movies 237
coolest locations movies have been filmed (unofficial) 243
coolest sci-fi space pilots & captains (unofficial) 306
coolest vampires (unofficial) 279
craziest movie races (unofficial) 217
deadliest movie aliens (unofficial) 303
iconic costumes (unofficial) 244
insane movie explosions! (unofficial) 247
longest-running comic books with movies 239
most bankable movie stars 248
most complex make-up (unofficial) 244
most evolved sci-fi characters (unofficial) 65
most expensive movies with special effects 246
most movies in a franchise 233
most recurring roles 250
movies based on historic events/ people's lives 242
movie vehicles (unofficial) 13
movie villains (unofficial) 232
natural disaster movies 151
sci-fi/fantasy movies 236
sports stars in movies (unofficial) 143
superhero movies 231
tallest actors of all time 251
toughest movie characters (unofficial) 277

unrecognizable stars (unofficial) 251

MUSIC
actors that are also singers/musicians (unofficial) 191
artist/group with the highest grossing tours 190
artists with the most web searches 2012 180
biggest pop music documentaries (movies) 243
biggest selling artists of 2012 174
biggest selling digital albums 2012 173
biggest selling digital songs 2012 175
biggest tour attendance 192
coolest official artist/group websites (unofficial) 181
groups/bands with the most followers on Twitter 185
groups with more than five members (unofficial) 193
highest earning bands/groups in 2012 187
highest earning solo artists in 2012 186
largest festivals 196
longest concerts (running time) 194
longest tours (amount of shows) 195
most amazing set/stage production (unofficial) 193
most downloaded songs ever 170
most epic music videos (unofficial) 189
most expensive music videos 188
most "Likes" on their official Facebook page 178
most popular music genre 171
most streamed artists 2012 176
most streamed song 2012 177
official music videos with the most YouTube "Likes" 182
official music videos with the most YouTube views 183
social networking-related music sites (unofficial) 179
solo artists with the most followers on Twitter 184
stand out festival sets (unofficial) 197
strangest places bands have played live (unofficial) 195

MYSTERIES
strangest aquatic mysteries (unofficial) 153

N

NATURE
amazing rock forms (unofficial) 164
largest craters 165
recurring phenomena (unofficial) 163

O

OLYMPICS
most successful Olympians 141
most successful Olympic nations 138
nations that have never won an Olympic medal 138

P

PEOPLE
heaviest people 271

heaviest strongest men 272
most intelligent people (highest IQ) 273
tallest people 270

PLANES
fastest in the air 10
giant machine disasters (unofficial) 15
most expensive planes to build 24
most habitable planets (unofficial) 299
planes with the largest wingspan 16
smallest man-driven machines (unofficial) 17

PLANETS, MOONS & THE SUN
coolest man-made things left on other planets & moons 289
fastest masses to orbit our sun 290
most recent total solar & lunar eclipses 294
planets'/dwarf planets' longest days 286
planets/dwarf planets nearest our sun 285
planets/dwarf planets with the most moons 286
smallest planets/dwarf planets in our solar system 287

PLATFORMS (GAMING)
bestselling gaming platforms 94
bestselling handheld platforms 97
bestselling home consoles 96
first ever gaming consoles 95

PREHISTORIC CREATURES
biggest fish 71
biggest in the air 68
coolest beasts unearthed (unofficial) 71
deadliest weapons (unofficial) 70
largest carnivores of them all 66
largest ocean reptiles 68
oldest surviving species 62

R

RIOTS
biggest riots 275

RIVERS
longest rivers 164

ROBOTS
battling movie robots (unofficial) 27

ROLLER COASTER
longest roller coasters 214
tallest roller coasters 204

RULERS & DITATORS
deadliest dictators 262
longest serving rulers 263
maddest rulers (unofficial) 264
most brutal assassinations (unofficial) 263
youngest rulers 264

S

SAILING

fastest around the world by sailboat (eastbound) 256
SATELLITES
first countries to launch orbital satellites 291
important satellites (unofficial) 285
SHARKS
most shark attacks 42
SHIPS & BOATS
coolest amphibious vehicles (unofficial) 21
giant machine disasters (unofficial) 15
highest passenger numbers 19
largest battleships 29
largest ships sunk by nature 154
most expensive private boats 23
smallest man-driven machines (unofficial) 17
SNAKES
longest snakes 40
SOCCER
fastest shots in soccer 105
SOLAR SYSTEM
biggest masses in our solar system 284
SPACE
bestselling published space stories (fiction) 305
biggest space computer game franchises 304
biggest space movie missions 307
biggest space programs 301
coolest sci-fi space pilots & captains (unofficial) 306
farthest a man-made machine has ventured 298
first living things sent into space 299
first rockets in space 300
future space projects (unofficial) 301
longest running TV shows set in space 303
mind-blowing space quotes 295
SPIDERS
largest spiders 41
SPORT
fastest machines in sport 126
fastest on land (unassisted by motors) 125
fastest on water (unassisted by motors) 124
highest scoring monster jam freestyle winners 128
illegal kicks in sport (unofficial) 107
largest attendance to sports with a swing 116
largest attendance to sports that kick 102
most damaging kick sports (unofficial) 104
most important kicks in sport (unofficial) 103
most important leaps in sporting history (unofficial) 109
most important swings in sport (unofficial) 113
most important throws in sport (unofficial) 119
most popular solo sports stars 140
most successful MMA fighters 142
oddest swing sports (unofficial) 115
greatest racing drivers (unofficial) 127

sporting tricksters (unofficial) 125
sports stars in movies (unofficial) 143
sports that propel the fastest 122

sports with the fastest swings 112
sports with the farthest throws 118
sports with the highest jumps 108
sports with the longest jumps 109
sports with the most dangerous jumps (unofficial) 111
teams with the coolest nicknames (unofficial) 137
teams with the largest stadium 136
weirdest swingin' sports (unofficial) 117
STADIUMS
biggest indoor arenas 220
biggest stadiums 220
STREAMING
most streamed artists 2012 176
most streamed song 2012 177
SUBMARINES
smallest man-driven machines (unofficial) 17
worst nuclear submarine disasters 30

T
TANKS
biggest tanks 26
coolest amphibious vehicles (unofficial) 21
smallest man-driven machines (unofficial) 17
TELESCOPES
largest telescopes 293
TEMPRATURE
coldest places 162
hottest places 162
TENNIS
fastest tennis serves 114
TELEVISION
biggest animated TV shows with movies 240
biggest live-action TV shows with movies 241
coolest sci-fi space pilots & captains (unofficial) 306
longest running TV shows set in space 303
THEME PARKS
most visited theme parks 221
TORNADOES
deadliest tornadoes 156
fastest cyclonic storms, hurricanes & typhoons 157
TOYS
biggest toys before the movie 238
TRAINS
most expensive railway systems 22
TUNNELS
longest tunnels 212
TWITTER

groups/bands with the most followers on Twitter 185
solo artists with the most followers on Twitter 184

U
UFOS
alien craft discovery claims (unofficial) 32
biggest "aliens invading earth" movies 302
strongest UFO encounter claims (unofficial) 305
UNIVERSE
biggest constellations 294
crazy space debris (unofficial) 291
farthest a man-made machine has ventured 298
mind-blowing space quotes 295
most habitable planets (unofficial) 299
most important astronomical events 293
mysteries of the universe (unofficial) 292

V
VEHICLES
biggest passenger carriers (unofficial) 15
coolest amphibious vehicles (unofficial) 21
fastest machines in sport 126
giant machine disasters (unofficial) 15
heaviest land transporters 14
movie secret agent/detective vehicles 33
movie vehicles (unofficial) 13
smallest man-driven machines (unofficial) 17
VOLCANOES
biggest volcanic eruptions 150

W
WALLS
longest walls 215
WATERFALLS
highest waterfalls 160
WATER SLIDES
highest water slide drops 205
WEALTH
artist/group with the highest grossing tours 190
biggest movie studios 247
billionaire owners & their hardware (unofficial) 25
highest earning bands/groups in 2012 187
highest earning solo artists in 2012 186
WIRE WALKS
highest wire walks 261

Y
YOUTUBE
official music videos with the most YouTube "Likes" 182
official music videos with the most YouTube views 183

PICTURE CREDITS

T: top B: bottom L: left C: centre R: right BG: background

All images supplied by © **Getty Images**

Except:

iStockphoto
Throughout: (Metal texture) © iStockphoto, P36-37: (TL) © iStockphoto

The Kobal Collection
P27: (BG) The Kobal Collection / Halcyon Company, The, (B) Touchstone Pictures / The Kobal Collection, P33: (B) The Kobal Collection / MGM / United Artists / Sony, P36-37: (TL) © iStockphoto, P39: (TR) The Kobal Collection / Universal Pictures, P57: (TC) Universal / Wing Nut Films / The Kobal Collection, P65: (BL) The Kobal Collection / 20th Century Fox, P66-67: (BC) & (TR) Amblin / Universal / The Kobal Collection, P90: (BG) The Kobal Collection / Walt Disney Pictures, P151: (B) The Kobal Collection / Sony Pictures Entertainment, P155 (BG) Earthship Productions / The Kobal Collection, P203: (C) The Kobal Collection / Warner Bros. / DC Comics, P217: (T) The Kobal Collection / Warner Bros., P229: (BG) The Kobal Collection / Marvel / Sony Pictures, P230: (BG) Marvel Enterprises / The Kobal Collection, P231: (L) The Kobal Collection / Marvel Enterprises, P232: (L) 20th Century Fox / The Kobal Collection, (BR) The Kobal Collection / Lucasfilm / 20th Century Fox, P233: (BG) Warner Bros. Pictures / The Kobal Collection, (B) Warner Bros. / DC Comics / The Kobal Collection, P234: (BG) New Line Cinema / The Kobal Collection, P235: (L) The Kobal Collection / Walt Disney, P236: (BG) The Kobal Collection / Walt Disney Pictures, (B) The Kobal Collection / Lucasfilm, P237: (C) Amblin Entertainment / The Kobal Collection, P238: (BG) The Kobal Collection / Paramount Pictures, P239: (B) Marvel Enterprises / The Kobal Collection, P240: (TR) The Kobal Collection / New Line Cinema, (BR) The Kobal Collection / 20th Century Fox / Groening, Matt, P241: (BC) NBC-TV / The Kobal Collection, (BR) Paramount Television / The Kobal Collection, P242: (BG) 20th Century Fox / Paramount / The Kobal Collection / Wallace, Merie W., (BL) The Kobal Collection / 20th Century Fox / Paramount, (BR) The Kobal Collection / Warner Bros., P243: (BL) New Line / Saul Zaentz / Wing Nut / The Kobal Collection, P244: (BL) The Kobal Collection / Columbia, P245: (BG) Walt Disney Pictures / The Kobal Collection, (BR) Warner Bros. Pictures / The Kobal Collection, P246: (L) Columbia Pictures / The Kobal Collection, (BC) The Kobal Collection / Walt Disney, P247: (TL) 20th Century Fox / The Kobal Collection, (BL) Lionsgate / The Kobal Collection, P248: (BG) Paramount Pictures / The Kobal Collection, P249 (BL) The Kobal Collection / Warner Bros., P250: (BR) 20th Century Fox / Marvel Entertainment / The Kobal Collection / Israelson, Nels, P251: (BL) The Kobal Collection / Universal Pictures, P252: (BR) The Kobal Collection / Marvel Productions, P253: (C) The Kobal Collection / Universal Pictures, (R) New Line / The Kobal Collection / Gordan, Melinda Sue, P268: (C) The Kobal Collection / Forward Pass, P376: (BL) Columbia Pictures / The Kobal Collection, (C) Marvel / 20th Century Fox / The Kobal Collection, P277: (BG) Marvel Enterprises / The Kobal Collection, (R) The Kobal Collection / Silver Pictures, P279: (BG) The Kobal Collection / Warner Bros/DC Comics, (BL) Lionsgate / The Kobal Collection, P280: (TL) The Kobal Collection / Lucasfilm / Paramount Pictures, (BL) Warner Bros. / The Kobal Collection, P302: (BG) The Kobal Collection / Paramount Pictures, (BL) Amblin Entertainment / The Kobal Collection, P303: (BL) The Asylum / The Kobal Collection, P306-307: (BG) The Kobal Collection / Paramount / Bad Robot, (BL) Lucasfilm / 20th Century Fox / The Kobal Collection, (C) The Kobal Collection / Lucasfilm / 20th Century Fox, (R) The Kobal Collection / Twentieth Century-Fox Film Corporation, P309: (L) The Kobal Collection / Twentieth Century-Fox Film Corporation, (CL) The Kobal Collection / Lucasfilm / 20th Century Fox, (CR) The Kobal Collection / Paramount / Bad Robot, (R) Marvel Studios / The Kobal Collection

Various
P103: (TR) © Al Messerschmidt Archive / Getty Images Sport, P133: (CL & R) Jay Nemeth/Red Bull Content Pool, (B) Joerg Mitter/Red Bull Content Pool, P196: (BL) © David Goddard / Getty Images Entertainment, P250: (BG) © 2012 Warner Bros. Ent. Inc. All Rights Reserved. P255: (B) Adarsh Padegal / Flickr RF

• •

ACKNOWLEDGEMENTS

Top 10 For Boys 2014 Produced by SHUBROOK BROS. CREATIVE

Writer & Researcher: Paul Terry

Editorial Director: Trevor Davies
Chief Sub-editor: Amanda Alcindor
Sub-editor: Claire Wilson
Proofreader: Hannah Verdier

Special thanks to...

Ian Turp & Marc Glanville at Getty Images

Phil Smith, Darren Osborne and Harry Rowland at Dot Gradations

Helena Kosinski at Nielsen Music

Jennifer Martin at Wright's Media

Andrew Minn at Prometheus Global Media

Billboard

Susanne Jursik at Red Bull

Jonathan Davies at Games Press

Dr. Andy Hughes

David Martill

Luke Hauser

Louise Ord

All lists credited to Billboard: Copyrighted 2013. PROMETHEUS Global Media. 96098:113JM

Box office information courtesy of The Internet Movie Database (http://www.imdb.com). Used with permission.

Benjamin Baker
Dylan Enskat
Alex Jackson
Elliott Jackson
Ollie Jackson
Freddie Kamasa
Frank McCormick
Jack McCormick
Henry Shubrook
Marley Whitington